The Parallel Curriculum

Carol Ann Tomlinson

Sandra N. Kaplan

Joseph S. Renzulli

Jeanne Purcell

Jann Leppien

Deborah Burns

The Parallel Curriculum

A Design to Develop High Potential and Challenge High-Ability Learners

A Service Publication of the
National Association for Gifted Children

CORWIN PRESS, INC.
A Sage Publications Company
Thousand Oaks, California

For information:

Corwin Press, Inc.
A Sage Publications Company
2455 Teller Road
Thousand Oaks, California 91320
E-mail: order@corwinpress.com

Sage Publications Ltd.
6 Bonhill Street
London EC2A 4PU
United Kingdom

Sage Publications India Pvt. Ltd.
M-32 Market
Greater Kailash I
New Delhi 110 048 India

Printed in the United States of America

Library of Congress Cataloging-in-Publication Data

The parallel curriculum: A design to develop high potential and
    challenge high ability learners / by Carol Ann Tomlinson ... [et al.].
        p. cm.
    Includes bibliographical references.
    ISBN 0-7619-4558-X — ISBN 0-7619-4559-8 (pbk.)
    1. Gifted children—Education—Curricula. 2. Curriculum
planning.   I. Tomlinson, Carol A.
    LC3993.2 .P34 2001
    371.95´3—dc21   2001005340

This book is printed on acid-free paper.

    05   10   9   8   7

_____

Acquiring Editor:	Robb Clouse
Corwin Editorial Assistant:	Erin Buchanan
Production Editor:	Diane S. Foster
Copy Editor:	Joyce Kuhn
Typesetter:	Marion Warren
Proofreader:	Jamie Robinson
Cover Designer:	Tracy E. Miller

Contents

Preface

This book represents three years of reflection and work by a group of educators toward the goal of developing a model to guide curriculum design for the journey toward expertise. Beyond that, it represents the thoughtful legacy of our field in its continual attempts to understand how best to help young people build self-actualized and productive lives.

It is our intent that the Parallel Curriculum Model represent a synthesizing of views and approaches to creating curriculum that leads toward expertise rather than reflecting any single view or approach. To that end, while we do not cite specific contributors from the field of gifted education, we acknowledge with a profound sense of heritage the work of all those who have pioneered our understanding of what it means to teach for expertise, those who have developed that understanding over the years, and those who continue to develop that understanding.

We are hopeful that the model represented here will extend the conversation about high-quality curriculum, but we do not suggest that this model replace existing models of curriculum development. Rather, we believe that the field of education benefits from a variety of models from which teachers and schools can select to most appropriately address both the learning needs of students and the ongoing professional growth of educators themselves. We know that no single model can fully attend to all needs—so to that end, we hope that the Parallel Curriculum Model will serve, at the very least, as a catalyst for vigorous conversation about what it means to develop curriculum leading to expertise for learners who will leave today's schools to live out their lives in tomorrow's world.

Acknowledgments

The development of this project has been dependent on the critical and creative exchanges of educators representing various roles and responsibilities, organizations, and relationships to the education of gifted students. In addition, the presentation of the Parallel Curriculum reflects the responses of educators who both design and implement curriculum. We express sincere appreciation to the many individuals who have been committed to supporting this curriculum project of the National Association for Gifted Children. They have willingly devoted time in a variety of ways to ensure its completion.

—Carol Ann Tomlinson, Sandra N. Kaplan, Joseph J. Renzulli,
Jeanne H. Purcell, Jann Leppien, and Deborah E. Burns

Reviewers

Carolyn M. Callahan, University of Virginia, Charlottesville
Mary Ruth Coleman, The Association for the Gifted, Council
    for Exceptional Children
Carolyn R. Cooper, Maryland Department of Education
Jerry Flack, University of Colorado, Colorado Springs
Nancy Hertzog, University of Illinois, Champaign
Leslie Kiernan, Association for Supervision and Curriculum Development
Sharon Lind, Lind Consulting, Kent, Washington
Sheri Nowak, Emporia State University, Emporia, Kansas
Patricia O'Connell Ross, U.S. Department of Education
Joyce VanTassel-Baska, College of William and Mary, Williamsburg, Virginia
Karen L. Westberg, University of St. Thomas, St. Paul, Minnesota

Dialogue and Exchange

Linda Burquett, Fairfax County Schools, Gifted Programs, Virginia
Jane Clarenbach, National Association for Gifted Children
Mary Ruth Coleman, The Association for the Gifted, CEC
Evelyn English, National Middle Schools Association
Bob Farrace, National Association of Secondary School Principals
J. Arthur Jones, Quality Education for Minorities Network
Leslie Kiernan, Association for Supervision and Curriculum Development
Janet Lieberman, National Council for the Social Studies
Jay McIntire, Council for Exceptional Children
Carolyn Pool, Association for Supervision and Curriculum Development
Peter Rosenstein, National Association for Gifted Children
Sylvia Seidel, National Education Association
Mary Shaughnessy, Fairfax County Schools, Gifted Program, Virginia

Respondents and Developers

Kathy Apps, Santa Ana Unified School District, California
Joanna Blakely, Newport Mesa Unified School District, California
Kay Brimijoin, Sweet Briar College, Virginia, Charlottesville
Nanci Cole, Garden Grove Unified School District, California
Nancy Craig, Sacramento Unified School District, California
Miriam Font-Rivera, University of Virginia, Charlottesville

Holly Gould, University of Virginia, Charlottesville
Wendy Hayes-Ebright, Long Beach Unified School District, California
Ellen Hench, University of Virginia, Charlottesville
Holly Hertberg, University of Virginia, Charlottesville
Marge Hoctor, California Association for the Gifted
Carol Horn, Fairfax County Public Schools, Virginia
Sandi Ishii, Garden Grove Unified School District, California
Lacy Peale, University of Virginia, Charlottesville
Debbie Peña, Garden Grove Unified School District, California
Cindy Strickland, University of Virginia, Charlottesville
Janice Strauss, Arlington County Public Schools, Virginia
Pat Thurman, Santa Ana Unified School District, California

Teachers (Pilot Classrooms)

Kim Dodds, San Juan Capistrano Unified School District, California
Irene Guzman, Santa Ana Unified School District, California
Kim Garcia, Santa Ana Unified School District, California
Lucy Hunt, Los Angeles Unified School District, California
Kristen Worden, Los Angeles Unified School District, California

About the Authors

 **Carol Ann Tomlinson**'s career as an educator includes 21 years as a public school teacher. She taught in high school, preschool, and middle school, and worked with heterogeneous classes as well as special classes for students identified as gifted and students with learning problems. Her public school career also included 12 years as a program administrator of special services for advanced and struggling learners. She was Virginia's Teacher of the Year in 1974. She is Professor of Educational Leadership, Foundations, and Policy at the University of Virginia's Curry School of Education; a researcher for the National Research Center on the Gifted and Talented; a co-director of the University of Virginia's Summer Institute on Academic Diversity; and President of the National Association for Gifted Children. Special interests throughout her career have included curriculum and instruction for advanced learners and struggling learners, effective instruction in heterogeneous settings, and bridging the fields of general education and gifted education. She is author of over 100 articles, book chapters, books, and other professional development materials, including *How to Differentiate Instruction in Mixed-Ability Classrooms, The Differentiated Classroom: Responding to the Needs of All Learners, Leadership for Differentiated Schools and Classrooms,* the facilitator's guide for the video staff development sets called *Differentiating Instruction,* and *At Work in the Differentiated Classroom,* as well as a professional inquiry kit on differentiation. She works throughout the United States and abroad with teachers whose goal is to develop more responsive heterogeneous classrooms.

 **Sandra N. Kaplan** has been a teacher and administrator of gifted programs in an urban school district in California. Currently, she is Clinical Professor in Learning and Instruction at the University of Southern California's Rossier School of Education. She has authored articles and books on the nature and scope of differentiated curriculum for gifted students. Her primary area of concern is modifying the core and differentiated curriculum to meet the needs of inner-city, urban, gifted learners. She is a past president of the California Association for the Gifted (CAG) and the National Association for Gifted Children (NAGC). She has been nationally recognized for her contributions to gifted education.

Joseph S. Renzulli is Professor of Educational Psychology at the University of Connecticut, where he also serves as director of the National Research Center on the Gifted and Talented. His research has focused on the identification and development of creativity and giftedness in young people and on organizational models and curricular strategies for total school improvement. A focus of his work has been on applying the strategies of gifted education to the improvement of learning for all students. He is a Fellow in the American Psychological Association and was a consultant to the White House Task Force on Education of the Gifted and Talented. He was recently designated a Board of Trustees Distinguished Professor at the University of Connecticut. Although he has obtained more than $20 million in research grants, he lists as his proudest professional accomplishments the UConn Mentor Connection program for gifted young students and the summer Confratute program at UConn, which began in 1978 and has served thousands of teachers and administrators from around the world.

Jeanne H. Purcell is the consultant to the Connecticut State Department of Education for gifted and talented education. She is also director of UConn Mentor Connection, a nationally recognized summer mentorship program for talented teenagers that is part of the NEAG Center for Talent Development at the University of Connecticut. Prior to her work at the State Department of Connecticut, she was an administrator for Rocky Hill Public Schools (CT); a program specialist with the National Research Center on the Gifted and Talented, where she worked collaboratively with other researchers on national issues related to high-achieving young people; an instructor of Teaching the Talented, a graduate-level program in gifted education; and a staff developer to school districts across the country and Canada. She has been an English teacher, community service coordinator, and teacher of the gifted, K-12, for 18 years in Connecticut school districts and has published many articles that have appeared in *Educational Leadership, Gifted Child Quarterly, Roeper Review, Educational and Psychological Measurement, National Association of Secondary School Principals' Bulletin, Our Children: The National PTA Magazine, Parenting for High Potential,* and *Journal for the Education of the Gifted.* She is active in the National Association for Gifted Children (NAGC) and serves on the Awards Committee and the Curriculum Committee of NAGC for which she is the co-chair for the annual Curriculum Awards Competition.

Jann Leppien served as a gifted and talented coordinator in Montana prior to attending the University of Connecticut, where she earned her doctorate in gifted education and worked as a research assistant at the National Research Center for the Gifted and Talented. She has been a teacher for 24 years, spending 14 of those years working as a classroom teacher, enrichment specialist, and coordinator of the Schoolwide Enrichment Model in Montana. She is past president of the Montana Association for Gifted and Talented Education. Currently, she is an Associate Professor in the School of Education at the University of Great Falls in Montana. She teaches graduate and undergraduate courses in gifted education, educational research, curriculum and assessment, creativity, and methods courses in math, science, and social studies. Her research interests include teacher collaboration, curriculum design, underachievement, and planning instruction for advanced learners. She works as a consultant to teachers in the field of gifted education and as a national trainer for the Talents Unlimited Program. She is coauthor of *The Multiple Menu Model: A Parallel Guide for Developing Differentiated Curriculum*. She is active in the National Association for Gifted Children (NAGC), serving as a board member and newsletter editor of the Curriculum Division, and a board member of the Association for the Education of Gifted Underachieving Students.

Deborah E. Burns earned her bachelor's degree in elementary education from Michigan State University in 1973. She pursued her graduate studies at Western Michigan University in clinical reading instruction and received her M.Ed. from Ashland College in 1978 in remedial reading, administration, and supervision. She pursued additional graduate studies at Ohio State University involving administration, special education, and gifted education and received her Ph.D. in educational psychology and gifted education from the University of Connecticut in 1987. She began her teaching career in 1973, as a Title I reading and mathematics teacher in a rural K-8 school in Michigan. She has worked as a K-8 classroom teacher, as a middle school language arts specialist, and as a program coordinator for a seven-district consortium. She has taught in preschool, summer, and Saturday programs, in resource rooms, a psychiatric ward, an orphanage, and at the university level. She has written grants, professional development modules, journal articles, assessments, program evaluations, curriculum units, and three books. She has also designed and implemented classroom-based research studies and conducted program and teacher evaluations. For the past 15 years, she has been employed by the University of Connecticut's NEAG

School of Education as a program director, an assistant professor, a research scientist, associate professor in residence, and most recently in Cheshire as curriculum coordinator for the district. She is an active member of the National Association for Gifted Children (NAGC) and has been a board member for the past five years. She is a member of the Curriculum Division and is co-chair of the annual Curriculum Awards Competition.

CORWIN
PRESS

The Corwin Press logo—a raven striding across an open book—represents the happy union of courage and learning. We are a professional-level publisher of books and journals for K-12 educators, and we are committed to creating and providing resources that embody these qualities. Corwin's motto is "Success for All Learners."

The Rationale for an Evolving Conception of Curriculum to Develop Expertise

The human enterprise is a quest for learning from what came before and improving upon what we have learned. In fact, those are arguably key goals of education itself—helping people understand the past in order to invent a future. So it is with this particular conceptualization of ways to think about crafting curriculum for gifted learners. It is an attempt to understand a heritage and use that as a platform for constructing ways of thinking that are at once more contemporary and more forward looking than the past alone allows.

A reasonable question prior to an examination of the model of curriculum development proposed in this book is "Why do we need to think differently about curriculum than we have in the past?" We suggest at least four reasons that seem compelling to us and certainly invite readers to add to the list.

Reasons for Curriculum Development

A Changing Society Can Change Students

Over the past few decades, both the nature of society and the nature of young learners in our society have changed dramatically. While there is room for debate about degrees of the changes and their positive or negative implications, we believe it is safe to say that our society is much more information saturated than in the past, is more consumer oriented, is more overtly pluralistic in viewpoints and ideas, and generally demands a faster pace of daily life and a greater capacity to adapt to change than was the case in past generations. It also requires workers to be both more specialized and more adaptable than in times past.

It is not surprising, then, that young people generally have less time to be inno-cent—they are less protected from difficult issues than in the past. It is not surpris-ing that many young people feel more separated from, and are less supported by, adults whose lives are busier and more compartmentalized than in earlier times. And it is not surprising that young people are more demanding and powerful con-sumers—including in regard to their education—than they have been traditionally.

While we believe there are constant elements in effective curriculum and instruction (described in later sections of the book), we also believe effective curric-ulum must be proactively responsive to the learner and his or her world. An appre-ciation of contemporary learners, their world, and the need to maximize the capac-ity of each learner leads us to make the following conclusions about curriculum design that have guided our work:

▶ Curriculum should guide students in mastering key information, ideas, and the fundamental skills of the disciplines

▶ Curriculum should help students grapple with complex and ambiguous issues and problems

▶ Curriculum should move students from novice toward expert levels of perfor-mance in the disciplines

▶ Curriculum should provide students opportunities for original work in the disciplines

▶ Curriculum should help students encounter, accept, and ultimately embrace challenge in learning

▶ Curriculum should prepare students for a world in which knowledge expands and changes at a dizzying pace

▶ Curriculum should help students determine constants in the past and in themselves while helping them prepare for a changing world

▶ Curriculum should help students develop a sense of themselves as well as of their possibilities in the world in which they live

▶ Curriculum should be compelling and satisfying enough to encourage stu-dents to persist in developing their capacities

Changing Views of Intelligence and Giftedness

Building on the work of their predecessors, psychologists like Robert Sternberg (1988), Howard Gardner (1993), and David Feldman (1992) have made convincing cases that we should understand intelligence more broadly and flexibly than we have in the past. That is, rather than "intelligence," there are "intelligences," and they are reflected in the full range of human endeavors. If that is the case, as psy-chologists have believed and demonstrated for the better part of the 20th century, then educators are remiss to ignore development of any of those intelligences in their students. In addition, intelligence is more fluid (less fixed) than we might have once imagined. Also, environment and opportunity can affect one's intelligence capacity. Therefore, education at all levels ought to be about providing environments and opportunities designed to maximize individual capacity. Further, intelligence is conceived and expressed somewhat differently in different cultures. Therefore, educators should be aware of varied cultural conceptions and expressions of intelligence and should design learning opportunities that both honor diverse perspectives and develop multiple manifestations of intelligence. Finally, as with other aspects of human growth, intelligence is developmental, and its development differs among individuals. Therefore, educators should be prepared for variability in the development of intelligence in individuals and ready to support a range of developmental stages and needs in a single learning environment.

Implications for educators are clear. Advanced levels of intelligence exist in a full range of human endeavors. Educators of the gifted are remiss if we overlook or undervalue development of potential in any of the intelligences. Even though analytical intelligence (Sternberg, 1988) or logical-mathematical and verbal-linguistic intelligences (Gardner, 1993) are brokers of opportunity in our society, human progress can be charted in all intelligence areas. Narrow views of intelligence limit our growth as individuals and as a whole. Further, restricted and rigid views of intelligence are likely unduly restrictive to members of groups whose cultures may emphasize intelligences that are typically not addressed in schools, blinding us to some cultures' perceptions of giftedness. Finally, even in a population we identify as gifted, intellectual development will vary, with some learners developing more rapidly or more slowly, with more or less scaffolding and support, and in a greater or lesser number of domains. If this is the case, it is not viable to think about a single curriculum or even a single approach to curriculum for learners with high potential. Rather, we must conceive curriculum that is ready to nurture incipient talent as well as precocity—within and among learners.

These beliefs about human intelligence lead us to make at least four key conclusions regarding curriculum design that have guided our work in developing the Parallel Curriculum Model presented in this book. First, because intelligence can be affected by environment and opportunity, curriculum for all learners should be rich in opportunity for learners to explore and expand a wide range of intelligences and abilities. Second, curriculum should be designed in ways that both identify and develop high capacity in the widest feasible range of intelligences. Third, curriculum should be flexible enough to address both variability in manifestations of high ability and variability in how talent develops over time in a broad range of learners and talent areas. Fourth, curriculum should plan for development of intelligences in ways that are valid for an intelligence area and domains in which it is expressed.

The Need to Explore Similarities and Differences in Curriculum for All Learners and for Gifted Learners

In the past, gifted education (at least in rhetoric) has taken a more constructivist approach to curriculum and instruction for gifted learners than has general education, which predicated curriculum largely on a behaviorist view. Based on profiles of high-ability learners and a sense of what it meant to be responsive to those profiles, the field of gifted education advocated curriculum rooted in discovery, manipulation of ideas, integration of subjects via exploration of common themes, a product orientation, and so on. In general education, careful presentation of material for practice and replication by students was the order of the day.

More recently, however, educators have begun to advocate constructivist, meaning-making, student-centered approaches to curriculum and instruction for all learners. While this evolution in thinking is certainly positive, it presents to the field of gifted education the challenge of clearly articulating both what we believe to be attributes of good curriculum and instruction for all learners and what we believe to be attributes of curriculum and instruction especially responsive to the needs of gifted learners. It is our strong conviction that clarifying the commonalities and the distinctive characteristics will support more effective and more defensible curriculum for all learners, including those with exceptional ability.

In this regard, three additional beliefs have guided our work in developing the model presented in this book. First, good curriculum for gifted learners is rooted in good curriculum. Second, the boundaries between high-quality curriculum for all learners and high-quality curriculum for gifted learners are blurred because of developmental and experiential variance among learners. Third, an effective model for developing defensible curriculum for advanced learners should help curriculum designers focus on high-quality curriculum for all learners, as well as helping curriculum designers attend to the specific needs of students who exemplify varying degrees of advanced potential or performance.

Those of us who have spent significant portions of our careers working with students whom we identify as gifted have no doubt that our classrooms include young people whose abilities and talents are already so advanced that, given the opportunity, they would humble us with their knowledge, ideas, and products. It is a great failing of contemporary education that so few of these students are recognized and nurtured in appropriate ways. We not only *believe* these students exist and need appropriate schooling; we *know* they do!

On the other hand, we also know that our classrooms and schools contain many students who likely will never be identified as gifted, but who also possess immense potential as learners, leaders, and producers. They, too, need appropriate schooling. For these students, that means, at least in part, the opportunity to work with rich and demanding curriculum that can bring to the surface potential and promise likely otherwise to remain dormant and hidden from view. Only by ensuring that the maximum number of learners consistently experience the highest quality curriculum, as well as appropriate coaching, mentoring, and support, will these individual students, and society as a whole, benefit from their possibilities.

It is our hope that the model presented in this book points the way to more effectively educating both groups—those whose abilities are already highly advanced, and those whose abilities are advancing. Only in this way can we "lead out" the best that is in each individual entrusted to us.

A Need to Honor the Past by Building to the Future

From its earliest days, educators of the gifted have challenged the status quo of teaching and learning in an attempt to ensure appropriate learning opportunities for highly able learners. From the days of Leta Hollingworth to the National/State Leadership Training Institute on the Gifted and Talented and proceeding to current leaders, the field of gifted education has often been a catalyst, and sometimes a gadfly, for curriculum and instruction that is both sound and dynamic. It is the legacy of this field to pioneer in teaching and learning. Educators of the gifted have often exemplified what they commend to the young people they serve—learning from the past, challenging assumptions, and building toward a more thoughtful future.

In that vein, we offer three assertions. First, roots of the past will be clearly evident in curriculum models of the future. Second, curriculum models for the future will differ from the past in ways that are very clear. Third, if the model we propose here has utility in the near term, the time will come when its role will be to join the root system of the past and invite other educators to challenge its assumptions in order to once again push forward the thinking of the field.

Theoretical Underpinnings of the Model

Delineating the underpinnings for a theory of qualitatively differentiated curriculum is a challenging task. First and foremost, the theory must be able to show how curriculum for advanced students extends beyond what constitutes appropriate curriculum for all students. Next, the theory needs to take into account differences between two general types of curriculum: required or prescribed curriculum and curriculum that has its roots in the interests and learning preferences of students. Finally, a theory that supports differentiated curriculum for gifted learners should provide authors of curriculum with enough guidance to help ensure that materials, tasks, and products exemplify the principles around which the theory has been developed.

Curriculum That Respects the Unique Characteristics of the Learner

A general principle of education is that curriculum should address and thus respect individual learner characteristics. Although this principle is not unique to gifted students, this group of learners, like other groups, presents characteristics to which appropriate curriculum must attend.

In a general way, we can characterize traits of all learners into three areas: abilities, interests, and learning preferences. Although the population of all students reflects a range of abilities and potentials in varied areas, the advanced level abilities and potentials that bring students to our attention as gifted provides a rationale for adjusting the level and complexity of materials and student tasks. While all students have or can develop a broad range of interests, some who have domain-specific talents develop strong and even passionate interests and sustain these interests for extended periods of time. Additionally, in regard to learning preferences, these students may prefer less structured kinds of learning experiences and environments and may prefer to pursue learning in more inductive or investigative ways than some other students will find comfortable.

An inescapable truth is that gifted learners themselves vary. Their abilities may be strong in one area or many. Their interests may be few or many, durable or transitory. The learning preferences they exhibit will be influenced by factors such as gender, culture, and general development. Further, their capacities may be blatantly evident or camouflaged. For those reasons, it is essential to stress the fact that no single "curriculum for gifted students" can adequately address the needs of all highly able learners.

Even a curriculum that appears to adhere to principles of curriculum design for advanced learners will need to be modified for the abilities, interests, and learning preferences of individual students. Even for students whom we might elect to call gifted and who have the capacity to excel as consumers, connoisseurs, and/or producers of knowledge, that potential will develop to differing degrees, on varying timetables, calling for assorted kinds of support, and in the full range of human endeavors. Curriculum designed to be a catalyst for developing advanced capacity in young people must be flexible enough to provide them with appropriate challenge and support at all points in their evolution as learners.

An examination of some of the key underpinnings of curriculum follows. The discussion provides an overview of theories and principles of knowledge and learning that ground effective curriculum design.

Theories of Knowledge

Untold numbers of books have been written about theories of knowledge, and various authors have posed several organizational systems for classifying knowledge and studying it in a systematic manner. Any one of these organizational systems might serve as a rationale underlying a particular approach to curriculum development. A theory of knowledge that is highly effective in providing a rationale for curriculum development for gifted learners would need to focus on both levels of knowledge and functions of knowledge in any given field.

Levels of Knowing

The American psychologist and philosopher, William James (1885) first suggested a theory of knowledge based on three levels of knowing. These levels are knowledge-of, knowledge-about (also referred to as knowledge-that), and knowledge-how. Before describing these levels, it must be pointed out that each of the three levels—and especially the second and third levels—exists on a continuum from the simple to the complex. It remains the responsibility of the curriculum developer to determine the degree of complexity within each level that might be appropriate for a given age group, readiness level, and individual. In the final analysis, it is the curriculum developer's understanding of the content field and instructional techniques, plus an understanding of human development, that will guide effective decision making with regard to the level of knowledge that might serve as appropriate content for a particular unit to be taught to a particular group and to individuals within that group.

Knowledge-of. This level of knowledge represents entry or awareness level knowing. It involves remembering, recalling, and recognizing but does not ordinarily include more complex sorts of thinking. Because there is certain information that students must simply "know" about any area of study, most curriculum development begins with the knowledge-of level. It is likely that most teachers feel comfortable with the facts and basic data of a topic, although determining which information is essential and which is less so is not always easy. At any rate, unless curriculum planning moves quickly beyond this lower level of knowing, students are unlikely to become engaged in the topic or to find what they learn to be useful or memorable.

Knowledge-about. Knowledge-about represents a more advanced level of understanding than merely remembering or recalling information that has been learned. While it builds upon remembering or recalling, it also includes more advanced levels of knowing, such as distinguishing, translating, interpreting, and being able to explain a given fact, concept, theory, or principle. Being able to explain something might also involve the ability to demonstrate it. At this level, basic "knowing" evolves into "understanding" and is much more durable, relevant, and powerful for the learner than is accumulation of information alone.

It is at the knowledge-about level that learners must begin to deal with the key concepts, principles, and skills of a discipline. In order to move from acquaintance with facts to mental facility and practical comfort in a field, students will need to *understand* the key concepts that organize the discipline, essential principles that govern the concepts, and ways in which professionals in the field do their work.

Many of us as teachers are uncertain of the key concepts, principles, and skills of the disciplines we teach. It is of great importance to student understanding, however, that we invest the time needed to discover these conceptual frameworks and that we learn to build curriculum solidly on those frameworks. Among sources to help teachers develop comfort with conceptual underpinnings of the various disciplines are college textbooks, educational standards documents developed by national professional groups, and books on conceptual teaching such *as Concept-Based Curriculum and Instruction: Teaching Beyond the Facts* (1998) by H. Lynn Erickson.

Knowledge-how. This level of knowing ultimately enables persons to make new contributions to their respective fields of study. It deals mainly with the *application* of methodology to generate new knowledge. At this level, the student is transformed from the role of lesson-learner or consumer of knowledge to the role of producer of knowledge. Once again, this level of knowing builds on knowledge-of and

knowledge-about a subject. Obviously, the more advanced knowledge-about information an individual commands the more likely he or she is to be able to generate
new ideas, procedures, and solutions to problems. Scholars generally view knowledge-how as the highest level of involvement in a field. It represents the kind of
work that is pursued by researchers, writers, and artists who are making new contributions to the sciences, humanities, and the arts.

While the majority of young learners do not reshape fields of human endeavor,
they can, nonetheless, begin to work like professionals in a field. This type of
authentic work is a part of the progression from novice to expert and should be central in curriculum design. Over time, teachers can become comfortable answering
the question "How do I create tasks that guide students in learning to work like a
historian (or artist, or mathematician, etc.)?"

Levels of Involvement

The theory of knowledge represented by James's three levels of knowing is similar to Alfred North Whitehead's (1929) concepts of romance, technical proficiency,
and generalization, which speak to levels of involvement with a subject or field.
According to Whitehead, we first develop an interest in or romance with a particular field. Many learners want to know about a variety of topics and fields as they
progress in their education (interest), and may, for a time, immerse themselves in
one or more of those areas (romance).

Some people follow up this romance by pursuing a field or career to the point of
becoming a proficient practitioner in the field. Most professionals within a field
reach their maximum involvement at this level.

However, there are some persons who go on to the generalization level, adding
new information and contributing new knowledge to the field they have chosen.
This third level is, in many respects, consistent with one of the major goals of special programming for gifted and talented learners. A major premise underlying
gifted education is that special programs or learning opportunities should contribute to the development of persons who may become the inventors, leaders, and creative producers of the next generation.

A theory of curriculum with the goal of developing high potential should place
a premium on the pursuit of authentic knowledge (that which is acknowledged and
used by experts in a discipline), and the application of authentic methodology to
problem areas within various content domains. In other words, such a curriculum
should focus on the kinds of complex structures, concepts, principles, and research
methods that characterize the firsthand inquirer. Instructional techniques should
emphasize high-level thinking skills, less structured teaching strategies, and a concern for controversial issues, values, and beliefs.

Curriculum to develop high potential should also reflect content selection and
procedures that will help maximize the transfer of knowledge, understanding, and
skill. The accelerated rate at which knowledge is currently expanding accentuates
the value of this principle. Futurists tell us that the amount of accumulated knowledge is expanding in geometric proportions, with hundreds, or sometimes thou-

sands, of new scientific and literary pieces published each day. These figures might suggest a seductive and potentially dangerous approach when it comes to curriculum designed to develop high ability. The fact that many bright students can learn more material faster lures us to a quantitative (more is better) approach to curriculum design. In fact, a more selective approach to curriculum design is called for to foster both understanding and transfer for such students.

Selected Concepts From Theories of Curriculum and Instruction

An important part of a rationale underlying the development of curriculum to develop high potential builds on the work of several persons who have made important contributions to general curricular and instructional theory. These include David Ausubel (1968), Albert Bandura (1977), Jerome Bruner (1960, 1966), Robert Gagné and Leslie Briggs (1979), Philip Phenix (1964), Hilda Taba (1962), and Benjamin Bloom and his colleagues (Bloom, Englehart, Furst, Hill, & Krathwohl, 1956). The work of these theorists is reflected in a blended way in most of the material that follows.

The Foundations of Enduring Knowledge

All of the disciplines and fields of human understanding rest on a foundation of enduring knowledge. This foundation consists of the key concepts, basic principles, and methodologies of a field. This foundation is the "engine" that drives the field forward to the acquisition of new knowledge and understanding. Although concepts, principles, and methods do change slowly over extended periods of time, they represent the enduring knowledge of mankind, as opposed to transitory topics or information. Concepts, principles, and methods should be viewed as tools that help the learner understand any and all selected topics of a content field. Thus, for example, understanding the concept of reliability is central to the study of psychological testing, and therefore may be considered an example of an enduring element of that field. The specific reliability of any given test, however, is more timely or transitory in nature because it changes over time (e.g., from test to test and from population to population). It is that kind of information that we can always "look up" and grasp because we have a basic comprehension of the more enduring concept of reliability. Further, knowledge of the structure of the field of psychometrics allows us to know how reliability is organized and stored so we can retrieve it.

Representative Topics

One of the biggest issues in curriculum theory is determining what should be taught—precisely what knowledge and understanding will best represent the essential structure of the discipline. In any given field, there is an almost endless amount of information, and it becomes the task of the curriculum developer to determine what knowledge is of most worth.

Philip Phenix (1964) suggests the study of what he calls representative topics. These topics are drawn from the content of a field and are highly representative of numerous other similar topics that can be found in the field. For example, a study of the cell as a system with interdependent parts paves the way for understanding systems of the body, the body as a system, ecosystems, and so on. This is the case because studying the cell as a system provides learners with knowledge, concepts, principles, and tools to facilitate understanding in a vast number of related topics. A teacher or curriculum developer realizes that students cannot meaningfully study all possible information and topics in a domain. Thus it becomes critical to select study topics that exemplify other topics in the domain, allowing for more effective and efficient exploration of and mastery in the domain. That is, we need to select topics for study that effectively illustrate the essential concepts and principles governing a field of knowledge, and the methodologies used to acquire knowledge in that field.

Process Development

While advanced level, in-depth coverage of representative topics is important in curriculum designed to develop high potential, an equally critical feature is development of process skills. Process skills allow students to do something with what they know—beyond storing and retrieving information. Process objectives include a wide array of skills including, but certainly not limited to, comprehension, application, analysis, synthesis, evaluation, inducing, deducing, seeking varied perspectives, empathy, being aware of and regulating one's own thinking, generating and maintaining standards of quality in work and thought, and persistence (Bloom et al., 1956; Costa & Kallick, 2000; Marzano, 1992; Wiggins & McTighe, 1998).

Because of the greater transferability of the process objectives than knowledge alone, it is important to use representative topics as vehicles to develop both core knowledge and fundamental process skills. Process development is discussed further in Chapter 2.

Focus on Methodology

Because of the goal of helping learners become producers of knowledge, a theory of curriculum design for developing high potential should place emphasis on appropriate use of methodology within content fields. Each content field is defined, in part, by the methods and techniques it uses to add new knowledge to the domain. Most knowledge experts consider the appropriate use of methodology to be the highest level of competence in a content field. Indeed, this is the level at which research scientists, composers, authors, and academicians typically operate as they make new contributions to their fields.

Although this level undoubtedly requires advanced understanding of a field, and sometimes requires use of sophisticated equipment, young students can successfully learn and apply some of the entry-level methodologies associated with most fields of knowledge (Bruner, 1960). Engagement with methodology should also help high potential learners develop a positive attitude toward the creative challenges of a domain. Further, focus on acquisition and application of methodology also necessitates more active learning and a hands-on involvement with a content field—generally considered to be among the hallmarks of effective instruction.

A Product Orientation

We believe that a theory of curriculum to develop high potential should consider goals or outcomes in terms of both concrete and abstract products. These two kinds of products generally work in harmony with one another and are separated here for discussion purposes only.

The concrete products consist of the acquisition of specific segments of knowledge, understanding, process, and methodological skills, plus a broad range of things actually produced by students (e.g., reports, research projects, stories, timelines, dances, musical compositions, and community service activities). It is important to emphasize that these concrete products are not intended to be ends in themselves. Rather, they are viewed as vehicles through which the various abstract products can be developed and applied.

Abstract products consist of more enduring and transferable outcomes of learning. Examples of abstract products are frameworks of knowledge, ideas, problem-solving strategies, attitudes, beliefs and values, and personal and social development. Abstract products also include aesthetic awareness and appreciation, the development of self-efficacy, and continuous movement toward self-actualization. In most cases, achieving the most mature level of abstract products takes many years. However, each curricular experience should make a contribution to one or a combination of these more enduring goals of curriculum. Taken collectively, the concrete and abstract products represent the overall goals of a theory of curriculum to develop high potential.

Effective Curriculum for All Learners

Leaders in education have distilled the field's heritage from research and experience to delineate the best of what we currently know about curriculum and instruction (e.g., Brandt, 1998; Costa & Kallick, 2000; National Research Council, 1999; Schlechty, 1997; Wiggins & McTighe, 1998). These leaders suggest that high-quality curriculum and instruction for all learners:

▶ Has a clear focus on the essential facts, understandings, and skills that professionals in that discipline value most

▶ Provides opportunities for students to develop in-depth understanding

▶ Is organized to ensure that all student tasks are aligned with the goals of in-depth understanding

▶ Is coherent (organized, unified, sensible) to the student

▶ Is mentally and affectively engaging to the learner

▶ Recognizes and supports the need of each learner to make sense of ideas and information, reconstructing older understandings with new ones

▶ Is joyful—or at least satisfying

▶ Provides choices for the learner

▶ Allows meaningful collaboration

▶ Is focused on products (something students make or do) that matter to students

▶ Connects with students' lives and worlds

▶ Is fresh and surprising

▶ Seems real, purposeful, useful to students

▶ Is rich

▶ Deals with profound ideas

▶ Calls on students to use what they learn in interesting and important ways

▶ Aids students in developing a fruitful consciousness of their thinking

▶ Helps learners monitor and adapt their ways of working to ensure competent approaches to problem solving

▶ Involves students in setting goals for their learning and assessing their progress toward those goals

▶ Stretches the student

Ascending Intellectual Demand in the Parallel Curriculum Model

While the vast majority of learners would benefit from curriculum and instruction characterized by the features noted above, it is also the case that learners vary in their cognitive development as well as in interests and preferred learning modes. There is a substantial body of theory and research to suggest that a student will learn best when curriculum and instruction are congruent with that learner's particular needs. Thus, while most, if not all, learners share a common need for high-level, meaning-focused curriculum and instruction, there will be variance in how students should encounter and interact with the curriculum.

It seems clear from the work of Vygotsky (e.g., 1962, 1978) that individuals learn when a teacher presents tasks to the student at a level of difficulty somewhat beyond the learner's capacity to complete the task independently. When a teacher presents tasks in the student's "zone of proximal development" and then scaffolds, coaches, or supports the student in successfully completing the tasks, the student's independence zone ultimately expands, necessitating new tasks at a greater level of demand. For advanced learners in a given area, the implication is that tasks will, of necessity, need to be more advanced than would be appropriate for students who are less advanced in their capacities at that time.

More recently, brain research (e.g., Howard, 1994; Jensen, 1998) suggests that students learn best when they are neither overchallenged nor underchallenged but, rather, when tasks are moderately challenging for the individual. When tasks are too difficult for a child, frustration results. When they are too easy, stagnation and apathy result.

In addition, there is ample evidence that intrinsic motivation and learning are improved by attending to a student's interests (e.g., Amabile, 1983; Collins & Amabile, 1999; Csikszentmihalyi, Rathunde, & Whalen, 1993). Studies also provide evidence that matching instruction to a student's preferred mode of learning, based on the student's style of learning, gender, culture, and intelligence preferences, enhances learning (e.g., Delpit, 1995; Dunn & Griggs, 1995; Grigorenko & Sternberg, 1997; Sullivan, 1993).

Thus the underpinnings of our current knowledge of teaching and learning suggest a need to ensure a basic curriculum for all learners focused on making sense of and applying the seminal ideas and skills of the disciplines—but adapted to address learner variability evident in the student population. For all learners, this means curriculum and instruction must be suited for the current readiness level of the learner, tap into and/or develop the student interests, and be offered in a mode of learning effective for the individual.

As students become more advanced in their knowledge, understanding, and skill in a domain, the challenge level of materials and tasks will necessitate escalation. In this book, we call that escalating match between the learner and curriculum "ascending intellectual demand."

Simply put, this model suggests that most, if not all, learners should work consistently with concept-focused curriculum, tasks that call for high level thought, and products that ask students to extend and use what they have learned in meaningful ways. As a student becomes more advanced, task "demand" will need to escalate to ensure ongoing challenge for that learner and to ensure continual progress toward expertise. This concept of "ascending intellectual demand" will be discussed and illustrated at many other points in the book.

One premise of the Parallel Curriculum Model is that students of a given age will exhibit development along a continuum of knowledge and skill in a given area, with some students far advanced beyond grade or age expectations, some moderately or slightly advanced, some in the general range of grade/age expectations, and some slightly, moderately, or acutely behind those expectations. A second premise of the model is that by offering each learner the richest possible curriculum and instruction at a level of demand appropriate for the learner, linked to learner interest and mode of learning, and escalating as the learner develops, we would assist each learner in developing his or her capacity to the maximum.

Student Affect and the Parallel Curriculum Model

In discussing curriculum design, it is easy to focus solely on student cognition or thought without acknowledging the integral role of student affect or feeling. Although it is beyond the scope of this book to explore in depth the profound role of affect in both student learning and development, it is also not wise to omit all reference to the very central role of affect in what and how students learn.

A lesson plan or unit design may look elegant on paper but in practice be of little worth if it fails to attend to the affective needs of the learners it is designed to reach. It is our belief that an effective teacher persistently develops a learning environment, designs curriculum, and uses instructional approaches with the goal of fostering both cognitive and affective growth in learners. Such teachers are:

▶ Reflective about the needs of each student and the class as a whole, continually seeking a deeper understanding of both individuals and the group

▶ Responsive in using what they learn about students to craft curriculum and instruction that are better matched to learner needs

▶ Respectful of students' common and distinct cognitive, physical, social, and emotional profiles

Teachers who are students of their students, as well as of their content, seek to ensure that all learners' classroom experiences lead to:

▶ Security, or the students' sense that the classroom is a safe place to be who they are, ask questions that matter to them, express their ideas, and make the errors that are an inevitable part of learning and growing

▶ Affirmation, or the students' sense that each of them is actively supported by the teacher and their peers in the classroom

▶ Validation, or the students' belief that each of them has a valuable and valued role in the classroom

▶ Affiliation, or the students' sense that each of them belongs to and fits in with the group

▶ Affinity, or each student's sense of kinship and common ground with the group (Mahoney, 1998)

Teachers who work actively to develop learning environments, curriculum, and instruction that honor the complete learner understand the pivotal role of each learner in achieving the goals of security, affirmation, validation, affiliation, and affinity. Thus these teachers continually guide their students to become more:

▶ Respectful of their own contributions, needs, ideas, and products as well as of the contributions, needs, ideas, and products of others

▶ Responsive in their work and relationships with others, as well as responsive to their own need for challenge and quality

▶ Reflective about what they learn, how their learning affects who they are, what they believe, what they can do, and how their attitudes and behaviors affect the development and options of other people

Teachers who continually strive to be reflective, respectful, and responsive, who support their students in developing those same traits, and who constantly assess the impact of environment, curriculum, and instruction on the security, affirmation, validation, affiliation, and affinity of each learner are far more likely to make a major, positive impact on the learning and lives of their students than are teachers who undervalue any of these factors.

A particular challenge for teachers in contemporary classrooms is ensuring that students from all cultures feel security, affirmation, validation, affiliation, and affinity in classrooms. Because so many teachers represent the majority culture in this country, and an increasing number of students represent a broad array of minority cultures, the challenge is both considerable and critical that teachers learn about and appreciate the cultures of their students; make classrooms flexible enough to be comfortable to a variety of learning modes; ensure that language does not construct insurmountable barriers to learning; consistently include in the curriculum materials, people, and perspectives that represent a broad range of cultures; and help students learn to value the contributions of multiple cultures to all of the disciplines.

Complex as it is to know, appreciate, and respond to all learners, doing so is an imperative in teaching. In no other way can we make learning personal and relevant to each student we teach. It is simply impossible to overstate the interconnectedness between cognition and affect in the classroom.

2

An Overview
of the Parallel
Curriculum Model

The model for developing curriculum presented in this book is called the Parallel Curriculum Model. It proposes the possibility of developing appropriately challenging curriculum using one, two, three, or four "parallel" ways of thinking about course content (Figure 2.1). The term "parallel" indicates several formats through which educators can approach curriculum design in the same subject or discipline. "Parallel" should not be taken to mean that the formats or approaches must remain separate and distinct in planning or in classroom use.

All curriculum takes its basic definition and purpose from what the Parallel Curriculum Model calls "The Core Curriculum" because this parallel reflects the essential nature of a discipline as experts in that discipline conceive and practice the discipline. A second parallel proposed by the Model is called "The Curriculum of Connections" and expands on the Core Curriculum by guiding students to make connections within or across disciplines, across times, across cultures or places, or in some combination of those elements. A third parallel in the Model is the "Curriculum of Practice," which guides learners in understanding and applying the facts, concepts, principles, and methodologies of the discipline in ways that encourage student growth toward expertise in the discipline. The fourth and final parallel proposed by the Model is "The Curriculum of Identity." Curriculum developed according to this parallel guides students in coming to understand their own strengths, preferences, values, and commitment by reflecting on their own development through the lens of contributors and professionals in a field of study. The Parallel Curriculum Model assumes that teachers may create appropriately challenging curriculum by using any one parallel (at appropriate levels of intellectual demand) or a combination of the parallels (at appropriate levels of intellectual demand) as a framework for thinking about and planning curriculum.

Figure 2.1. The Parallel Curriculum: A Model for Curriculum Planning

The Core or Basic Curriculum	The Curriculum of Connections	The Curriculum of Practice	The Curriculum of Identity
The Core Curriculum is the foundational curriculum that establishes a rich framework of knowledge, understanding, and skills most relevant to the discipline. It is inclusive of and extends state and district expectations. It is the starting point or root system for all of the parallels in this model.	This curriculum is derived from and extends the Core Curriculum. It is designed to help students encounter and interact with the key concepts, principles, and skills in a variety of settings, times, and circumstances.	This curriculum is derived from and extends the Core Curriculum. Its purpose is to help students function with increasing skill and confidence in a discipline as professionals would function. It exists for the purpose of promoting students' expertise as practitioners of the discipline.	This curriculum is derived from and extends the Core Curriculum. It is designed to help students see themselves in relation to the discipline both now and with possibilities for the future; understand the discipline more fully by connecting it with their lives and experiences; increase awareness of their preferences, strengths, interests, and need for growth; and think about themselves as stewards of the discipline who may contribute to it and/or through it. The Curriculum of Identity uses curriculum as a catalyst for self-definition and self-understanding, with the belief that by looking outward to the discipline, students can find a means of looking inward.
The Core or Basic Curriculum: • Is built on key facts, concepts, principles, and skills essential to discipline • Is coherent in its organization • Is purposefully focused and organized to achieve essential outcomes • Promotes understanding rather than rote learning • Is taught in a meaningful context • Causes students to grapple with ideas and questions, using both critical and creative thinking • Is mentally and affectively engaging and satisfying to learners • Results in evidence of worthwhile student production	The Curriculum of Connections is designed to help students think about and apply key concepts, principles, and skills: • In a range of instances throughout the discipline • Across disciplines • Across time and time periods • Across locations • Across cultures • Across times, locations, and cultures • Through varied perspectives • As impacted by various conditions (social, economic, technological, political, etc.) • Through the eyes of various people who affected and are affected by the ideas • By examining links between concepts and development of the disciplines	The Curriculum of Practice asks students to: • Understand the nature of the discipline in a real world application manner • Define and assume a role as a means of studying the discipline • Understand the impact of this discipline on other disciplines and other disciplines on this discipline • Become a disciplinary problem solver rather than being a problem solver using the subject matter of the discipline • Understand and use the discipline as a means of looking at and making sense of the world • Develop a means of escaping the rut of certainty about knowledge • Comprehend the daily lives of workers or professionals in the discipline: working conditions, hierarchical structures, fiscal aspects of the work, peer or collegial dynamics • Define and understand the implications of internal and external politics that impact the discipline • Value and engage in the intellectual struggle of the discipline • Function as a producer in the discipline • Function as a scholar in the discipline	The Curriculum of Identity asks students to: • Reflect on their skills and interests as they relate to the discipline • Understand ways in which their interests might be useful to the discipline and ways in which the discipline might serve as a means for helping them develop their skills and interests • Develop awareness of their modes of working as they relate to the modes of operation characteristic of the discipline • Reflect on the impact of the discipline in the world, and self in the discipline • Think about the impact of the discipline on the lives of others in the wider world • Take intellectual samplings of the discipline for the purpose of experiencing self in relation to the discipline • Examine the ethics and philosophy characteristic of the discipline and their implications • Project themselves into the discipline • Develop self in the context of the discipline and through interaction with the subject matter • Develop a sense of both pride and humility related to both self and the discipline

A Look at the Four Curriculum Parallels

Before taking a look at the four approaches to curriculum that the Parallel Curriculum Model proposes, it is important to specify three assumptions of the model.

▶ *There is no such thing as "the" gifted learner.* Some young people whom we might call gifted will manifest talents and abilities. Other young people of similar promise may have latent talents and abilities. Some may have strengths in multiple areas. Others will have a single area of strength. Some highly able young people will be afire with motivation to learn. Others will underachieve. Further, the students will differ in the degree to which they have realized their abilities, readiness for school tasks, personal interests, manners of learning, and attitudes about school. Some gifted learners will achieve in spite of us, some because of us, and others will not achieve because we do not reach them. Some students who are not identified as gifted at a given point in school will later encounter opportunity, support, passion for learning, or some other catalyst for growth that propels them to become remarkable contributors to society. We are wise, therefore, to look at curriculum that taps the potential of many learners.

▶ *Curriculum and instruction for gifted learners must be flexible enough to address the broad array of needs represented in that population.* There can be no "standard" curriculum that will develop the possibilities in the very non-standard population of learners. While there are principles that guide effective curriculum and instruction for all learners, and principles that guide effective curriculum and instruction for learners whose giftedness is evident, there is no single curricular or instructional approach that will be adequate for all high potential learners. Any model of curriculum development that seeks to serve the broad population in which high potential learners exist will have to promote flexibility to match curriculum to learner.

▶ *Teachers who are effective in developing high potential will be curriculum decision makers.* Such teachers will, of necessity, develop comfort and competence in their subject areas and have a broad understanding of high-quality curriculum. Further, they will develop expertise in applying principles of high-quality curriculum and instruction in ways that develop the unique capacities and interests of the range of advanced learners.

With these underlying beliefs, the model proposed here is heuristic rather than algorithmic. That is, it attempts to provide useful guidelines for thinking about what and how we teach a broad range of learners who display, or might display, high potential. It does not purport to be a recipe. It cannot be prescriptive. Recall that the parallel curricula described in the Parallel Curriculum Model can be used in any order. In addition, it is important to recall that the parallels in the Parallel Curriculum Model can be used singly or in combination. Drawing on the flexibility of the model in response to the current cognitive and affective status of a given learner allows curriculum designers to generate learning experiences that are genuinely responsive to learner readiness and interest.

We invite teachers and other educators to think about the Parallel Curriculum Model, try it out, critique it—and ultimately, add to it and reshape it. This is the only approach to teaching that can both identify and develop the wide-ranging capacities of learners and of the educators who work with them. We begin with an introduction to the Model's four parallels. Later chapters will provide specific guidance in applying the parallels to curriculum design.

The Core Curriculum

The Nature of the Effective Core Curriculum

The Core Curriculum is the starting point for all effective curricula. The Core Curriculum is defined by the nature of a given discipline. The purpose of the Core Curriculum is to ensure that students develop a framework of knowledge, understanding, and skills that prepare the students for a journey toward expertise in a subject area or discipline. National, state, and/or district learning goals for students should be reflected in the Core Curriculum. Figure 2.2 capsules the intent of the Core Curriculum Parallel.

Among the driving questions posed by the Core Curriculum are the following:

▷ What does this information mean?

▷ Why does this information matter?

▷ How is the information organized to help people use it better?

▷ How do these ideas make sense?

▷ What are they for?

▷ How does this thing work?

▷ How can I use these ideas and skills?

The Core Curriculum:

▶ Stems from the key facts, concepts, principles, and skills essential to a discipline and reflects what experts in the discipline find most important

Figure 2.2. The Intent of the Core Curriculum Parallel

The Core or Basic Curriculum

The Core Curriculum is the foundational curriculum that should establish a rich framework of knowledge, understanding, and skills most relevant to the discipline. It is inclusive of and extends state and district expectations. It is the starting point or root system for the parallel curricula.

The Core or Basic Curriculum:

- Is built on key facts, concepts, principles, and skills essential to the discipline
- Is coherent in its organization
- Is purposefully focused and organized to achieve essential outcomes
- Promotes understanding rather than rote learning
- Is taught in a meaningful context
- Causes students to grapple with ideas and questions, using both critical and creative thinking
- Is mentally and affectively engaging and satisfying to learners
- Results in evidence of worthwhile student production

▶ Is coherent in its organization so that it helps students build knowledge, understanding, and skills systematically and organize what they learn in ways that develop students' abilities to remember, make meaning, and use what they know in unfamiliar situations

Our best understanding of teaching and learning suggests that virtually all students should work with a core curriculum characterized by this sort of quality and purpose. However, as students demonstrate advanced or advancing talent, ability, and/or interests in particular facets of the Core Curriculum, those students will need to work at escalating levels of intellectual demand in order to experience challenge and to have the opportunity to develop their capacities.

Ascending Intellectual Demand and the Core Curriculum

"Ascending intellectual demand" is always relative to the need of a particular learner. In relation to the core curriculum, ascending intellectual demand can be achieved in many ways, among them the following:

▶ Using more advanced reading, resources, and research materials

▶ Adjusting the pace of teaching and learning

▶ Working at greater levels of depth, breadth, complexity, and/or abstractness

▶ Applying ideas and skills to contexts quite unfamiliar and dissimilar from those applications explored in class

▶ Designing tasks that are more open-ended or ambiguous in nature and/or that call on students to exercise greater levels of independence in thought and scholarly behavior as learners and producers

▶ Developing rubrics for tasks and/or products that articulate levels of quality that include expert-level indicators

▶ Encouraging collaborations between students and adult experts in an area of shared interest

▶ Designing work that requires continuing student reflection on the significance of ideas and information, and causes students to generate new and useful ways to represent ideas and information

Close-Ups of the Core Curriculum

Elementary

Ms. Lance wants to organize and extend expectations for teaching and learning the district's standards. For example, science standards direct that students study living things in their environment. She and her students use the concepts of change and interaction to further organize, explain, clarify, and exemplify the standard. Two of the key principles she introduces are "Change is a result of interactions" and "Interactions can result in change." Her students will take part in an ongoing "mental treasure hunt" to look for evidence within their study of living things that support these principles. The teacher will use a large wall chart to display student examples and evidence from their study and research. As the year goes on, Ms. Lance will use a second chart to record examples and evidence of the same principles at work in other science topics the students study. The framework will also be useful to guide the work of students who do extended readings in science on topics in which they have particular interest or skill.

Secondary

Students in Mr. Rose's high school biology class explore biology through a conceptual framework. They are looking at ways in which the four key scientific processes of observation, classification, verification, and explanation are used in the study of physical science, biochemistry, cells, tissues, individuals, populations, and ecosystems. Individually and as a class, students look for similarities and differences in uses of the four processes in the seven "segments" of biology.

In addition to this comparative analysis, Mr. Rose introduced the concepts of "change" and "interaction" and the principles "Change is a result of interactions" and "Interactions result in change." Students are expected to extend their analysis of the seven segments of biology by using information they learn to prove or exemplify these two principles. A further challenge to the students is that they synthesize their learning over the course of the year to effectively debate the inevitability of change.

The Curriculum of Connections

The Nature of the Curriculum of Connections

This parallel of the Model is designed to help students discover and learn from the interconnectedness of knowledge. The Curriculum of Connections builds directly on the Core Curriculum and thus emphasizes the key facts, concepts, principles, and skills of a discipline. It extends the Core Curriculum, however, by inviting students to move their growing understandings and skills into arenas not necessarily directly addressed by the Core Curriculum (see Figure 2.3).

The Curriculum of Connections may ask students to see how particular concepts, principles, and/or skills are manifest in other facets of a discipline, across disciplines, in other times or time periods, in other places, or in some combination of those possibilities. It may also ask students to look at how the concepts, ideas, or skills influenced and are influenced by various people, varying perspectives, and/or different conditions (such as economic, political, social, or technological circumstances).

Asking students to explore and describe connections within a discipline typically aids them in building depth of knowledge about a discipline (such as social studies) or among its subdisciplines (such as anthropology, sociology, or political science). Asking students to make connections across disciplines (such as art, social studies, literature, and history) typically aids them in building breadth of knowledge.

Further, it is useful to recall that essential concepts rooted in the Core Curriculum can guide both intra- and interdisciplinary studies. For example, looking at the concept of "obsolescence" in subsets of social studies such as economics, political science, and archaeology should yield a deeper understanding within a discipline. Looking at the concept of "obsolescence" across architecture, literature, and ecology should yield a broader understanding of the concept. In addition, skills can guide explorations in the Curriculum of Connections. For instance, the skill of "hypothesizing" takes on varied nuances of meaning in different subjects, while also helping students generalize about the skill.

Among the driving questions of the Curriculum of Connections are the following:

> ▷ How do the ideas and skills I have learned work in other contexts?
>
> ▷ In what other contexts can I use what I have learned?
>
> ▷ How does looking at one thing help me understand another?
>
> ▷ How do different settings cause me to change or reinforce my earlier understandings?
>
> ▷ How do I adjust my way of thinking and working when I encounter new contexts?
>
> ▷ How do I know if my adjustments are effective?
>
> ▷ Why do different people have different perspectives on the same issue?
>
> ▷ How are perspectives shaped by events and circumstances?
>
> ▷ In what ways is it beneficial for me to examine varied perspectives on a problem or issue?
>
> ▷ How do I assess the relative strengths and weaknesses of differing viewpoints?

Among its goals, the Curriculum of Connections helps students:

▶ Discover key ideas in multiple contexts and examine their similarities and differences as a result of variance in context

▶ Apply skills in varied contexts, becoming familiar with both clear and subtle differences in the applications that allow the learner to modify his or her approaches in productive ways

▶ Use ideas and information from one context to ask more fruitful questions about other contexts

▶ Use ideas and information from multiple contexts to generate new hypotheses or theories

▶ Make analogies or other comparisons between and among contexts to extend understandings

▶ Develop ways to see unfamiliar things in familiar ways

▶ Develop an awareness of and appreciation for multiple perspectives on issues and problems

▶ Evaluate the relative strengths and weaknesses of various approaches to problems and issues taken by groups and individuals with varying perspectives

▶ Understand the role of individuals in the evolution of the disciplines and of the issues embedded in the disciplines

Figure 2.3. The Intent of the Curriculum of Connections Parallel

The Curriculum of Connections

The Curriculum of Connections is derived from and extends the Core Curriculum. It is designed to help students encounter and interact with the key concepts, principles, and skills in a variety of settings, times, and circumstances:

The Curriculum of Connections is designed to help students think about and apply key concepts, principles, and skills:

- In a range of instances throughout the discipline
- Across disciplines
- Across time and time periods
- Across locations
- Across cultures
- Across times, locations, and cultures
- Through varied perspectives
- As impacted by various conditions (social, economic, technological, political, etc.)
- Through the eyes of various people who affected the ideas
- By examining links between concepts and development of the disciplines

Ascending Intellectual Demand and the Curriculum of Connections

As is the case with the Core Curriculum, we would assume that the vast majority of students should be guided in making connections in learning across times, places, subjects, perspectives, and so on. Thus it is not the idea of curricular connections that is uniquely appropriate for advanced learners but, rather, matching the degree of intellectual demand made by materials, tasks, and products to the advanced level of the learner. Here again, it is necessary to recognize that "gifted learners" range through a broad spectrum of intellectual demand, based on factors such as degree of aptitude, depth of interest, prior experience, affective state, and so on.

Most of the more generic routes suggested for creating ascending intellectual demand in the Core Curriculum can also be used to develop ascending intellectual demand in the Curriculum of Connections. In addition, more specific approaches such as the following are useful in increasing the "degree of challenge" of tasks in the Curriculum of Connections because of their alignment with the goals of this parallel.

▶ Applying understandings or skills in contexts that are markedly unfamiliar

▶ Generating defensible criteria against which students then weigh diverse perspectives on a problem or issue

▶ Developing solutions, proposals, or approaches that effectively bridge differences in perspective and still effectively address the problem

▶ Making proposals or predictions for future directions based on student-abstracted patterns from the past in a particular domain

▶ Searching for legitimate and useful connections among seemingly disparate elements (e.g., music and medicine, or law and geography)

▶ Looking for patterns of interaction among multiple areas of connection (e.g., ways in which geography, economics, politics, and technology tend to affect one another)

▶ Looking at broad swaths of the world through a perspective quite unlike the student's own (e.g., how an age mate from a culture and economy very unlike the student's would react to the student's house, slang, religion, clothing, use of time, music, interactions with adults, plans for the future, and so on)

▶ Seeking out and evaluating unstated assumptions that are beneath the surface of decisions, approaches, and so on

▶ Developing systems for making connections, achieving balanced perspectives, addressing problems, and so on

▶ Making connections and developing approaches or systems that indicate a higher standard of quality (e.g., insightful, highly illustrative, highly synthetic, or unusually articulate or expressive) rather than a less demanding but still positive standard of quality (e.g., appropriate, accurate, feasible, informed, or defensible)

Close-Ups of the Curriculum of Connections

Middle School History

In Mrs. Bernstein's middle school history class, making connections is an ongoing emphasis for all students. Throughout the year, three concepts are used to organize the curriculum: culture, continuity, and diversity. At the end of the second quarter, all students will work with projects that ask them to use these concepts to compare their own culture with that of Russia. Many students will select or develop a family that is similar to theirs but that lives in Russia. The students will then select or develop ways to show how the geography in which the two families live is alike and different. They'll also show how music, technology, religion, and jobs have changed for their own family and for the Russian family in the past 25 years. In the end, they'll write about ways in which continuity and diversity are evident in the two cultures over the past two-and-a-half decades.

In addition to the project that helps them see how culture, diversity, and continuity work across cultures, each of the students keeps a journal that relates the three concepts of culture, continuity, and diversity to (a) the students' other classes and (b) the world around them (e.g., music, home, current events, movies, reading, etc.). Later in the year, each of the students will select a history-related topic of interest for an independent study, using that study as a way to demonstrate how the key concepts connect the topic to the whole-class study and to other phenomena the students have observed and recorded in their journals.

Fourth Grade Science

Mrs. Gomez works with a group of fourth graders identified as gifted in science. She meets with them three times a week for an hour each time in a class designed to extend their science curriculum. In a pull-out science class, she uses the Curriculum of Connections to help students link what they are learning in their regular classroom science curriculum to a broader set of understandings and applications. In their regular classroom, they have been studying the topic of weather.

Mrs. Gomez first worked with the students to help them see how weather is part of a "system." Students and teacher examined weather systems and other systems (e.g., family systems, the school as a system, and body systems) to propose statements they believed would be true about systems in general (principles). They then tested and refined the principles by looking at weather systems in their area.

Now Mrs. Gomez and her fourth graders are looking at connections between weather systems and ecosystems in several very different parts of the world (the Sahara Desert, Antarctica, and a South American rainforest). Their goal is to generate and test principles that would show the relationship between weather systems and ecosystems in general—and between weather systems and particular elements in ecosystems (animals, plants, rocks, and food chains). Students will gather data from a number of sources to test their hypotheses, work with the teacher to develop a systematic way of evaluating their data, and ultimately present a science newsletter that will be available online and in the library for other students to use as a resource in their study of weather. The newsletter will stress linkages between (a) the concept of systems as applied to weather systems and ecosystems and (b) the scientific processes of data gathering and analysis in understanding the linkages.

Mrs. Gomez took the topic-based classroom curriculum and helped her students look at it through a conceptual lens, stressing the key concept, "system." Then she used the Curriculum of Connections to help students generalize their knowledge and extend it through linkages made to unfamiliar geographic settings and two applications: weather systems and ecosystems—the former more familiar to the students and the latter less so.

The Curriculum of Practice

The Nature of the Curriculum of Practice

As is the case with the previous parallel in this curriculum model, the Curriculum of Practice derives from and extends the Core Curriculum. Its purpose is to help students extend their understandings and skills in a discipline though application of those understandings and skills in ways as much as possible like those of a professional in that discipline. This parallel of the curriculum model focuses on and guides the student in the journey from novice to expert production in a field. In the process, it asks students not only to engage in the work of professionals but also to examine the habits, affect, and ethics that permeate the work (see Figure 2.4).

Humans learn through guided experience, and thus human progress is marked by our apprenticeships to practice in all areas of importance to the human race. In fact, for many students—especially those who respond best to practical and contextual learning—doing is more compelling than attending. When the doing takes on the nature of the discipline, these students are likely to learn far more, and far more efficiently, than through more didactic approaches. The Curriculum of Practice provides an opportunity for students to learn and test the key ideas and skills of the discipline. It also exercises their facility and adaptability with those ideas and skills. The relevance, complexity, curiosity, and contributory power of knowledge are best distilled as students become practitioners in a domain.

At some points, the Curriculum of Practice might ask students to function as a scholar, developing an appreciation for the contribution of individuals to the body of knowledge, skills, tools, and methodologies of a domain. At other points, the Curriculum of Practice might ask students to function as an expert practitioner, actually using the body of knowledge, skills, tools, and methodologies of the domain. In this latter category, many students will be developmentally ready only to *simulate* the role of an expert, using knowledge, skills, tools, and so forth as a scholar to develop fuller understandings of the domain. In less frequent instances, students may actually *be* experts, using knowledge, skills, tools, and so forth as a disciplinarian to contribute to the domain. In addition, the intended flexibility of the Parallel Curriculum approach suggests that Curriculum of Practice for the same student(s) might begin with the approach of "scholar" and evolve into work of an "expert practitioner." A student's cognitive and affective development should signal which of the two approaches or combination of approaches is best suited to that particular learner at a particular time.

Figure 2.4. The Intent of the Curriculum of Practice Parallel

The Curriculum of Practice

The Curriculum of Practice is derived from and extends the Core Curriculum. Its purpose is to help students function with increasing skill and confidence as professionals in a discipline would function. It exists for the purpose of promoting expertise as a practitioner of the discipline.

The Curriculum of Practice asks students to:

- Understand the nature of the discipline in a real world application manner
- Define and assume a role as a means of studying the discipline
- Understand the impact of this discipline on other disciplines and other disciplines on this discipline
- Become a disciplinary problem solver rather than being a problem solver using the subject matter of the discipline
- Understand and use the discipline as a means of looking and making sense of the world
- Develop a means of escaping the rut of certainty about knowledge
- Comprehend the daily lives of workers or professionals in the discipline— working conditions, hierarchical structures, fiscal aspects of the work, and peer or collegial dynamics
- Define and understand the implications of internal and external politics that impact the discipline
- Value and engage in the intellectual struggle of the discipline
- Function as a producer in the discipline
- Function as a scholar in the discipline

Among the driving questions of the Curriculum of Practice are the following:

▷ What are the theories that govern the knowledge of the discipline?

▷ How do practitioners organize their knowledge and skills in this discipline?

▷ How do the concepts and principles that form the framework of the discipline get translated into practice by those in the discipline?

▷ What are the features of routine problems in the discipline?

▷ How does the practitioner know which skills to use under given circumstances?

> ▷ What strategies does a practitioner use to solve nonroutine problems in the discipline?
>
> ▷ How does a practitioner sense whether approaches and methods are effective in a given instance?
>
> ▷ What constitutes meaningful evidence versus less significant information in this instance?
>
> ▷ On what basis does a practitioner in the discipline make educated guesses?
>
> ▷ On what basis does a practitioner in the discipline draw conclusions?
>
> ▷ What are the methods used by practitioners and contributors in the field to generate new questions, new knowledge, and solve problems?
>
> ▷ What are indicators of quality in the discipline?
>
> ▷ According to what standards does the discipline measure success?

Among its goals, the Curriculum of Practice helps students:

▶ Experience learning in context

▶ Expand their experiences in the field, leading to greater comfort and confidence in and identification with the field

▶ Develop clarity about the key concepts and principles in the field

▶ Develop awareness of problems in the field, and ways of identifying problems in the field

▶ Organize their understandings in ways useful for accessing information on, thinking about, and acting upon tasks, problems, and dilemmas in the field

▶ Recognize key features of a variety of problems in the field

▶ Distinguish and develop meaningful patterns of information in the field

▶ Distinguish between relevant and less critical information for particular tasks in the field

▶ Develop fruitful strategies for addressing problems in the field

▶ Monitor their thinking and problem-solving strategies effectively

▶ Become acquainted with and ultimately use key tools in the field

▶ Become acquainted with and ultimately use resources and methods professionals in the field use to teach themselves

▶ Expand their fluency and flexibility as problem solvers in the field

▶ Establish awareness of indicators of quality in the field, including those that distinguish between competence and elegance in the field

▶ Develop and pursue a sense of the possibilities that the field holds for them as individuals

▶ Develop awareness of where practitioners work and how those settings impact both the nature of the work and the practitioner him- or herself

Ascending Intellectual Demand and the Curriculum of Practice

It seems evident that virtually all students need opportunities to study and experience what it would be like to be a practitioner, problem solver, and contributor to a variety of fields or disciplines. Clearly, many students find school more inviting and its goals more compelling when it is clear to the students that what they are learning is of use to them in the world both now and in the future. Much knowledge and most understandings and skills are more durable for the learner when they are applied to real situations and problems. Thus the Curriculum of Practice is of value to virtually all students in schools. As has been the case in past parallels of the Model, the "match" between a task and student's capacity, readiness, and proclivities will be used to determine appropriate challenge.

Ascending intellectual demand can, as in the Core Curriculum and Curriculum of Connections, be achieved through the generic channels of increased complexity, adjusted pace, degree of independence required, amount of task ambiguity, level of materials, and so on. In general, functioning as a *scholar* calls on the student to do *expert-like* work, whereas functioning as an expert *practitioner* requires of the student *expert-level* work—the latter clearly being at a greater level of intellectual demand. However, because expertise is evolutionary, even expert-like work (the work of a scholar) can be designed at varied levels of challenge.

In addition, ascending intellectual demand in the Curriculum of Practice can be achieved by asking students who are ready to do so to accomplish the following:

▶ Distinguish between rules of practice often learned in text and lecture approaches in school and those that seem relevant in tackling authentic problems of the discipline

▶ Develop a language of reflection about problems and scenarios in the field

▶ Develop, through application, personal frameworks of knowledge and understandings related to the field

▶ Test those frameworks of knowledge and understanding through repeated field-based tasks and refine them as necessary

▶ Compare standards of quality used by practitioners and contributors in the field to those typically used in school as they relate to problem solving in the field

▶ Establish goals for their own work at what they believe to be the next steps in quality for their own growth and assess their own work according to those standards

▶ Submit best-quality exemplars of their work to experts in the field for expert-level feedback

▶ Work with problems currently posing difficulties to experts in the field

▶ Seek understanding and resolution of problems currently posing difficulties to experts in the field

▶ Develop and use mechanisms for getting in-process feedback as they work on complex problems

▶ Engage in persistent, prolonged, written reflection about their own work and thinking in the field with analysis of patterns and critique of the evolution of those patterns

▶ Compare and contrast their own approaches to discipline-based dilemmas, issues, or problems with those of experts in the field

Close-Ups of the Curriculum of Practice

High School Art

In the state where Ms. Black and her art students live, a recent tragedy took the lives of many people, young and old. Throughout this year, her Honors Arts students will work as a group of artists with talents in varied facets of art to create a memorial exhibit in honor of those who died and as a way of helping those who survived. The year-long focus is an example of the Curriculum of Practice.

Students will begin, as professional artists in a similar situation might, by trying to understand the tragedy and how it affected people's lives. To start that journey, they will read in a variety of genres about similar tragedies and discuss what they learn. They will study about and interview other artists who have used their art to develop memorials or to express feelings of loss. They will interview those who experienced loss in the event, and those who survived it. They will examine other memorials and memorial exhibits at first in a general way and later in the mode of expression of greatest interest to them as individuals or small groups (e.g., sculpture, photography, and dance). Throughout their work, Ms. Black will guide students in analyzing a range of art that illustrates aspects of grief, faith, conflict, and other elements related to their thinking.

Working together, students establish shared goals for the exhibit and a sense of how each part of the exhibit will contribute to the whole. They will also have to find a venue for the exhibit, understand the requirements of the venue, and align those with goals and timelines they have established for their work.

Ultimately, students, either individually or in small groups, will design a portion of the memorial exhibit in their chosen area of expression. To do so, they will consult with practicing professionals in their area of expression in order to make decisions about design and use of materials likely to facilitate their wishes for the exhibit. They must then collaborate continually with other individuals and groups in the classroom to ensure the creation of a coherent exhibit that communicates effectively. Throughout the span of work on their personal expressions, they receive consistent feedback from professionals in the field designed to help them push forward their skills and thinking as artists. In the end, they will work with an exhibitor to set up the exhibit and will take turns being in the exhibit area to talk with visitors.

Students will keep "sketchbooks" or portfolios of their drafts or iterations of their ideas for the exhibit. Throughout the year, students will meet regularly with others working in the same mode of expression, their teacher, and practitioners in their domain to discuss their work, examine their work in light of key concepts and principles of their form of art, problem solve, and compare methods of working and problem solving among themselves and with the professionals.

Elementary Social Studies

After a study of the American Revolution as part of the Core Curriculum, Mrs. Yee's students scanned a collection of major national newspapers and news magazines for the purpose of identifying contemporary revolutions. Next, students classified their examples as social, political, or economic revolutions. With the teacher's guidance, students then conducted a comparative analysis of the origin and effects of the contemporary revolutions and the American Revolution.

The final outcome defined for the learning experience was for students to apply their discipline-related knowledge and understanding to a present-day conflict. The essential question guiding student work was "How can knowledge of the American Revolution be used to help us understand and respond to revolution in today's world?" Students selected from a variety of contemporary revolutions to which they applied insights about causes of, reactions to, and effects of the American Revolution as a means of thinking about causes of, reactions to, and potential effects of a contemporary cultural change.

Middle School Math

Ms. Harrington's students always work on a long-term, real-world problem as a part of a middle school curriculum that introduces skills and concepts of algebra and geometry. Participation in the problem-solving project also helps students extend and apply previously learned skills in the basic mathematical operations. This year, students will study a traffic problem that became evident at the construction site for a new high school down the highway from their middle school. Working with this problem, the students will function as traffic engineers and use a variety of math skills that draw on their various mathematical strengths and interests.

First, both architects and highway engineers talked with the students about the problems they encounter daily, the mathematics-related knowledge they draw on to address the problems, and the methods and tools they use to solve the problems. Later, students consulted with the architects of the school, using site blueprints to get a sense of traffic patterns on the school site. Several times during the year, students shadowed and interviewed highway department engineers who design structures to guide traffic patterns.

Based on what they were learning from the architects and engineers, students examined the high school site at various times of the day to conduct traffic flow surveys relative to the new school entrance. They developed several problem scenarios they believed could be created by the current situation, consulting again with highway department engineers to learn how to depict the scenarios in a way that would be appropriate for presentation to professionals.

In time, the students met with and presented their concerns along with supporting mathematical data to the highway department officials, who concurred that there was a potential problem they had not anticipated. They invited the students to further study the problem and propose solutions they felt would be most effective and efficient in addressing the problem.

As the year progressed, students visited the site many more times, gathered a variety of data, devised a range of potential solutions, assessed each for a variety of factors including safety, best use of space, cost versus safety factors, convenience for commuters not entering the school, convenience for those entering the school, and aesthetics. Engineers, landscape designers, and other experts continued to meet with the students to provide feedback on their plans and to offer suggestions for ways in which professionals would depict and present the suggestions. Their teacher continually worked with them to refine their use of mathematical language, define and articulate key principles and skills of math that were useful to them in various scenarios, and focus on strategies for effective application of math to the scenarios.

As the year ended, students made their recommendation to highway department officials and school board members. Their proposal was accepted and implemented prior to the opening of the new school the following year. In addition, students developed a series of materials (print, poster, video) called "Math Works" in which they depicted how various professionals use math as a way of thinking about their work, how "math in the world" is and isn't like "math in a book," and connections the students made among math operations, principles, and concepts in differing applications.

The Curriculum of Identity

The Nature of the Curriculum of Identity

As is the case with the Curriculum of Connections and the Curriculum of Practice, the Curriculum of Identity is derived from and extends the Core Curriculum. This parallel exists to help students think about themselves, their goals, and their opportunities to make a contribution to their world—now and in the future—by examining themselves through the lens of a particular discipline (see Figure 2.5).

Each discipline has a particular function in helping humans make sense of the world in which they live. Because of the focus of each discipline, that discipline employs ways of thinking and ways of working that are notably different from all other disciplines. Each discipline looks at issues and problems that are, in some key ways, different from the issues and problems of greatest interest to the other disciplines. Thus each discipline has a unique capacity to shape the world, and that capacity has evolved through a unique history of human contribution.

While a goal of the Curriculum of Connections is to help students see linkages between and among disciplines (and parts of single disciplines), a goal of the Curriculum of Identity is to help students explore in depth the nature of particular disciplines as the disciplines relate to their own lives. Further, the goal is to help students understand themselves and their possibilities more fully by looking at their own interests and abilities in comparison with various relatively unique disciplines. The Curriculum of Identity helps students integrate rather than dichotomize cognitive and affective development. This parallel helps students think about (a) how their lives are shaped by the discipline, (b) challenges and conflicts that may exist as one moves through stages of development in a field, (c) varied levels of contribution one may make to a field (and to oneself through work in the field), (d) both difficulties and successes possible within a field, and (e) what it means for a person to both represent and be represented by a chosen field.

Among the driving questions in the Curriculum of Identity are the following:

> ▷ What do practitioners and contributors in this discipline think about?
>
> ▷ To what degree is this familiar, surprising, and/or intriguing to me?
>
> ▷ When I am intrigued by an idea, what do I gain from that, what do I give as a result of that, and what difference does it make?
>
> ▷ How do people in this discipline think and work?
>
> ▷ In what ways do those processes seem familiar, surprising, and/or intriguing to me?

▷ What are the problems and issues on which practitioners and contributors in this discipline spend their lives?

▷ To what degree are those intriguing to me?

▷ What is the range of vocational and avocational possibilities in this discipline?

▷ In which ones can I see myself working?

▷ What difficulties do practitioners and contributors in this discipline encounter?

▷ How have they coped with the difficulties?

▷ How do I think I would cope with them?

▷ What are the ethical principles at the core of the discipline?

▷ How are those like and unlike my ethics?

▷ Who have been the "heroes" of the evolving discipline?

▷ What are the attributes of the "villains"?

▷ What do I learn about myself by studying these attributes?

▷ Who have been the "villains" of the evolving discipline?

▷ What do I learn about myself by studying about them?

▷ How do people in this discipline handle ambiguity, uncertainty, persistence, failure, success, collaboration, and compromise?

▷ How do I handle those things?

▷ What is the wisdom this discipline has contributed to the world?

▷ How has that affected me?

▷ To what degree can I see myself contributing to that wisdom?

▷ How might I shape the discipline over time?

▷ How might it shape me?

An analogy may be made between the Curriculum of Identity and rotations of medical students through various facets of medical practice. In the course of the rotations, two goals are achieved. The medical students come to understand many facets of medical practice more thoroughly and to understand in which of those facets of medicine they have particular talent, interest, and we hope, passionate commitment to contribute. While they develop cognitive preparedness in many facets of medicine, the students also develop an affective awareness of which of the practices is the best fit for them as individuals—a sense of which of the practices can become an extension of themselves and a link between themselves and the wider world.

Figure 2.5. The Intent of the Curriculum of Identity Parallel

The Curriculum of Identity

This curriculum is derived from and extends the Core Curriculum. It is designed to help students see themselves in relation to the discipline both now and with possibilities for the future; understand the discipline more fully by connecting it with their lives and experiences; increase awareness of their preferences, strengths, interests, and need for growth; and think about themselves as stewards of the discipline who may contribute to it and/or through it. The Curriculum of Identity uses curriculum as a catalyst for self-definition and self-understanding, with the belief that by looking outward to the discipline, students can find a means of looking inward.

The Curriculum of Identity will ask students to:

- Reflect on their skills and interests as they relate to the discipline
- Understand ways in which their interests might be useful to the discipline and ways in which the discipline might serve as a means for helping them develop their skills and interests
- Develop awareness of their modes of working as they relate to the modes of operation characteristic of the discipline
- Reflect on the impact of the discipline in the world and of self in the discipline
- Think about the impact of the discipline on the lives of others in the wider world
- Take intellectual samplings of the discipline for the purpose of experiencing self in relation to the discipline
- Examine the ethics and philosophy characteristic of the discipline and their implications
- Project themselves into the discipline
- Develop self in the context of the discipline and through interaction with the subject matter
- Develop a sense of pride and humility related to both the self and the discipline

Among its goals, the Curriculum of Identity helps students:

▶ Sample the discipline in order to understand themselves in relation to it

▶ Project themselves into the discipline both intellectually and through working like a practitioner in it

▶ Develop an appreciation of the potential of one or more disciplines to help people—including themselves—make sense of their world and live more satisfying and productive lives

▶ Recognize connections between their own cultural heritage and the evolution of the field, past and future, as well as connections between their cultural heritage and their interests in the field

▶ Reflect on and identify their skills, interests, and talents as they relate to one or more disciplines

▶ Understand how they might shape and be shaped by ongoing participation in a discipline

▶ Develop a clear sense of what types of lives practitioners and contributors to a discipline lead on a day-to-day, as well as on a long-term, basis

▶ Explore the positive and negative impacts of the discipline on the lives of people and circumstances in the world

▶ Examine their own interests, ways of thinking, ways of working, values, ethics, philosophy, norms, and definitions of quality by examining those things as reflected in the discipline

▶ Understand the excitement that people in a discipline have about ideas, issues, problems, and so on and how those things energize contributors to a discipline

▶ Understand the role of self-discipline in practitioners and contributors to the discipline and reflect on their own evolving self-discipline

▶ Think about how creativity is manifest in the discipline, when, why, and about what that helps them understand their own creativity

▶ Develop both a sense of pride and a sense of humility related to self and the discipline that relates to accomplishments both past and future

Ascending Intellectual Demand and the Curriculum of Identity

Once again, it seems clear that virtually all students should have the opportunity to understand how disciplines shape and are shaped by human beings and the world. Virtually all students should have opportunities to examine themselves in relation to a discipline to get a clearer sense of their talents, interests, values, and goals. And surely, virtually all students would benefit in many ways from consistently working in school as much as possible like a practitioner in a discipline so that schoolwork is connected to real events, problems, skills, ideas, and opportunities. Thus again, there is no basis for assuming that the Curriculum of Identity is uniquely appropriate for highly able learners. Rather, it is the "match" between the degree of intellectual demand and the readiness and interests of a student that will result in appropriate challenge.

Once again, ascending intellectual demand can be achieved in the Curriculum of Identity through the descriptors of ascending intellectual demand in the section on the Core Curriculum (that is, matching the degree of task complexity, ambiguity, independence, material difficulty, pace, and so forth with the need of the student). In addition, ascending intellectual demand in the Curriculum of Identity can be achieved by students through means such as these:

▶ Looking for and reflecting on "truths," beliefs, ways of working, styles, and so on that typify the field

▶ Looking for "roots" of theories, beliefs, and principles in a field and relating those theories, beliefs, and principles to the time when they "took root" in one's own life

▶ Looking for and reflecting on the meaning of paradoxes and contradictions in the discipline or field

▶ Conducting an ethnography of a facet of the discipline and reflecting on both findings and personal revelations

▶ Engaging in long-term problem solving on an intractable problem in the discipline that causes them to encounter and mediate multiple points of view and reflecting systematically on the experience

▶ Researching and establishing standards of quality work as defined by the discipline, applying those standards to their own work in the discipline over an extended time period, and reflecting systematically on the experience

▶ Collaborating with a high-level professional or practitioner in the field in shared problem solving and reflection

▶ Challenging or looking for limitations of the ideas, models, ways of working, or belief systems of the discipline

▶ Looking for parallels (or contrasts) in personal prejudices, blind spots, assumptions, habits, and those evident in the field

▶ Studying and reflecting on one discipline by using the concepts, principles, and modes of working of another discipline, reflecting on the interactions and insights gained

Close-Ups of the Curriculum of Identity

Fifth Graders in Social Studies

Mr. Yin is working in a resource room for students identified as gifted for six weeks. All of the students have a keen interest in history. In their regular classroom, they are currently studying the time period leading up to the Civil War. Their resource room curriculum will guide them in thinking about the Underground Railroad as a way of understanding themselves and the time period more fully. Students will read from a variety of both primary and secondary sources to understand perspectives of slaves, freed slaves, slave owners, Northerners opposed to slavery, and other groups during the pre-Civil War time.

Students will keep a journal with three sections. In one section, they will record ideas, information, and conclusions as a historian would—trying to use data to present a verifiable and balanced view of events. In a second section, they will write from the perspective of a person in a role they are assigned and on whom they do research (for example, a slave or an abolitionist). In the third section, they will write about their own thoughts and feelings on the time period and people they are learning about, the work and responsibilities of a historian, and courage across time, including courage demonstrated in their own lives.

At the end of their study, students will participate in panel discussions among members of various groups from the pre-Civil War era, historians who chronicled the time period, and contemporary students. They will discuss what people can learn from the time period, how people can have confidence in what they learn, and how people can shape their lives with what they learn from history.

High School English/ Writing

In Ms. Mitchell's 11th-grade English class, writing is a centerpiece of the curriculum. All students work to meet certain prescribed writing standards, and all students regularly take part in writing process workshops. Students also select a kind of writing for further exploration. Amy and Darius selected a genre in which they have a personal interest—Amy as a writer of short stories and novels, Darius as a playwright.

Amy and Darius will study writers relevant to their preferred genres—looking at how these people became writers, how their careers have evolved over time, what has been positive for them in their writing lives and what has been costly, what advice they give aspiring writers, and particularly how their writings reflect the authors' cultures, values, and worldviews. The overarching question Amy and Darius are addressing is "What does it mean to be a writer?" Ultimately, they will each develop a way of answering this question as it relates to the writers they have studied and to themselves as present and future writers. Their reflections will be crafted in the genre(s) they share and the group of writers investigated. Ultimately, the two students should have a fuller sense of what it means for others to be writers but also ways in which the pursuit of writing is (or is not) a good match for their own interests, habits, perspectives, and temperaments. They should also develop insights into ways in which the pursuit of writing might contribute to their own lives and ways in which they might contribute to writing as a field.

A Curriculum Combining Parallels

The parallels in the Model are clearly related. While they can be used separately as a focus of curriculum for an individual, small group, or entire class, it makes good sense to combine the parallels for a curriculum that has great richness and broad reach. Because the Parallel Curriculum Model assumes that the Core Curriculum is the basis for all other curricula, the Core Curriculum is always evident in any combination. It can combine with any or all of the other parallels. The level of intellectual demand should be matched to student need, as is the case in using the parallels individually. One such example follows.

Beth was a fifth grader with strong ability in reading, thinking, and research, as well as a passion for history and historical fiction. She spent a year in the special class for students identified as gifted that she attended each day, working with a personalized curriculum that combined several of the parallels. She began with the concept of "interconnectedness" as it related to the Civil War. In her small town, she discovered a cemetery containing several graves of young women about her age, all of whom died during the Civil War. The question she began pursuing was "In what ways were the lives of young people affected by the Civil War?" She quickly found an interconnection between disease and the Civil War.

Beth used primary documents at the local courthouse to find out about the young people whose graves had captured her attention. In time, she found relatives of the young women still living in her area. Through interviews with these relatives, experts on the Civil War, additional primary documents and numerous secondary sources, she reconstructed events that dominated the lives of the young women.

She presented her findings in a formal paper to the local historical society where she received encouragement for her work together with suggestions for the next steps she might take. As her research continued, she translated her findings to a work of historical fiction that she created reflecting the lives of the young women in the graveyard—meeting regularly with professional writers who held scheduled meetings to discuss her work.

Beth's story was published, as was a reflective piece on the journal she'd kept throughout the year that captured what she had learned about herself as she worked like a historian and then like a writer of historical fiction.

Beth's year-long curriculum reflected key elements of the Core Curriculum, the Curriculum of Connections, the Curriculum of Practice, and the Curriculum of Identity. While the Curriculum of Connections and the Curriculum of Practice took center stage in her year-long efforts (that actually expanded through the summer and into the following year), elements of the Core Curriculum—dealt with effectively in her regular classroom—served as the catalyst for her work. Further, her teacher encouraged her to keep a reflective journal as she worked. The teacher systematically provided her with questions for reflection such as those key to the Curriculum of Identity, helping this relatively young student become much more aware of who she was and what she valued through her experience in two fields of study.

Looking Ahead in the Book

While we hope you've found the conceptual framework and overview of the Model interesting, we know that the key to making the Model useful for educators is carefully explaining its parts in a way that invites classroom application. The remainder of the book has that as its goal. Chapter 3 provides an overview of curriculum design to help establish a common vocabulary and framework for curriculum development in general. Chapters 4 through 7 then use that framework in conjunction with the four parallels of the Parallel Curriculum Model to provide both guidance in applying the Model and images of what the Model might look like in action. Chapter 8 examines flexible uses of the Parallel Curriculum Model. The chapters are not meant to be recipes or to provide rigid structures for using the Model to create curriculum. In fact, we are convinced that there are no recipes for thoughtful curriculum, and no recipe followers who develop dynamic classrooms. Instead, we offer these chapters as a way to test and extend your thinking about curriculum design—a professional art form as ill suited to paint-by-number approaches as are the fine arts.

3

The Essentials of Curriculum Design

This chapter is *not* about the Parallel Curriculum Model. Rather, it establishes a common vocabulary between authors and readers so that there is a shared basis for discussing each of the parallels in later chapters. In other words, this chapter is a quick review of (a) what it means to develop a curriculum at a very basic level and (b) the components that are generally a part of teacher planning in the effective curriculum. With that foundation in place, the remainder of the book—and work done by teachers who draw on its ideas—is more firmly grounded in the fundamentals of teaching and learning.

Key Components of Comprehensive Curriculum Design

In its simplest form, the teaching-learning process involves interactions among three elements. The constellation of these elements and interactions among them can be represented by a triangle (see Figure 3.1).

The top of the triangle represents humankind's accumulated knowledge within and across disciplines. The other two points of the figure represent students and teachers. Lines drawn between the three points refer to interactions between the elements.

The line segment between the teacher and the content suggests multiple decisions the teacher must make in regard to what he or she will teach at a given time. That includes teachers' ongoing acquisition of content knowledge and evolving insights about the meaning of the content, the numerous decisions teachers make about the appropriateness of the content for varied learners, and the lesson and unit planning needed to manage the learning process.

The line segment between the teacher and the student represents the array of links a teacher must make with students. It includes gathering information about

Figure 3.1. The Process of Education

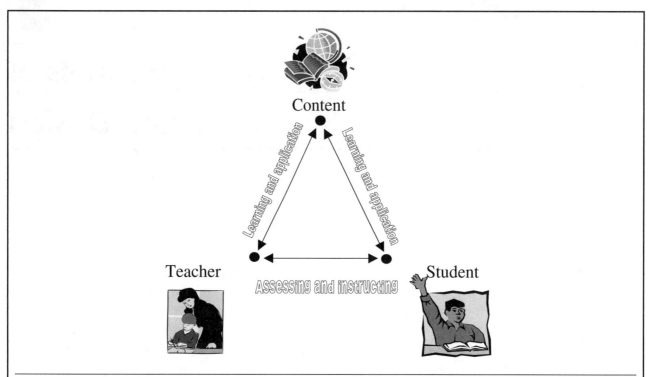

student learning needs as well as about students as members of a group and as individuals, assessment, reflections on what appears to be successful and unsuccessful for individuals and the class as a whole, and evolving teacher sophistication in understanding and responding to student "signals."

Finally, the interactions symbolized by the student-content line segment involve what we think of as teaching and learning. It includes teacher decisions about how to teach, how to ensure that students learn, and how to set up and manage a classroom for effective and efficient learning. It also suggests the role of the student in attending to and making sense of ideas, developing skills, transferring new knowledge, and contributing to effective classroom functioning.

The field of education often uses the term "curriculum"—or "curriculum and instruction"—to refer to the purposeful, proactive organization, sequencing, and managing of these interactions across the three classroom elements: the content, the teacher, and the student. The curriculum is a multifaceted plan that fosters these connections.

Although a curriculum writers can make decisions independently about what to teach, how to teach it, and when to teach it, this scenario rarely occurs. In most instances, curriculum is developed only after a lengthy process that involves teachers, state department of education personnel, content area specialists, and community members about which knowledge is most vital for students to acquire.

Some call this agreed-on or designated body of knowledge and skill the "basic" or "general" curriculum; others refer to it as the "grade-level" or "mandated" curriculum. In its most skeletal form, the general curriculum often merely lists the knowledge and skills that students in various grade levels are expected to acquire—perhaps represented in a scope and sequence chart.

Seldom is this sort of general curriculum document more than a beginning in the curriculum development process. Typically, this sort of framework provides little more than a list of "ingredients," and often an incomplete one at that. To assume that curriculum development ends with this document is equivalent to putting flour, a sack of apples, a couple of cups of sugar, a stick of butter, and a tin of cinnamon on the table and telling diners they have apple pie. Meaningful curriculum design includes much more than listing the raw ingredients!

Comprehensive curriculum plans typically include decisions about components such as content knowledge to be acquired (including, but not limited to, prescribed standards), representative topics, assessments, an introduction to a topic or idea, teaching activities, learning activities, grouping strategies, products, resources, extensions, and differentiation strategies.

This chapter provides an overview of one approach to the curriculum design process. It contains: (1) an explanation of key features of a comprehensive curriculum plan, (2) a description of exemplary characteristics for each of the components within this plan, (3) a rationale for developing high-quality curriculum, (4) an example of the curriculum design process in action, and (5) an explanation of the relationship between this curriculum design framework and the four curriculum parallels described in subsequent chapters: the Core Curriculum, Curriculum of Connections, Curriculum of Practice, and Curriculum of Identity.

Components of a
Comprehensive Curriculum Plan

Through explanations and visuals, this section of the chapter proposes elements likely to be a part of planning high-quality curriculum. These elements represent our current professional understanding of what it means to plan well so students can learn well.

There may be times when a teacher has legitimate reasons not to attend to one or more of the elements we propose here. There are likely to be instances in which teachers would add elements to the ones we've chosen to present. Further, the curriculum planning process may not always follow a linear process. That is, a teacher may not begin by thinking about content or standards, move directly to thinking about an assessment plan, select an introductory activity, and so on. Early planning may actually begin with an idea for a powerful student product or by examining available resources for the unit, for example. Our goal in presenting elements of

Figure 3.2. Key Components of Comprehensive Curriculum

Curriculum Component	Definition	Exemplary Characteristics
Content (Standards)	Content is what we want students to know, understand, and do as a result of our curriculum and instruction. Standards are broad statements about what grade-level students should know and be able to do.	Exemplary standards incorporate "big ideas," enduring understandings, and skills of a discipline. Additionally, they provide clarity, power, and authenticity for teacher and students.
Assessments	Assessments are varied tools and techniques teachers use to determine the extent to which students have mastery of learning goals.	Well-designed assessments are diagnostic, aligned with the learning goals, and provide a high ceiling, as well as a low baseline, to ensure that all students' learning can be measured. They are used before, during, and after instruction. High-quality assessments inform instruction.
Introductory Activities	An introduction sets the stage for a unit. Components may include (1) a focusing question, (2) a needs assessment to determine students' prior knowledge, interests, and learning preferences, (3) a teaser or "hook" to motivate students, (4) information about the relevance of the goals and unit expectations, (5) information about expectations for students, and (6) consideration of students' interests in or experiences that connect with the unit topic.	A high-quality introduction will include all six elements, as well as an advance organizer that provides students with information that they can use to help assess their acquisition of the unit's learning goals.
Teaching Strategies	Teaching strategies are methods teachers use to introduce, explain, demonstrate, model, coach, guide, transfer, or assess in the classroom.	Beneficial teaching methods are closely aligned to learning goals, varied, promote student involvement, and provide support, feedback, and scaffolding for learners.
Learning Activities	A unit's learning activities are those cognitive experiences that help students perceive, process, rehearse, store, and transfer knowledge, understanding, and skills.	Effective learning activities are aligned with the learning goals and efficiently foster cognitive engagement (i.e., analytic, critical, practical, and creative thinking) integrated with the learning goal.
Grouping Strategies	Grouping strategies refer to varied approaches a teacher can use to arrange students for effective learning in the classroom.	Well-designed grouping strategies are aligned with the learning goals. Effective grouping strategies are varied and change frequently to accommodate students' interests, questions, learning preferences, prior knowledge, or learning rate, and zone of proximal development. Group membership changes frequently.

Products	Products are performances or work samples created by students that provide evidence of student learning. Products can represent daily or short-term student learning, or can provide longer-term, culminating evidence of student knowledge, understanding, and skill. High-quality products often double as assessment tools.	Powerful products are authentic, equitable, respectful, efficient, aligned to standards, and diagnostic.
Resources	Resources are materials that support learning during the teaching and learning activities.	Exemplary resources are varied in format and link closely to the learning goals, students' reading and comprehension levels, and learning preferences.
Extension Activities	Extension activities are preplanned or serendipitous experiences that emerge from learning goals and students' interests.	Powerful extension activities provide for student choice. They relate in some way to the content/standards, are open ended, authentic, and generate excitement for and investment in learning.
Modifications for Learner Need	Teachers can enhance learning by optimizing the match between the curriculum and students' unique learning needs. One kind of modification represented in the Parallel Curriculum Model is referred to as "Ascending Intellectual Demand."	Well-designed modification strategies are closely aligned with the learning goals and students' interests, questions, preferred learning modes, product preferences, prior knowledge and/or learning rate.

curriculum is not to restrict or prescribe teacher planning but, rather, to prompt reflection on those elements which, used in concert and with finesse, can strengthen what and how we teach, with the goal of strengthening student learning. In addition to a text explanation of the components, Figure 3.2 lists key components of a comprehensive curriculum, defines them, and suggests some characteristics of exemplars of each component.

1. Content/Standards

Content is what we specify students should come to know, understand, and be able to do as a result of their participation in a lesson, unit of study, or a year in the classroom. Content emerges from a variety of sources. Certainly content arises, to some degree, from a teacher's growing comfort with and expertise in a domain. When we understand a field deeply and richly, we know what matters most in it! There is no substitute for a teacher's developing expertise in the subject matter he or she teaches.

In addition, content may be spelled out in district curriculum plans and documents in the form of learning objectives, benchmarks, goals, or learner outcomes. Certainly, textbooks play a role in determining the content of the curriculum.

Currently, standards documents often specify what a grade-level student should learn or be able to do. The variety of quality among standards documents is strongly correlated to the kind of content knowledge valued by the constituency group involved in developing the standards.

In general, the most effective standards documents help teachers focus on the essential structure of a discipline and the "big ideas" within that discipline. Thus high-quality standards documents specify the concepts, principles, and skills that give the particular discipline its power and authenticity. Hilda Taba (1962) made clear the distinctions among different categories of knowledge in her seminal work *Curriculum and Practice* (see Figure 3.3).

When teachers are provided with guidelines for content—whether from standards documents, lists of objectives or benchmarks, texts, or some combination of sources—it's critical for the teacher to determine the degree to which the content seems comprehensive (vs. a disjointed series of facts and skill, for example), coherent (each portion flows from previous portions), authentic (characteristic of content used by a professional in the domain), and relevant (evident in its usefulness to students). When some or all of these characteristics are lacking, it is the teacher's job to supply missing elements in order to improve student learning. To do less is to present students with fragmented learning options that are low on meaning and with information that is difficult to care about, retain, or use.

There is little doubt that content is the most important of the key features of a curriculum plan because it provides teachers with a clear understanding of what students are supposed to learn as a result of their participation in a lesson, unit, or course of study. Without clear content, a curriculum unit dissolves quickly into a collection of disjointed activities unlikely to support meaningful learning across all students in the classroom. In addition, effective content delineates a learning sequence that fosters development of ascending levels of expertise as students progress through the grades.

2. Assessment

Effective standards documents also contain information that helps teachers align content standards with appropriate assessment strategies and criteria for mea-

Figure 3.3. Hilda Taba's Knowledge Categories

Knowledge Category	Definition and Examples
Fact	A specific detail; verifiable information or data *Example: The capital of New York is Albany.*
Concept	A class of things; a category with common elements *Examples: capital, city, nation*
Principle	A fundamental truth, law, rule, or doctrine that explains the relationship between two or more concepts *Example: Capital cities are often located along major transportation routes. Social, economic, political, and geographic factors influence the location of a capital city.*
Skill	A proficiency, an ability, or a technique; a strategy, a method, or a tool *Example: Locate capital cities using longitude and latitude. Use a map key to identify the symbol for capitals.*
Attitude	A belief, disposition, appreciation, or value *Example: Develop an appreciation for the cultural heritage of capital cities.*
Problem Solving, Transfer, and Application	The ability to use knowledge to address a goal that may not be immediately be understandable *Example: Examination of issues that might arise when a capital needs to be relocated.*

suring student growth over time. Assessments are tasks assigned to students in order to determine the extent to which they have acquired the knowledge and/or skills embedded within a performance standard or content goal. Assessment tasks provide tangible evidence of student understanding and growth before instruction begins (preassessment), as instruction progresses (formative assessment), and at the end of a segment of instruction (summative assessment).

Preassessment data allow a teacher to know how much content students know at the outset of a unit so that the teacher can make appropriate lesson plan adjustments. Little useful learning occurs when a teacher "teaches" something to a student that the student already knows. Likewise, a student generally cannot learn what a teacher teaches if that student has significant gaps in background knowledge, understanding, and/or skill. Used effectively, preassessment eliminates "blind teaching" and encourages teachers to expand beyond one-size-fits-all instruction.

Formative assessment should occur throughout a unit of study. Data from this kind of assessment helps teachers know who is mastering ideas and skills and who may need additional assistance to achieve competency with the content goals.

Summative assessments help teachers understand who has mastered content and skills objectives at a designated "ending point" of instruction. In the classroom, summative assessment at the end of one lesson or unit will often inform a teacher's planning for the next lesson or unit, because—at least in a well-constructed curriculum—the latter flows from the former. Nonetheless, summative assessment also has more of a "high stakes" character than do preassessment or formative assessment. In the classroom, summative assessment may have a major impact on a report card grade. Beyond the individual classroom, summative assessment can affect such decisions as promotion to the next grade, college acceptance, access to special classes or programs, and even judgments about the quality of instruction at a grade level or in a school.

An assessment usually involves the development of a behavior or product that results from the student's interaction with content. The process of assessment is depicted in Figure 3.4.

Figure 3.4. The Assessment Equation

PARTICIPANT + CONTENT + TASK +

COGNITIVE PROCESSING = ASSESSMENT

The following task, designed for use in a three-week high school unit on tragic heroes and the hero quest, illustrates the relationship among the components of an assessment. The task is a culminating (summative) assessment, and the purpose was to determine (a) how much content students had acquired and (b) the extent to which students were able to transfer concepts across genres.

Over the past few weeks we have explored the mythical journeys of heroes such as Jason, Perseus, and Odysseus. We have also examined the pattern of the archetypal quest that was put forth by Joseph Campbell in Hero With a Thousand Faces. *In this book, Campbell describes the major phases of the heroic journey: departure, initiation, and return. Examine three current story plots that contain heroes who undertake personal quests. These can be movies, fairy tales, or your own personal journey. In a format of your choice (e.g., short paper, PowerPoint presentation, or brief documentary), explore the similarities and differences among the heroes and plot lines in the three stories that you select.*

Using the assessment equation from Figure 3.4, the mythology assessment can be analyzed to reveal its component parts, as shown in Figure 3.5.

The student is provided with an assessment task. As a result of his or her involvement with the task, the student is required to think about key content. The

Figure 3.5. Applying the Assessment Equation

PARTICIPANT (student) + **TASK** (documentary)

+ **CONTENT** (archetypal quest pattern and three current story lines)

+ **COGNITIVE PROCESSING** (finding similarities) = **ASSESSMENT**

---

student's interaction with the knowledge is the basis for the product. In turn, the teacher uses the product to evaluate the student's understanding of the targeted knowledge.

This same process is also embedded in an assignment. The difference between an assessment and an assignment is that an assessment implies a decision-making function and suggests how a teacher can assist learners and modify instruction.

The key to designing an assessment is aligning the task, the knowledge, and the product format. Teachers must choose cognitive processes and a product format that clearly reveal students' understanding of the knowledge they are to acquire. Part of the alignment difficulty stems from the fact that the knowledge is "hidden" or "disguised" in the product. Teachers need to be confident, for example, that a nutrition poster will reveal a student's knowledge of the food pyramid or that a concept map reflects a student's accurate understanding not only of the major concepts covered in a curriculum lesson or unit but also of the relationships between and among them.

Teachers and students benefit from using a variety of assessment formats. Some possible assessment formats are listed in Figure 3.6.

Superior assessments have several attributes. They are reliable, valid, efficient, equitable, seamless, and motivating. *Reliable* assessments provide a consistent and "stable" reading of a student's knowledge and/or skill acquisition from one occa-

Figure 3.6. Sample Assessment Formats

Sample Assessment Formats		
Oral Questions	Conversations	Recitations
Tests	Essays	Behaviors
Observations	Portfolios	Performances
Think-Alouds	Concept Maps	Lab Reports
Ongoing Records of Progress	Competency Checklists	Auditions
Conferences	Products	Journal Entries

sion to the next. A reliable thermometer works in a similar fashion every time it registers 100° Celsius when submerged in boiling water.

Valid assessments measure what they say they measure. Have you ever taken a test that dealt with only a few pages of the textbook and none of the notes? Have you ever created a project for a class when you had no clear sense of what knowledge, insight, or skill it should represent? These were likely not valid assessments because they did not measure the content taught.

Assessments need to be *efficient* for students and teachers. The effort expended by the student to respond to the task and the effort expended by the teacher to assess the task and provide positive and corrective feedback must balance with the time required for both student and teacher.

Finally, assessments must be *equitable, seamless,* and *motivating.* Assessments can be subject to rater bias based on such things as a student's personality or access to state-of-the-art technology. It is, therefore, advisable to use objective rating scales, rubrics, or checklists to evaluate student performances to increase the likelihood of equity in scoring and feedback. *Seamless* assessments are those that are imperceptibly woven into instruction. They provide teachers with honest "snapshots" of student growth over time. Finally, superior assessments *motivate* students. They invite and encourage students to explore an area or topic thoughtfully and to work for a high level of quality.

3. Introductory Activities

Introductory activities are created by the teacher and are offered to students in order to acquaint them with the new curriculum, its content, and teacher expectations for students' work and production during the unit. Introductory activities should do far more to motivate and orient students to what lies ahead than traditional one-sentence introductions such as "Please open your books to page 23."

A comprehensive introduction can actually contain a variety of elements that help orient, engage, and motivate learners. First, a focusing question derived from a standard or overarching principle embedded within a unit can promote curiosity in students, and help both teachers and students maintain a focus on meaning that is central to the unit. Focusing questions for the unit on tragic heroes might be "What is meant by the phrase 'tragic hero'?" "Who are tragic heroes?" "Is anyone you know a tragic hero?" "What are the common characteristics of their journeys toward self-understanding?"

Second, a "teaser" or "hook" can be highly motivating for students, and may point to the relevance of upcoming content as well. A primary teacher had "Paul Bunyan" come to her class to talk about how it felt when people exaggerate about you all the time. This brief dramatic monologue absolutely hooked her students on tall tales and established some key understandings for the young learners as well. A science teacher introduced the concept of inertia by skillfully pulling the tablecloth off of a table set with flowers and good china. Again, this strategy captured the students' curiosity even as it began to plant the seed for further exploration.

Third, an effective introduction may enable students to attach their own past knowledge, experience, interests, and/or strengths to the new content. Interest checklists, charts that guide students in listing what they already know about a topic and questions they have about the topic, and invitations for students to suggest ways in which they might like to explore the topic or express their learning are just a few ways teachers commonly use introductory activities to help students connect with new content or a new topic.

An effective introduction to a unit may also help students understand the purpose of the unit, the direction it will take, and expectations for high-quality work during the unit. A concept map of ideas in the unit, unit schedule or calendar of events, and presentation or review of rubrics or checklists for quality can assist in these goals.

While there is no formula for introducing content effectively, a powerful introduction can have a long life and a very positive impact on learning. For that reason, it's worth a teacher's time to ask the following questions: How will I let students know the content of the unit is going to be worthwhile, interesting, and exciting? How will I establish curiosity or a desire to know in the students? What will I do to help students connect with the content or unit? How will I orient them to the learning journey we will take together? How do I begin to let them know they can be successful in this study? How can I tap into my students' prior experiences in a way that connects the study to their lives?

4. Teaching Methods

One of the most important tasks in designing curriculum is the selection of teaching activities, sometimes referred to as methods or pedagogy. A teaching method is a strategy or technique, selected purposefully, that educators use to instruct students or connect them with the content. These strategies forward the learning goals within a curriculum unit and place the teacher in the role of facilitator, trainer, coach, or model of learning.

There are many useful teaching methods. Figure 3.7 contains just a sampling of them. The table contains two columns. The first column identifies a teaching method, and the second provides a succinct definition. The "Benefits" section of the second column includes information about value in benefits for students appropriately using the teaching strategy. Strategies nearer the top of the chart are likely to be more teacher centered and require less student inquiry or independence. As the chart continues, the strategies become more student centered, and require more inference and independence on the part of students. Teachers will also have to adjust the level of teacher support, scaffolding, and coaching for various students, depending on factors like complexity of content, student familiarity with the strategy, and student independence in thought and work.

Teacher comfort and competence with each method is valuable, but more valuable is a teacher's ability to match the instructional technique with learning goals and to provide structure, guidance, and support for student success. Within a curriculum unit, teaching methods should be varied, aligned with learning goals and

(Text continued on page 56)

Figure 3.7. Selected Teaching Methods

Teaching Method	Definition and Benefits
Lecture	A deductive teaching strategy that consists of a carefully sequenced, illustrated oral presentation of content that is delivered to small and large groups of students; an oral presentation interspersed with opportunities for reflection, clarification, and sense making *Benefit: Effective, short-term acquisition of new content knowledge*
Drill and Recitation	A teaching strategy that helps students memorize and recall information with accuracy and speed *Benefit: Accuracy and speed in student's recall of factual-level information*
Direct Instruction	A method of teaching that consists of a teacher's systematic explanation of a new concept or skill followed by guided practice under a teacher's guidance *Benefit: Efficient and equitable knowledge acquisition*
Strategy-Based Instruction	A method for teaching a cognitive strategy or procedure; the teacher explains and helps students acquire the strategy, models the strategy, and provides guided practice and feedback to students as they internalize the strategy *Benefits: Strategy acquisition; improved student efficiency and self-efficacy related to skill performance*
Assisted Instruction in the Content Areas	A range of methods to support or scaffold students' reading of nonfiction material in various content fields *Benefits: Strategy acquisition; improved student efficiency and self-efficacy related to skill performance*
Graphic Organizer	An instructional strategy that uses visual diagrams to help students understand content and thinking strategies *Benefit: Enhanced ability to organize, interpret, and understand contents and skills*
Coaching	A teaching method in which teachers make criterion-referenced observations about a student's performance and provide immediate, specific feedback in order to improve the student's performance *Benefit: Proficiency with respect to physical or cognitive skills*
Concept Attainment	A method teachers use to help students understand the essential attributes of a category or concept; to achieve this goal, the teacher systematically leads students through a controlled discussion during which students compare and contrast characteristics of examples and non-examples of the category or concept *Benefit: Acquisition of new categories, concepts, and macro concepts (e.g., vegetable, adjective, tragic hero, compromise)*
Synectics	A teaching method in which teachers and students share or develop metaphors, similes, and/or analogies that build a bridge between students' prior knowledge or experience and new learning *Benefits: Acquisition of new knowledge, enhanced creative expression, and/or increased ability to generate creative solutions to problems*

Demonstration/ Modeling	A teaching method in which the teacher's actions and behaviors serve as an example for students who, in turn, are able to replicate the actions and behaviors in other contexts
	Benefit: Acquisition of behaviors, skills, and dispositions
Socratic Questioning	An instructional strategy in which the teacher poses a carefully constructed sequence of questions to students to help them improve their logical reasoning and critical thinking about their position on an issue; can be used as a technique to bridge students' current level of understanding with new knowledge that students need to acquire
	(Model tailored for older students in middle school and beyond)
	Benefits: Acquisition of content related to social issues; enhanced ability to think issues through logically
Visualization	An instructional strategy in which the teacher encourages the students to pretend and imagine; students do not speak. They can be asked to see themselves performing a skill or participating in an event at some time in the future, etc.
	Benefits: Literal comprehension and transfer of procedures, reduced anxiety, increased likelihood of goal attainment
Role Playing	The involvement of students as participants and observers in a simulation of a real-world situation
	Benefits: Growth and understanding as it relates to content; students' understanding of others' beliefs and values; problem-solving skills
Cooperative Learning	A teaching activity in which the teacher purposively uses small group interaction to forward new learning and accomplish academic and social tasks
	Benefits: Collaboration among students; deeper thinking and understanding; enhanced feelings of empathy for others
Jurisprudence	A teaching strategy in which teachers provide students with the opportunity to collaborate in order to develop cases and persuasive arguments on all sides of an issue, a controversy, or a decision
	Benefits: Critical thinking, analysis, evaluation, synthesis, oratory, and persuasive writing
Simulation	An inductive teaching method in which students assume roles of people engaged in complex, real-life situations
	Benefit: Increased likelihood that concepts and principles induced from the simulation will be transferred and applied to the real world
Inquiry-Based Instruction	An inductive teaching strategy in which the teacher poses a task, problem, or intriguing situation, while students explore the situation across small changes in the data set, and generate insights about the problem and/or solutions
	Benefits: Increased self-awareness; awareness of different points of view; enhanced curiosity; increased understanding of concepts and principles; enhanced ability to solve problems

(Continued)

Figure 3.7. Continued

Problem-Solving and Problem-Based Learning	An inductive teaching method in which the teacher presents an ill-structured, novel, and complex problem for students to investigate and solve collaboratively with teacher guidance and coaching *Benefits: Acquisition of new knowledge, concepts, and principals; enhanced problem-solving ability*
Shadowing Experiences	A teaching strategy employed by a teacher in which a student, or small group of students, receive short-term exposure to selected fields or disciplines. A teacher may involve a student for several hours or several days *Benefits: Increased ability to use the tools and methodology of the discipline; increased understanding of the life of the practicing professional; a deepening awareness about the fit between a learner's profile and the targeted field or discipline*
Mentorship	A teaching method in which a student spends a period of time collaborating with an expert in the field in order to learn the content, methodology, and day-to-day activities of the practicing professional *Benefits: Enhanced content area knowledge; increased ability to use the tools and methodology of the discipline; increased understanding of the life of the practicing professional; a deepening awareness about the fit between a learner's profile and the targeted field or discipline*
Independent Study	An instructional strategy in which the teacher encourages individuals or small groups of students to explore self-selected areas of study *Benefits: Enhanced motivation, content area knowledge, and methodological skills*

students' learning needs, and promote student engagement and higher order thinking. In addition, these methods promote optimal student learning when they provide for scaffolding, monitoring, adjustment, and feedback.

5. Learning Activities

Learning activities are tasks for students designed to develop the knowledge, understanding, and skills specified in the content goals. They should help students perceive, process, rehearse, store, and transfer new information and skill.

Many practitioners equate learning with listening or observing. In these classrooms, children are expected to learn because they read a page, listen to a lecture, or complete an experiment. In actuality, these approaches may help students *perceive* information, but there is little assurance that students who stop with these approaches have really "learned."

Learning that results in deep understanding requires activities that call on students to engage thoughtfully with the new information. Analytical, critical, and creative thinking skills require students to "do something" with the new information. When students are required to use and process information, they have to perceive it *and* manage it mentally. This sort of cognition not only supports learning but also memory retrieval. Cognitive tasks, then, work "double time" for the learner. Some cognitive tasks that can be used as the pivotal elements in learning activities are categorized and defined in Figure 3.8.

As is the case with high-quality teaching methods, high-quality learning activities are aligned with content goals and teaching methods. Moreover, they must link to students' prior knowledge and the learning strategies they have already acquired. Finally, learning activities must be efficient for students and their use must fit within the time frame for a curriculum unit.

Figure 3.8. Cognitive Processes That Can Be Used to Design Learning Activities

Thinking Skill	Definition
Analytical Thinking Skills	**Various cognitive processes that deepen understanding of knowledge and skills**
Identifying characteristics	The ability to identify distinct, specific, and relevant details that characterize an object, an event, or a phenomenon
Recognizing attributes	The facility to discern and label general or common features of a set of objects
Making observations	The capability to perceive and select attributes of an object or experience
Discriminating between same and different	The ability to make fine discriminations among objects, ideas, or events
Comparing and contrasting	The facility to see similarities and differences among objects, events, and people
Categorizing	The ability to group objects or events according to some preconceived classification scheme
Classifying	The capability to extract relevant attributes of a group of objects, people, or phenomena that can be used to sort or organize the same
Ranking, prioritizing, and sequencing	The facility to place objects, events, or phenomena in hierarchical order according to some quantifiable value
Seeing relationships	The ability to see a connection or interaction between two or more objects or phenomena

(Text continued on page 60)

Figure 3.8. Continued

Finding patterns	The ability to perceive and extract a repeating scheme in objects or phenomena
Determining cause and effect	The ability to see and extract the most powerful reasons, or results for a given event or action
Predicting	The ability to see patterns, compare and contrast, identify relationships, determine cause and effect, and anticipate likely events in the future
Making analogies	The ability to identify a relationship between two familiar items or events and similar items and events in order to problem-solve or initiate creative productivity
Critical Thinking Skills	**Various thinking skills that are used to analyze and evaluate data and evidence in order to develop, judge the effectiveness of, or respond to an argument or position**
Inductive thinking	The ability to draw an inferential conclusion based on repeated observations that yield consistent but incomplete data
Deductive thinking	The ability to draw a logical conclusion from premises
Determining benefits and drawbacks	The ability to weight the advantages and disadvantages of a given idea or action
Determining reality and fantasy	The ability to distinguish between that which is fanciful and that which is true or actual
Identifying value statements	The ability to recognize statements that reflect appraisals of worth that cannot be supported through objective means
Identifying points of view	The ability to recognize that individuals and groups may have values and beliefs that influence their perspective on issues
Determining bias	The ability to ascertain information that is value laden
Identifying fact and opinion	The ability to distinguish between statements that can be proven and statements that reflect personal beliefs or judgments
Judging essential and incidental evidence	The ability to assess information and categorize it into useful and less useful categories
Identifying missing information	The ability to determine essential information that is not given or provided
Judging the accuracy of information	The ability to determine the precision of evidence that is presented
Judging the credibility of a source	The ability to assess whether the given information is believable, valid, and worthy to be considered

Recognizing assumptions	The ability to distinguish between information that is commonly accepted as true and information that is conjecture
Determining the strength of an argument	The ability to extract the reasons for an argument and evaluate the evidence as worthy
Identifying exaggeration	The ability to extract statements that magnify or overstate what is accepted as fact
Executive Processes	**Various cognitive skills that are involved in organizing, synthesizing, generalizing, or applying knowledge**
Summarizing	The ability to reduce a written or oral narrative to its essential components
Metacognition	The ability to consciously monitor, describe, and reflect upon one's thinking
Setting goals	The ability to set desirable outcomes in any situation
Formulating questions	The ability to develop relevant and precise queries related to any endeavor
Developing hypotheses	The ability to use prior observations to develop a possible explanation for an apparent relationship between two variables
Generalizing	The ability to use repeated, controlled, and accurate observations to develop a rule, principle, or formula that explains a number of situations
Problem solving	The ability to describe a problem, identify an ideal outcome, and to select and test possible strategies and solutions
Decision making	The ability to create and use appropriate criteria to select the best alternative in a given situation
Planning	The ability to develop a detailed and sequenced series of actions to achieve an end
Creative Thinking Skills	**Various cognitive skills that are involved in creative production**
Fluency	The ability to generate numerous ideas or alternatives to solve a problem that requires a novel solution
Flexibility	The ability to generate a wide variety of ideas to solve a problem that requires a novel solution
Originality	The ability to generate novel or unique alternatives to solve a problem that requires a novel solution

(Continued)

Figure 3.8. Continued

Elaboration	The ability to create a large number of details that explain a novel solution to a problem
Imagery	The ability to visualize a situation or object and to manipulate various alternatives for solving a problem without benefit of models, props, or physical objects
Using idea/product modification techniques	The ability to use techniques such as substituting, combining, adapting, modifying, making larger or smaller, putting to new uses, eliminating, reversing, or rearranging parts to make a more useful whole
Listing attributes	The ability to identify appropriate improvements to a process or product by systematically considering modifications to the original product's attributes
Brainstorming	The ability to work with others to withhold judgment while identifying varied, innovative, and numerous alternatives for solving a problem
Creative problem solving	The ability to identify, research, and plan to solve a problem that requires a novel, systematic solution

Burns, D. (1993). *A six-phase model for the explicit teaching of thinking skills.* Storrs, CT: University of Connecticut, National Research Center on the Gifted and Talented. Used with permission.

6. Grouping Strategies

Grouping strategies enable teachers to arrange students in configurations most likely to enhance the acquisition of content and skills. Teachers can employ a wide range of grouping strategies among which are whole group instruction, cooperative and collaborative groups, flexible small groups, partner checks, book buddies, lab partners, and discussion groups.

At times, it makes most sense for a whole class to work as a unit. At other times, it is wise for students to work alone. Often, it makes sense for small groups of students to work together on part or all of a task. In this latter instance, a flexible teacher will sometimes group students with similar readiness levels, interests, or approaches to learning. On other occasions, however, the teacher will purposefully construct groups in which students bring to the group differing readiness levels, interests, or approaches to learning. Sometimes, the teacher will select student groupings but at other times ask students to decide on group membership. At still other times, the teacher will assign students to groups randomly.

Decisions about grouping should be based on content goals and the needs of students and should include both the directions and support necessary to ensure that students know how to work successfully in the particular grouping. Effective use of varied groupings enables teachers to observe students in a variety of settings and enables students to see themselves in varied contexts, thereby increasing the chance that they will have ongoing opportunities to work in ways that both tap their strengths and help them strengthen areas of weakness.

7. Products

A well-designed product assignment produces tangible evidence of student learning. As such, it is an assessment tool. On the other hand, a product is also part of a learning activity. This is the case because most learning activities ask students to make, write, or do something both to help students process ideas and use skills and to provide evidence of what the student has learned. Thus products are strongly linked both to learning activities and to assessments. We have elected to include a category called "products" rather than embedding the discussion of products in either learning activities or assessments. That decision reflects a belief in the power of effective student products to motivate learners, distill content, and inform teachers.

Teachers use products to measure student growth over time, to monitor and adjust instruction in order to promote student success, and as a basis for evaluating students. Students use products to communicate their understanding of the learning objectives. Products can be short term—that is, provide evidence of learning over a class period or a few class periods. They can also be longer term—that is, culminating work that brings together knowledge, understanding, and skill from an extended time such as a unit, a grading period, or even a semester or a year. This book addresses both short- and long-term products in the discussion of each of the parallels in the Parallel Curriculum Model.

Products can take many forms: tests, worksheets, journals, performances, problem solving solutions, explanations, reflections, and many others. Exemplary products are closely aligned to content goals, authentic (i.e., represent ways in which a professional in a domain would work), efficient, equitable, and diagnostic. They provide an opportunity for students to link their own interests and talents with content goals or to extend their range of interests and abilities. Good product assignments include very clear expectations for the knowledge and understanding that must be represented in the product, skills that must be used in completing the product, and habits of work that students should use to complete the product. Figure 3.9 provides a variety of student products.

8. Resources

A resource is a source of knowledge for teachers and students. Resources are used to accomplish the goals within a curriculum, and they can be used by students independently or require teacher interpretation and assistance. Effective resources should provoke thinking and promote clarity of understanding about content goals. Resources are used primarily during the teaching and learning activities but also

Figure 3.9. Selected Products

Selected Products				
Advance organizer	Costume	Illustrated story	Pamphlet	Sculpture
Advertisement	Critique	Interview	Pantomime	Set design
Animation	Dance	Invention	Paragraph	Short story
Annotated bibliography	Debate	Investment portfolio	Pattern	Silk screening
Argument	Diagram	Journal	Photo essay	Simulation
Assignment	Diary	Landscape design	Photo journal	Skit
Audiotape	Dictionary	Learning profile	Play	Slide presentation
Biography	Diorama	Lecture	Picture dictionary	Small-scale model
Blueprint	Display	Lesson	Picture book	Social action plan
Board game	Dramatic monologue	Letter	Poem	Song
Book jacket	Drawing	Limerick	Portfolio	Sonnet
Bulleted list	Economic forecast	Line drawing	Poster	Stencil
Bulletin board	Editorial	List	Pottery	Summary
Compact disc	Elegy	Magazine article	PowerPoint presentation	Survey
Calendar	Essay	Map	Prediction	Table
Campaign	Etching	Maze	Protocol	Terrarium
Card game	Experiment	Memorial	Proposal	Textbook
Census	Fable	Memoir	Puppet	Timeline
Ceramics	Fact file	Montage	Puppet show	Theory
Chamber music	Fairy tale	Movie	Questions	Think piece
Character sketch	Family tree	Museum exhibit	Radio show	Topographical map
Charcoal sketch	Festival	Musical composition	Reader response	TV documentary
Chart	Filmstrip	Newspaper	Relief map	TV newscast
Choral reading	Glossary	Notes	Reflection	Video
Chronology	Graph	Observation log	Reflective essay	Video game
Collage	Graphic organizer	Oil painting	Research report	Vocabulary list
Collection	Greeting card	Oral history	Rubbing	Weather instrument/log
Comic strip	Haiku	Oral report	Rule	Web
Computer game	HyperCard® stack	Outline	Science fiction story	Worksheet
Computer program	Hypothesis	Overhead transparency	Scrapbook	Wrapping paper design

can be used during assessments, introductions, product development, and extension activities.

Resources can be categorized into two basic types: human and non-human. A sample of resources is listed in Figure 3.10. Exemplary resources are varied and closely linked to the learning goals, reading levels, cognitive strengths, and learning needs of the students who will use them.

9. Extension Activities

Extension activities are preplanned or serendipitous experiences that teachers orchestrate for individuals, small groups, or the entire class and that expand the basic unit plans. They emerge from the unit's content goals as well as student interests and

Figure 3.10. Resources

Human	Non-Human	
	Print	*Non-Print*
Content-area experts		
Older students		
Younger students	Biographies	Software
Other students in the classroom	Poems	Artifacts
Parents	Plays	Tools
Other teachers of that grade	Diaries	Inventions
Community members	Magazine articles	Technology
Teachers from other grade levels	Journals	Antiques
Other school personnel	Web	Posters
University personnel	College textbooks	Paintings
Business personnel	Newspaper	Dioramas
Service organization personnel	Emails	Models
Retired senior citizens	Nonfiction	Realia
	Fiction	Photographs
	Historical fiction	Observations
	Literary analysis	Experiments
	Manuals	Situations
	Maps	Events
	Survey data	Globes
	Tables	Videotapes
	Charts	Exhibits
	Anthologies	Costumes
	Textbooks	Designs
	Historical documents	Equipment
		Music

make content goals broader and richer. Extension activities can occur at any time during a unit. They may be of short duration (e.g., working with an interactive Web site or listening to a community speaker) or may require more extensive time (e.g., conducting an independent study, participating in a Web quest, or staging a performance). Extension activities may take place in class, at home, or both.

Teachers provide opportunities for extension activities for many reasons. First, extension activities promote the transfer and application of content goals to real-world contexts and problems. Second, they provide an opportunity to blend students' interests and areas of expertise with content goals. Third, they can link content goals in one discipline to other disciplines or to other topics within the same discipline. Extension activities also can help students gather ideas for writing, products, or problem solving. They enable students to apply new information, understanding, and skills. In addition, extension activities can be highly motivating.

High-quality extension activities have several attributes. They are (a) linked to content goals, (b) open ended, (c) authentic, (d) student centered, (e) guided, and (f) generate excitement for learning. Because of the flexibility of addressing interests of individual learners or small groups of learners, extension activities can be one way to address varied learner needs in the classroom. That is, when used to tap into or extend particular interests of learners, extension activities are much like the 10th curriculum element that follows.

10. Modifications Based on Learner Need

Teachers can greatly enhance student learning by improving the match between learners' unique characteristics and various curriculum components. Among student characteristics that affect learning, and that teachers should therefore address in curriculum planning, are students' interests, their readiness to learn particular content at a particular time, and their preferred modes of learning.

This book addresses modifications based on (a) student interest largely (but not exclusively) in sections on extension activities, (b) learning mode in discussions of teaching and learning activities, products, and extension activities, and (c) learner readiness, sophistication, or level of expertise, largely in sections on modification based on learner need. Although interest, readiness, and learning mode are all important and certainly interconnected, this book addresses readiness or sophistication largely in a separate section because the goal of the book is to address what it means to teach all learners in meaning-rich ways but to do so at levels of challenge appropriate for various learners at various points in their cognitive development.

The most effective and efficient modifications in response to learner need are proactive rather than reactive on the part of the teacher. That is, the teacher assesses and observes students to understand as fully as possible their readiness for current curriculum goals, their interests, how they learn best, their sense of self-efficacy, and their motivational patterns. In addition to learning about learners through preassessment tools, teachers can see important differences emerge from class discussions, student products, day-to-day interactions among students, teacher-student conversations, homework, and a range of other daily data sources. Using that information, the teacher is able to develop more than one path to critical learning goals.

Based upon the analysis of preassessment data and other observations, teachers adapt one or several of the components of instruction to accommodate the differences identified as potentially significant in student learning. Among the elements of instruction that can be altered in response to learner need are the following: learning goals, learning materials, methods of assessment, teaching methods (including opportunities for small group reteaching or small group advanced teaching), learning activities, grouping strategies, products, rubrics, resources, coaching or scaffolding, pacing, working arrangements, and extension activities. Naturally, not all components of instruction need to be altered at a given point. The goal is to modify those curricular elements that encourage each student to learn as much as possible and as efficiently and effectively as possible.

The concept of Ascending Intellectual Demand in the Parallel Curriculum Model is one type of modification based on learner need. It suggests the importance of a teacher monitoring the sophistication of a student's knowledge, understanding, and skill as it inevitably develops along a continuum of knowledge, understanding, and skill from fledgling or novice to expert. As the student shows increased sophistication or complexity in thought and work, the teacher modifies one or more curricular elements in response to student growth—not so much to change the core goals of the curriculum as to increase the intellectual demand in how the student works with the curriculum. This is necessary in order to continue challenge in accordance with student growth. The goal is for students to work at continual intellectual ascent in response to increased intellectual demand encountered in materials, tasks, products, pace, and so on. The intent of "ascending intellectual demand" is to ensure continual learner challenge and growth.

A Capsule of Components of Comprehensive Curriculum

A well-designed curriculum contains content/standards, referred to as content goals or learning goals; assessments, designed to chart student growth and inform instruction; an introduction, designed to motivate and orient students; varied teaching methods, aligned with learning goals and designed to present those learning goals effectively to students; learning activities, aligned with learning goals and designed to ensure cognitive engagement of students with those learning goals; grouping strategies that are varied and align both with the learning goals and students' learning needs; short- and long-term products that students create to demonstrate their understanding of the learning goals; and a variety of resources to support and extend the teaching and learning activities, extension activities, and modification of curricular elements in response to learner need, including ascending intellectual demand.

A well-designed curriculum should establish a rich framework of knowledge, understanding, and skills most relevant to the discipline. It includes and extends both district expectations and state frameworks or standards. A well-designed curriculum benefits school districts, teachers, and schools.

It benefits the school district because it:

1. Articulates, in writing, a defensible, coherent educational plan
2. Promotes consistency of implementation.

It benefits students because it:

1. Supports equality of educational opportunity by including all students as targets of powerful learning
2. Supports excellence through increasing levels of intellectual demand
3. Elevates thinking (analytical, critical, and creative) by focusing on appropriate learning activities
4. Sequences a continuum of learning experiences, PreK-12, that leads learners naturally from novice to expert in each discipline; it helps students organize and build knowledge
5. Is engaging; it beckons students into a content area through inviting problems, issues, and dilemmas central to a discipline
6. Engages students with meaningful products that represent the work of professionals in the discipline
7. Makes explicit what constitutes evidence of effectiveness; it clarifies, for students and teachers, a clear set of expectations

It benefits teachers because it:

1. Helps them understand what goes into a curriculum unit
2. Promotes the linkage among the components of instruction
3. Elevates the art of lesson planning and decreases teacher reliance on textbooks
4. Establishes educational priorities; makes teaching and learning more efficient and effective
5. Invites professional collaboration in order to make sense of the curriculum
6. Makes planning orderly and effective

Remodeling a Study Unit Using the Comprehensive Curriculum Framework: One Teacher's Approaches

Beginning with this chapter and subsequent ones that examine the four parallels of the Parallel Curriculum Model, you will see how "Lydia Janis," a fictionalized fifth grade teacher, uses five approaches to curriculum development to craft the same social studies unit on the Civil War for her students. In this chapter, she uses a "remodeling" approach to revise her original textbook unit. That is, rather than merely following the textbook's directions, she uses the components in the curriculum design process discussed earlier in this chapter to enhance the quality of her unit. As the chapters progress, she will redesign her fifth grade Civil War unit using each of the four parallels in the Parallel Curriculum Model. A note to keep in mind: Even though Lydia is a fictionalized teacher, the work presented as hers in the remainder of this book was actually developed by teachers using the thought processes described for each of the five approaches to curriculum design—first, the remodeling approach and then the approaches suggested, respectively, by the Core Curriculum Parallel, the Curriculum of Connections, the Curriculum of Practice, and the Curriculum of Identity.

Additional, but briefer, examples that illustrate the four parallels are also woven into the text of the next four chapters. These scenarios provide a glimpse of how the basic curriculum components might be designed to accomplish the unique goals of each of the four parallels. These examples were chosen to represent a variety of grade levels and content areas in order to broaden the reader's perspective on applying the parallels. It is our hope that the format will be helpful to readers in comparing and contrasting these ways of thinking about curriculum design.

Figure 3.11 reviews the steps that Lydia follows in remodeling her unit from one that simply covers standards and the text to one that is more coherent, more likely to help students understand and retain what they encounter, and more inviting to the young learners with whom she works. Although not every teacher who engages in the basic remodeling process will work with each of these steps, and while it is not necessary that they always be followed in the precise order used here, Lydia addresses all the steps, and in the order noted, so that her example is a match for the explanation of the curriculum design components that precedes the teaching scenario.

Setting the Course: Aligning Text and Standards

Lydia Janis gathered the student's textbook, teacher's guide, and the notebook containing her state and district's Grade 5 social studies standards and related curriculum guide. She laid them on her dining room table and began her work. First on her list was an examination of the unit's learning standards and objectives.

Figure 3.11. Lydia's Steps in the Curriculum Remodeling Process

Step	Activity
1	Consult national, state, and local curriculum frameworks
2	Compare textbook objectives with state and local standards to ensure alignment
3	Design assessments (i.e., pre, ongoing, and post) that embed the targeted knowledge and contain the desired level of understanding
4	Establish clear learning objectives that build state and local learning goals and consider the learning needs of students
5	Develop an aligned set of introductory activities
6	Select teaching methods that align with the content and students' learning needs
7	Determine the learning activities and align them with the teaching activities and learning goals
8	Consider possible grouping formats
9	Target a variety of student products that align with the learning goals to assess student progress
10	Identify and locate resources
11	Consider possible extension activities
12	Consider modifications, including ascending intellectual demand, for students as they advance toward expertise

Lydia's state and local objectives were well aligned, eliminating a great deal of time that she might have had to spend aligning those two documents. In Lydia's state, the social studies curriculum incorporates four strands: history, government, economics, and geography. These four strands encompass 266 learning standards, K-12. Lydia's district decided that the fifth grade social studies curriculum would involve the study of history, with minor emphases on government, economics, and geography. The Grade 5 social studies curriculum committee divided the school year into seven related curriculum units focused on these emphases. These units included the following topics: indigenous people, exploration, colonization, revolution, formation of a new nation, our expanding nation, and the Civil War. Each unit varied in length, depending on the number of learning goals to be achieved, but generally lasted from three to five weeks.

After the social studies curriculum committee developed the list of units within each grade level, they worked together to select the learning standards related to each unit. As a result of this decision, Lydia's district developed a curriculum map that contained 25 learning standards for Grade 5. To improve transfer of learning, many of these standards were addressed in more than one grade level and within more than one curriculum unit.

Lydia's first task was to review the curriculum map and the grade level and unit learning goals in light of what she and her students needed to accomplish in social studies over the course of the year. She realized that she had approximately four weeks to address 12 social studies standards within the context of the Civil War. These standards, taken from *The Connecticut Framework: K-12 Curricular Goals and Standards* (Connecticut State Department of Education, 1998a), included the following:

1. Demonstrate an in-depth understanding of major events and trends in U.S. history (history)
2. Analyze data in order to see persons and events in their historical context; understand causal factors and appreciate change over time (history)
3. Examine current concepts, issues, events, and themes from historical perspectives and identify conflicting ideas from competing narratives or interpretations of historical events (history)
4. Explain reasons for conflict and the ways conflicts have been resolved (history)
5. Explain how economic factors influenced historical events in the United States (history)
6. Display empathy for people who have lived in the past (history)
7. Describe and analyze, using historical data and understandings, the options available to parties involved in contemporary conflicts or decision making (history)
8. Identify and evaluate various perspectives associated with places and regions (geography)
9. Evaluate situations involving conflicts between citizens' rights and propose solutions to these conflicts (government)
10. Use maps, globes, models, graphs, charts, and databases to analyze distributions and patterns (geography)
11. Identify governmental activities that affect the local, state, national, and international economy (economics)
12. Explain how specialization leads to more efficient use of economic resources and economic growth (economics)

Upon reading this list, Lydia concluded that the unit's standards did indeed capture the principles that students should understand about this period in United States history.

Next, Lydia compared the district curriculum guide with the teacher's guide that accompanied her textbook. She located the two chapters in her textbook devoted to the Civil War and searched for the section that described the learning goals. This section was labeled *Lesson Objectives*. She noted 15 learning objectives for the two chapters.

Lydia spread out the list of textbook objectives next to the list of standards that she located in her district's curriculum guide. She then listed in parentheses beside each textbook objective the number of the standard to which the objective seemed to connect. She wanted to make sure that her textbook addressed each of the standards.

1. Analyze the differences between the North and South (**4**)
2. Describe how some enslaved people fought against slavery (**4**)
3. Identify the difficulties faced by free African Americans (6)
4. Identify leading abolitionists and describe their fight against slavery (*1*, 8, 9)
5. Explain how the movement for women's rights began (3, 6, 8, 9)
6. Describe the compromises over slavery that temporarily prevented the South's secession (*1*, **4**)
7. Analyze the reasons that the South seceded (**4**)
8. Describe how the Civil War began (*1*, 5, 12)
9. Compare and contrast the strengths of each side (*1*, 2)
10. Explain how technology changed the way wars were fought (2, 10)
11. Analyze the effect of the Emancipation Proclamation on both the North and the South (3, **4**)
12. Describe how women on both sides supported the war effort (3)
13. Evaluate the effects of the war on the North and South (2)
14. Describe Sherman's march (*1*, 10)
15. Describe Lee's surrender at Appomattox (*1*)

She was not altogether surprised when she discovered that many of her textbook objectives related in some way to the first and fourth standards on her list. Six of her textbook objectives were related to the first standard (indicated in italics in the parentheses), and five were related to the fourth standard (indicated in bold in the parentheses). "That's good," she thought. "Students need to know the major events and trends surrounding the Civil War. They also need to know that the Civil War is really about a conflict."

The other thing that really pleased Lydia was the fact that her textbook appeared to cover all but two of the standards, 7 and 11. "Number 11 is about economics," Lydia thought to herself. "I will talk about the different economies of the North and South when we examine causes of the Civil War." She wasn't sure yet how to incorporate Standard 11. On a sticky note she jotted down, "Remember to help students see how government activities can affect the local, state, and national economy." She put the sticky note in her teacher's edition. "This note will remind me," thought Lydia.

Satisfied that the content of the textbook aligned fairly well with her standards, Lydia turned her attention to the other components of her instruction.

Revising the Teacher's Guide Assessment

When Lydia analyzed the assessment section that accompanied the teacher's guide, she found that the assessments addressed only 4 of the 15 objectives for the two textbook chapters. A closer analysis of the student's book revealed that the review section for each lesson was more closely aligned to the objectives but that these review sections went only as far as rephrasing each learning objective as a question for the students to answer. Other options for student assessment were sparse or omitted. One-word or short phrases were the only responses required of students. When a review question seemed to support higher level thinking from students (e.g., Why did Lincoln announce the Emancipation Proclamation after the Battle of Antietam?), Lydia discovered that the answer to the question need only be paraphrased from the original text (e.g., "President Lincoln also found a way to inspire his troops. Five days after Antietam, Lincoln issued the Emancipation Proclamation.").

She realized she needed to create her own assessments. Her first decision was to create a pre- and a postassessment that mirrored each other. Using these assessments as bookends before and after instruction, Lydia would be able to measure each student's growth and progress with regard to her content. To assess student growth with respect to the objective "Describe how the Civil War began," Lydia chose a simple, open-ended question. Using a graphic organizer that resembled a flow chart, Lydia asked her students to respond to the following prompt: "Use this diagram and your knowledge of the Civil War to list, in order, the major events and people that led up to the beginning of the Civil War." She created a very simple, five-point rubric, reprinted below in Figure 3.12, to evaluate student responses.

The impact of the change she made in assessment strategies was powerful. Not only was she able to assess changes over time in an individual student's growth in critical knowledge, she had also developed a rubric that could be revised easily to fit a number of different objectives and contexts. Also, the use of the preassessment provided Lydia with important information about students' prior knowledge—information she could use to save valuable time for teaching the remaining units in her textbook.

Lydia was aware that the use of preassessment took some time during the course of a four-week unit. However, she believed the time allocated to preassessment was well spent because it provided previously hidden information about students' prior

Figure 3.12. Rubric to Evaluate Students' Flow Chart

				HIGHLY	
SOCIAL STUDIES RUBRIC: FLOW CHART OF MAJOR EVENTS LEADING UP TO THE CIVIL WAR					
Key Feature	*NOVICE*	*COMPETENT*	*INFORMED*	*HIGHLY INFORMED*	*EXPERT*
Accuracy	Two or fewer major events noted; 2 or more inaccuracies are evident; formatting is incorrect	At least 3 major events are noted; 2 inaccuracies are evident; the formatting has minor mistakes	At least 4 major events are noted; 1 inaccuracy is evident; formatting is correct	More than 5 major events are noted; minor inaccuracies are evident; formatting is correct	More than 6 major events are noted; no inaccuracies are evident; formatting is correct

knowledge and because it created an advance organizer for students by alerting them to the major goals within the unit. Lydia continued to develop open-ended questions and related rubrics for the remaining objectives in the textbook unit, attempting to pull together objectives when feasible to help herself and students see connections among them. She was pleased with her progress so far.

Planning the Introduction to the Unit

The teacher's guide provided suggestions for introducing the unit, including: showing students early photographs from the mid-1800s, asking them what they already knew about the guarantees of freedom provided by the U.S. Constitution, talking about bugles and what they symbolize, discussing quotations from the Emancipation Proclamation, and thinking about the similarities and differences in the lives of farmers, soldiers, merchants, slaves, and slave holders. Lydia recognized that many of these ideas were potentially powerful, but there were too many of them, and they were too splintered and discrete. Looking in the textbook chapters for introductory activities that would capture her students' interest, she decided to use the photographs in the text. She would ask students to scan the photographs for interesting and familiar elements. Students would then participate in small group discussions guided by questions Lydia provided to help them begin to focus on unit objectives.

To create a more motivating introduction to the unit for her students, Lydia created three additional introductory activities. She visited her school library and borrowed a copy of *The Boy's War: Confederate and Union Soldiers Talk About the Civil War.* She would use this book as a motivational tool and as part of her daily read-aloud to her students. As she read, she would ask students to sketch scenes, events, characters, and impressions from the book in order to improve their mental images of the historical period.

Next Lydia printed a list of learning goals and expectations for the four-week unit to share with her students. She knew it was important that students understand what was expected of them from the very beginning of the unit in order to increase their ownership in learning. She would use this list as her advance organizer for the unit. Then Lydia would preassess students' knowledge using the assessment questions and rubrics described in the previous section. Prior to the preassessment, Lydia planned to explain to them what a preassessment was, why she was administering one, and what she hoped to learn from their early responses to her questions.

Determining Teaching Methods and Learning Activities

Lydia wanted to be sure her teaching activities would introduce, explain, scaffold, organize, and demonstrate new knowledge and skills as well as engage students with the new material. In essence, she would be a bridge builder between learners and the new knowledge they needed to acquire. Good teachers, she knew, challenge learners to think their way through new content, but good teachers never present insurmountable obstacles to the acquisition of knowledge and skills.

When Lydia reviewed the teaching activities in her textbook, she realized that, for the most part, students were expected to acquire new knowledge by independent reading, with only a few clarifying questions posed by the teacher or the textbook every two to three pages. Although the textbook provided a great deal of information for elementary teachers who may not have majored in the social sciences, there was little support for the learner who may be unfamiliar with the content or the structure of textbook learning. There were few focusing questions, little use of headings, and no use of boldface to mark new vocabulary or concepts.

There seemed to be little role for the teacher in forwarding the learning of her or his students. Was Lydia's only job to maintain classroom discipline and on-task behavior, assign pages to be read each day, and ask the questions printed in the side margins of the teacher's manual? How were students to cope with the new knowledge that was so tersely presented in the textbook? Lydia made a decision not unlike those she had made before. She had to provide the scaffolding that the textbook lacked in order to help her students understand the new content they were to acquire.

She would use the writing in the student's textbook to inform her own knowledge base, but instead of expecting her students to absorb the new content by themselves, she would create a structure to help them analyze the text's content. Lydia chose focusing questions, strategy-based teaching, graphic organizers, and cooperative learning as teaching methods to provide this structure. She would also incorporate teaching methods to help novice textbook readers develop effective techniques for reading nonfiction.

First, she created focusing questions for each major section in the two textbook chapters. Then, she identified the kind of analytic thinking needed to process the text's information and answer the focusing questions. Third, she developed a skill strategy to help her students learn how to use this analytic thinking skill. Fourth, she created a graphic organizer that required the use of this analytic thinking skill to answer the focusing question. For example, to help students acquire knowledge about the major differences between the North and the South, Lydia created two related focusing questions:

1. What were the differences between the economies of the North and the South prior to the Civil War?
2. How did these differences contribute to the start of the Civil War?

Next, Lydia located the four pages in the student's textbook that explained differences between the North and the South prior to the Civil War. To help students identify the related factors, she realized her students must use two thinking skills: (a) comparing and contrasting and (b) finding the main idea. She created two skill strategies and two graphic organizers similar to those shown in Figures 3.13 through 3.16.

Figure 3.13. Skill Strategy for Comparing and Contrasting

1. Identify the purpose for comparing and contrasting.
2. Identify the objects, elements, persons, or events to be compared and contrasted.
3. Identify the attributes of each object, element, person, or event that relates to the purpose of the comparing and contrasting.
4. Note the relevant information.
5. Develop a related graphic organizer.
6. Identify a trend or pattern across the attributes or items.
7. Draw conclusions based on the evidence as it relates to the purpose for comparing and contrasting.

Figure 3.14. Graphic Organizer to Support Student Comparing and Contrasting

Purpose: *Compare and Contrast the Economies of the North and the South*

Factors	North	South
Workers	Worked in factories	Farmhands, slaves
Workplaces	Factories	Plantations
Resources	Coal, wood, iron, machines	Slaves, land, cotton, farms
Products	Ships, cloth, machines, guns, trains	Cotton
Profit	More money, more people	More land, more slaves

Conclusion: Slaves in the South worked on plantations. Free people in the North worked at lots of different factory jobs. These differences made people in the North and South feel differently about issues.

Figure 3.15. Skill Strategy for Finding the Main Idea

1. Identify the purpose for finding the main idea.
2. Identify passages related to this purpose.
3. Read the passage and identify relevant details related to the purpose.
4. Determine commonalties among the details.
5. Restate the commonalties as an overarching statement.
6. Connect the identified main idea to the original purpose.

Figure 3.16. Graphic Organizer to Support Finding the Main Idea

Purpose: To discover what key factors led to the Civil War and how these factors are connected

Main Idea: Four different factors led to the Civil War. These factors made Northerners and Southerners dislike and mistrust one another. They couldn't find a solution.

Factor #1—Two very different economies
Supporting Detail

Factor #2—Views about states' rights
Supporting Detail

Factor #3—Missouri Compromise
Supporting Detail

Factor #4—Slavery
Supporting Detail

Lydia knew these graphic organizers were aligned with the major thinking skills needed to understand the factual textbook content and would support students' knowledge acquisition. Students would work with these graphic organizers in small groups, scaffolded by each other and Lydia's strategy-based teaching, coaching, feedback, and questions regarding their work, to dissect and analyze textbook passages as they developed answers to the questions focused on literal comprehension.

Although these changes promoted greater student understanding, they were by no means the only teaching strategies Lydia used during the course of the unit. She also developed brief oral presentations and taught specific strategies for improving students' reading of nonfiction and their literal comprehension skills.

The development of the focusing questions, skill strategies, and graphic organizers required two hours of additional time. Lydia quickly realized, however, that her time had been well spent. Now that she had these skills strategies and graphic organizers, she could use them in numerous other units and subject areas, whenever students needed to analyze information in order to acquire new knowledge.

During this phase of textbook analysis and remodeling, Lydia also analyzed the learning activities embedded in the unit. After she reviewed the textbook learning objectives, she searched the related student pages to identify the means by which students were to acquire this new knowledge. She recalled that there were only two ways for students to acquire new information—either they read the textbook or they listened to the teacher's explanations and presentations. Further, she remembered that the text activities only called for the cognitive processes of recall and paraphrasing on the part of her students.

Lydia knew that this kind of learning was short lived. Knowledge that was memorized and paraphrased rarely entered a student's long-term memory. Not content with these results, Lydia was glad she had remodeled the teaching methods to support students' analytic thinking instead of restricting her focus to rote learning. To help her students come to a deep understanding of new knowledge, to retain, retrieve, and transfer new knowledge, she had to require students to use literal comprehension skills and analytic thinking. She couldn't assume her students already knew how to use these skills, and the textbook didn't teach them how. Instead, she decided to create and teach skill strategies that explained how expert readers and thinkers find the main idea, compare and contrast, note details, sequence ideas, and draw conclusions.

The graphic organizers she had created to support her teaching activities would be useful aids to scaffold students' literal comprehension and analytic thinking with the textbook content. She realized her revisions would contribute greatly to her students' evolving abilities to read nonfiction material in a variety of content areas.

To find time in the unit to complete these important activities, Lydia had to delete some of the textbook activities with less potential to help students make meaning of the events they were studying. These activities included learning the lyrics to "Battle Hymn of the Republic" and "Dixie," making a paper quilt containing Civil War themes, and creating a bulletin board of famous quotations from the Civil War.

Finding Resources for the Unit

Lydia spent time looking over the list of resources provided in the teacher's edition. They included photographs of log cabins, slaves, cotton fields, and famous people such as Fredrick Douglass, Sojourner Truth, Jefferson Davis, Harriet Tubman, and Abraham Lincoln; excerpts from primary source documents; and portions of newspaper articles and speeches. Songs, paintings, and political cartoons were also available to students via the teacher's guide. One of the strongest sections of her teacher's book was the bibliography that contained lists of historical fiction and nonfiction related to the war.

Lydia was confused about the number and variety of resources presented in her teacher's edition. The quantity of resources seemed overwhelming, and many of them did not seem a match for the factual objectives the book specified for the unit. For example, some of the resources were appealing, but they seemed to pull her away from her learning goals. It was interesting to her that the resources suggested in the book somehow seemed richer than the textbook content and objectives. She didn't want to change the unit objectives to match the resources unless she more fully understood the connections. Next summer, she decided, she'd revisit this issue and try to align the potential of the resources with the unit objectives. For now, she would be content to focus on and assess the original objectives along with her students' growth in reading nonfiction, literal comprehension, and analytic thinking. She continued to use the student edition of the textbook as a major resource.

Lydia supplemented the textbook with a list of learning objectives that she rewrote in students' language. She would distribute the list to her students. She also made lists of focusing questions for each section of the text, created skill strategies for key skills, developed graphic organizers to support students in understanding and applying the skills, and duplicated these for distribution to students at appropriate times.

She also purchased colored Post-it® notes and a large supply of colored highlighters. Finally, she duplicated some important textbook sections. She would use these copies along with the Post-it® notes and highlighter pens to help her students learn to note key ideas, supporting details, evidence, main ideas, and conclusions and how to jot down important thoughts and questions as they read.

These resources seemed a good match for both the content and skills goals she had adopted for the unit. She was satisfied that the resources would help her students be more thoughtful about the content of the text and more effective readers and analysts of nonfiction materials.

Developing Products for the Unit

Now Lydia was ready to review the product mentioned in the teacher's guide. Options included short answers to review questions worksheets with short answers, a bulletin board, a scrapbook, quilts, discussions, a debate, short answers to teacher's oral questions, character sketches, letters, editorials, charts and timelines, and a skit. She decided she wanted to select only those product ideas that aligned with her objectives and would not require a great deal of class time.

Lydia thought a combination of short- and long-term products would work well for her students. She had already decided to create a 15-item set of open-ended questions for the unit's pre- and postassessment. These questions related tightly to focusing questions she had developed for each section of the text and for classroom discussions. She decided to continue to use the review at the end of each section of the chapter because these questions also linked closely with the focusing questions and the main ideas in the text. The questions could be answered in writing by individuals or during whole class or small group discussions.

Still sensing a need to move beyond the factual level recall required in these assignments, however, Lydia considered the long list of optional products in her teacher's manual. She knew she couldn't assign all of them, and besides, many of them seemed a poor match for the unit's goals. She selected development of a timeline because it related closely to several of the text objectives. It would also allow her to use some newly acquired software to integrate technology into student learning—a key initiative in her district.

Lydia also decided to use a long-term collaborative project for her students that could serve as a culminating product. If she selected carefully, the product would be useful to her students in synthesizing all the events, people, and perspectives that played a role in the Civil War. She chose a mural that would depict, in chronological order, key issues, events, and people of the time period. Her directions for the mural would guide student thinking as they worked in small groups to complete the product. The directions would need to ensure a clear connection between the learning objectives and precisely what she asked the students to do.

At this point, Lydia Janis had remodeled her unit to make it more coherent, challenging, and aligned with her learning objectives. Her work should be more effective in helping students understand content and issues related to the Civil War, retain what they study, and develop the skills of effective readers and thinkers.

Modifying Basic Plans in Response to Learner Needs

Although the vast majority of learners would benefit from the curriculum Lydia has remodeled, it is also the case that her students, as is the case with most groups of learners, vary markedly in their prior knowledge, experiences, readiness to learn, interests, and modes of learning. Thus, while all learners share a common need for quality curriculum, Lydia knew there would be times when she would modify her curriculum plans to accommodate the learning needs of the diverse students in her classroom. She decided to continually monitor students' work and conversations for indications of their needs and repeatedly invite them to let her know what was working for them and what was not working so well in their classroom.

Strategies that Lydia would use to modify her basic unit plans to ensure that learning was a good fit for all of her students include the following:

▶ Conducting reteaching sessions on topics or skills for students who have difficulty mastering them

▶ Providing audiotapes of the chapter along with an outline of the unit for students who have difficulty reading the textbook alone or who are highly auditory learners

▶ Offering a chance for students to work alone or with partners on some tasks

▶ Varying the amount of support she offers to students during various tasks based on their individual needs

▶ Setting up the classroom so that students sometimes have the freedom to choose where to sit and their work surfaces and materials

▶ Maintaining centers on topics of interest to her learners

▶ Supplementing her oral presentations with overhead transparencies, advance organizers, and opportunities for small group discussions of content

Lydia already knew where several of these strategies would be useful. In fact, she realized, she had built several of them into the unit as she had remodeled it.

First, Lydia's plans called for preassessment of her students. That would help her detect various levels of prior knowledge about the Civil War among her students, and she could respond to what she learned at the outset of the unit by varying homework based on learner need and by excusing students already demonstrating mastery from some of the reading and writing tasks.

Second, her teacher-created graphic organizers would help many of Lydia's learners understand how to find main ideas, supporting details, and cause and effect. However, for students who already possessed these skills, she would encourage them to develop their own ways to show their analysis of text and events and to depict examples of cause and effect in their studies.

Third, the class textbook was written at a fifth grade reading level. This would be advantageous for some of her grade-level readers. On the other hand, a few students would need assistance in reading this book. She would use reading squads with those students, enabling them to read aloud, hear others read aloud, hear her read aloud, and use tape-recorded readings. For her more advanced readers, she would select some additional, more complex nonfiction materials about the Civil War to provide challenge.

Looking Back and Ahead

In her remodeling effort, Lydia Janis has ensured that her fifth grade Civil War Unit is richer and tighter than it would have been if she had moved her students through text material. To revisit an earlier analogy, she resisted the temptation to serve a list of ingredients and call it a meal. Instead, she blended and combined the ingredients to create a meal. She has systematically addressed the key components of effective curriculum. Her plans are thoughtful and thorough, although she understands she may modify them again as the unit unfolds—particularly in light of her ongoing assessment of her students' successes and needs. Lydia also knows, even as she is pleased with these new unit plans, that her teaching of the unit this year will point her toward changes she can make in the unit next year to make it more effective still. She understands that her goal is not to "finish" writing the unit but, rather, to learn more about teaching each time she uses it and to convert what she learns into refined ways of practicing her profession.

Lydia's work to this point is fundamentally sound but not especially sophisticated. As subsequent chapters explore the Parallel Curriculum Model and its four parallel ways of thinking about curriculum design, you'll see Lydia's thinking evolve. You should see several things as you read. First, the fundamental components of curriculum design are evident in all four parallels. The elements of curriculum don't disappear when a new curriculum model appears. Second, you'll see Lydia's curriculum become richer and more compelling as she restructures it using the four parallels of the Parallel Curriculum Model. We hope you'll see the possibilities offered by this new model and its four parallels to develop high potential in a broad range of young learners, including those who are already advanced. It is the premise of this book that educators—as all professionals—must continually look for avenues to make good practice better.

4

The Core Curriculum Parallel

The Comprehensive Curriculum Framework described in Chapter 3 provides a structure for designing a well-aligned and motivating set of teaching and learning activities stemming from clear objectives and carefully correlated assessments. With proper professional development and collegial collaboration, this framework supports teachers as they decrease reliance on the textbook-driven or activity-oriented curriculum and move toward one that is based on clear content standards and is cognitively engaging.

The framework itself is flexible enough to support either lesson remodeling or the development of comprehensive curriculum units that supplement existing textbook chapters for students at any grade level and within any subject area. The key components and the accompanying set of best practices provide a set of guidelines that encourage an evolution of the lesson planning and unit development process. In addition, the framework makes provisions for ensuring that teaching/learning plans are a good fit for the range of students in the classroom.

Yet in a book that proposes and describes four additional approaches to or frameworks for curriculum design, two questions immediately arise. First, if the Comprehensive Curriculum Framework is a defensible and effective method for delivering high-quality learning experiences, why does this book contain descriptions of four other approaches to curriculum development? Second, what are the differences among these four approaches; do they provide elements that contradict, complement, or supplant the key features of the Comprehensive Curriculum Framework?

In order to provide at least a partial answer to these questions, this chapter has been divided into four sections. The first section presents a rationale for having four approaches to curriculum design rather than adhering consistently to only one approach. In the second section, readers are given a definition of the first curriculum parallel proposed in this book, the Core Curriculum Parallel, and an explanation of its purpose and function. The third section explains procedures for modifying the key curriculum components in order to align them with the goals and purposes of the Core Curriculum Parallel and includes an exploration of the nature of "ascending intellectual demand" within the Core Curriculum Parallel. The fourth section revisits our fictionalized teacher, Lydia Janis, and provides a description of the decisions she used when recrafting her curriculum using the goals and purposes of the Core Curriculum Parallel.

Why Four Approaches to Curriculum Design? Isn't One Good Enough?

It's difficult to argue with the merits of using the components of the Comprehensive Curriculum Framework either for developing exemplary curriculum or for evaluating and improving existing curriculum. The value of designing or selecting clear learning objectives, related assessments, motivating introductory experiences, powerful teaching and learning activities, and appropriate resources, products, and extension activities is apparent and universal across the writings of our most honored curriculum theorists and researchers. In addition, the features mentioned above, and the accompanying characteristics and indicators of exemplary design, provide ideal criteria to guide the process of curriculum development. Why, then, might it be useful for an educator to have a working knowledge of other curriculum design approaches? Might additional approaches simply add to the confusion, invite competition, and decrease the likelihood of successful implementation?

Perhaps the best way to answer these questions is by relating two anecdotes that are familiar to many of us. They serve as metaphors and windows that allow us a clear perspective on changes in the curriculum development process over time. Have these events ever happened to you? Consider the learning you acquired as a result of these or similar experiences.

Metaphor #1: The Novice-Expert Continuum

You read an interesting book, short story, magazine article, or poem. A few days later, a friend or colleague mentions having read the same piece of writing. The two of you spend the next 15 minutes discussing the text. As you end the conversation, it occurs to you that you thought you had a sound understanding of that piece of writing before discussing it with your friend, but now you aren't so sure. Your companion mentioned aspects of the writer's style, perspective, and the text's content that you hadn't considered. It occurs to you that the conversation with your friend has deepened what you believed was already a comprehensive understanding of the topic.

That conversation with your friend caused you to see the text in new ways. You know more now because you had an experience that allowed you to reflect, recognize a gap between what was evident and what was assumed, learn, and, as a result, deepen your initial understanding. Sometimes, conversations cause us to see things with new eyes. Sometimes, solitude, analytic thought, time, distance, perspective, a simple question, or the acquisition of additional knowledge causes that change. Whatever the cause, the effect is the same. Our knowledge base and the depth of our understanding can grow and deepen as a result of our thinking and learning experiences. When this happens, we are often intrigued with the possibilities that this new knowledge offers and with the new doors that it opens.

Curriculum writing, like learning, is the result of a dynamic interaction between a person's cognitive faculties, his or her professional experiences with learners and colleagues, and an existing or new body of content knowledge. The lesson plan or unit that we write and implement today, with pride, may look different to us in a few years. Our students and our teaching circumstances often change and vary throughout our career. Our understanding of our students and of the topics that we teach often deepens as a result of our own professional learning. When this happens, we may experience a sense of dissatisfaction with curriculum that used to be a source of gratification. Like a shoe that no longer fits, we may outgrow what used to be a perfectly comfortable set of lesson plans in search of a larger, more expansive curriculum that permits us to travel farther, under different circumstances, or for diverse purposes.

That reaction is similar to the one many of us have when we unearth a lesson plan or longer piece of curriculum that we wrote years ago and haven't seen since. Our response is often one of surprise, an initial sense of puzzlement when we see our names on something we can't remember writing. We are often amazed at the lack of depth, the missing information, the gaps, or the inconsistencies in a lesson that at one time seemed so right, so complete, and so compelling.

Our own professional growth and hard work become the source of our dissatisfaction and a catalyst for change. Sometimes, a colleague provides an extra push, sometimes, it's a book, new research, or our students' reactions or comments. Either way, the inevitable happens. As teachers become more experienced, more reflective, and more knowledgeable, as they evolve from novices to veterans, expertise is enhanced. Although experience and tenure do not guarantee the development of expertise, the teacher who values and pursues lifelong learning and professional growth inevitably opens the door to new encounters, perspectives, knowledge, and needs as time passes. This growth process can affect our content knowledge, pedagogical expertise, and changes in priorities with regard to what students need from teachers and what students need to learn. These changes can also cause dissatisfaction with a curriculum framework that, on earlier occasions, seemed exemplary and comprehensive. As we become wiser and more experienced, our view of the curriculum, and of knowledge and the relationship among topics, disciplines, and learners often expands. When this happens, it is valuable to have other alternatives for thinking about the curriculum. Not only can alternative options satisfy our need to grow professionally, they can, like a stimulating conversation with a thoughtful friend, be a catalyst for that growth.

Metaphor #2: Form Follows Function

Increasing levels of curriculum expertise do not necessarily imply that eventually we should abandon one framework in search of another. Nor does it imply that if we search long enough, we will discover or develop one framework that is far superior to any other. Instead, growth in expertise usually produces a broader, not just a different, perspective. Instead of evaluating different approaches and finding some exemplary and others lacking, growth in curriculum expertise usually results in a more utilitarian view of various curriculum approaches; one is not necessarily better than another. The various approaches simply serve different purposes and address different needs.

This principle about curriculum design, that form follows function, helps explain the reason why this book shares four such approaches or frameworks for use in curriculum design or remodeling. As defined in this book, a model is a format for curriculum design. It is a special configuration of key curriculum components within the Comprehensive Curriculum Framework designed to meet special needs and purposes. It is the unique arrangement and fabrication of these components that results in the development of a curriculum that is singularly tied to the four special purposes of the four different curriculum frameworks or approaches described in this book.

Metaphor #3: Architectural Design

Just as a curriculum is a purposeful design, written by educators to build connections among teachers, learners, and content knowledge, a commercial architect drafts a blueprint for a building design that forges strong connections among service providers, their service, and the community at large. Just as the development of a curriculum requires the use of a framework comprised of interconnected components, an architectural design requires the combined use of a set of architectural components to construct a sound and functional building. Just as the basic framework of a commercial building remains constant while the form of the building varies according to its function, the key curriculum components and framework remain constant while the form and model (i.e., the special configuration) of these components vary according to the function and purpose of the curriculum.

Imagine that the comprehensive curriculum components are comparable to the basic components of a building: the foundation, the sill plate and flooring, the electrical system, the plumbing, the heating and cooling system, trusses, roof, windows, doors, and rooms. Depending on whether commercial architects are designing a hospital, a restaurant, a library, or a fire station, they would vary the configuration, or form, of these basic components to serve the specific needs of the service providers, the clients of these service providers, or the nature of the services. The special configuration of these architectural components may change the number of rooms, the height of the ceilings, the nature of the flooring, or the thickness of the pipes, but the basic architectural components still exist, as they do in all comprehensive curriculum.

Just as the nature and characteristics of these components vary according the purpose of the building, the basic curriculum components vary according to the purpose of the curriculum. Each of the four curriculum parallels described in this book follows the same basic curriculum design structure and incorporates the use of the key curriculum components. However, just as architectural form follows the function of a building, the choice to use a particular curriculum framework requires a conscious decision based on the needs of the learner and the purpose for which the curriculum is designed.

What Is "Core" in the Core Curriculum Parallel?

Let's begin with a word association. When you hear the word "core," what expressions spring to mind? If you said apple core, the core of the matter, core of the Earth, or the core of a nuclear reactor, you probably identified the most common associations for this term. In addition, some other synonyms for core are kernel, heart, gist, essence, basic nature, crux, and fundamental.

As these words imply, the Core Curriculum Parallel provides a format and set of procedures that help curriculum developers get to the core, fundamental, or essential knowledge and meaning of a discipline as they teach topics in that discipline. They see a benefit in using the topic studied to help students become proficient not only with information about the topic but also about the major concepts and principles in the discipline from which the topic is derived.

With this approach, a unit may focus learning on a specific topic, such as radish plants, the Civil War, *Romeo and Juliet,* or Beethoven, but that focus would not be an end in and of itself. Instead, a study of fast-growing radish plants is used to forge an understanding of the basic concepts, principles, and skills that cut across the study of all plants and across all topics in botany or biology, knowledge that is core to the discipline in which the topic resides. In the case of radish plants, the learning activities may focus attention on the life cycle, food production, or roles of ecosystem members. The topic being studied—in this case, radishes—serves as a representative topic, not a stand-alone subject, to help learners understand the basic structure of a discipline.

As the Comprehensive Curriculum Framework serves to elevate curriculum development by helping teachers move from coverage of sometimes disjointed information and skills to a richer, more coherent curriculum, so the Core Curriculum Parallel should again "lift" curriculum design to a higher level of quality. The Core Curriculum Parallel exists to move curriculum developers from a well-aligned plan for teaching to one that retains alignment while getting at the core knowledge, structure, and purpose of a discipline.

Because of its goal of helping teachers and students come to understand what constitutes the core knowledge, structure, and purpose of a discipline, the Core Curriculum Parallel suggests that teachers and students continue to ask a set of questions likely to help reveal those things (see Figure 4.1).

These additional questions probe the content more deeply. They help provide answers to the "So what?" and "Who cares?" questions that can plague teachers in a classroom inhabited by restless young minds. More to the point, these questions demand complex thinking, manipulation of ideas, awareness of patterns—and they have real implications for helping students move from novice-level consumers of someone else's information to more sophisticated meaning-makers who deal with

Figure 4.1. Focusing Questions of the Core Curriculum Parallel

- What does this information mean?
- Why does this information matter?
- How is the information organized to help people use it better?
- Why do these ideas make sense?
- What are these ideas and skills for?
- How do these ideas and skills work?
- How can I use these ideas and skills?

the fundamental concepts, principles, and skills of a discipline. Simply put, there is no such thing as an expert in a domain who lacks an understanding of the core organization, purpose, and meaning of that domain. If we are serious about helping more students develop their potential—and about helping more high potential learners maximize that potential—we have to teach them in ways that help them systematically develop and strengthen their understanding of the frameworks of meaning and skill that characterize experts in a discipline.

Within the Core Curriculum Parallel, knowledge is selected for teaching and learning based on its ability to cause a series of chain reactions that link learners to the key concepts and principles of the discipline as a whole. Just as the core in a nuclear reactor contains pellets of a special kind of uranium, capable of causing multiple nuclear reactions, the careful selection of specific aspects of knowledge within a curriculum unit can create a critical mass capable of causing its own kind of chain reaction. However, instead of choosing U-235 over U-238 because of its special capacity for splitting atoms, curriculum designers who use the Core Curriculum Parallel choose knowledge that transcends a topic and links learners to the very core of the discipline. Like the free neutrons in U-235 that bombard and split surrounding uranium atoms to release large sums of energy, the careful use of specific knowledge categories provides a powerful source of energy. The energy inherent in a deep understanding of concepts, principles, and methodological skills can promote a chain reaction that enables students to use their knowledge of one topic to understand the overarching structure of an entire discipline.

What Is the Purpose of the Core Curriculum Parallel?

Using the Core Curriculum Parallel benefits teachers and students in at least six noteworthy ways. First, the Core Curriculum Parallel promotes student understanding of the meaning and structure of a discipline. Second, it makes new learning in the same discipline easier and more efficient for students. Third, it directly promotes students' proficiency, skillfulness, independence, and self-efficacy in the discipline and thus promotes movement toward expertise. Fourth, use of this parallel helps teachers develop their own frameworks of meaning in the areas they teach—a proficiency often lacking at the end of undergraduate and even graduate education. In fact, the extent to which teachers are provided such frameworks by districts or professional groups, or to which teachers develop these frameworks on their own, often predicts the nature and quality of content that teachers present to their students. Fifth, curriculum developed with the approach suggested by the Core Curriculum Parallel meets the demand of employers and universities for individuals who independently use higher level thinking processes in response to complex materials and problems in a society marked by an explosion of new information. Finally, using the Core Curriculum addresses issues of equity and opportunity to learn for all students, regardless of their age, economic situation, or intellectual development. It also relates directly to Jerome Bruner's (1960) concept of a curriculum spiral. As originally defined by Bruner, a spiraled curriculum is one that treats all learners, regardless of age or cognitive ability, as active inquirers capable of understanding the major concepts, principles, and skills of a discipline, given age-appropriate curriculum. The major concepts, principles, and skills are revisited across grade levels to ensure a deeper understanding of the complexities of these facets of knowledge as a child becomes more intellectually advanced. From Bruner's perspective, the aim of education is to teach the basic structure of academic disciplines in a way that fosters understanding, regardless of the sophistication of the learner: "Good teaching which emphasizes the structure of a subject is probably even more valuable for the less able student than for the gifted one, for it is the former rather than the latter who is most easily thrown off track by poor teaching" (p. 9).

To guide teachers and students in achieving these benefits, the Core Curriculum Parallel directs teachers and other curriculum developers to ensure that the curriculum does the following:

▶ Stems from the key facts, concepts, principles, and skills essential to a discipline and reflects what experts in the discipline find most important

▶ Is coherent in its organization so that it helps students systematically build knowledge, understanding, and skills and organize what they learn in ways that develop students' abilities to remember, make meaning, and use what they know in unfamiliar situations

▶ Is designed to cause students to consistently use high levels of critical and creative thinking, as well as metacognition (thinking about their thinking), to grapple with ideas and problems

▶ Is taught in contexts that are authentic to the discipline and meaningful to students and in ways that are mentally and affectively inviting to students

▶ Engages students in worthwhile use of the understandings and skills central to the discipline

How Are the Key Curriculum Components Reconfigured to Achieve the Goals of the Core Curriculum Parallel?

It should be evident that the Core Curriculum Parallel retains the beneficial features of the Comprehensive Curriculum Framework discussed in Chapter 3 and moves beyond them to promote a higher level of quality in the curriculum we develop. The next section examines the key curriculum components as they would exist to address the particular purposes of the Core Curriculum Parallel. Brief examples from various grade levels and subject areas illustrate key points. The final section then explores Lydia Janis's second curriculum planning session, this time using the Core Curriculum Parallel to design her Civil War unit.

A practical question emerges: What does it mean to teach according to the nature of the discipline—to use the key facts, concepts, principles, and skills as organizers for curriculum development? We'll propose some answers to that question as we have a second curriculum planning session with Lydia. Interspersed with descriptions of her unit planning using the Core Curriculum Parallel are explanations of how the key components are modified in this second approach to planning the fifth grade Civil War unit. Figure 4.2 serves as an advance organizer for the remainder of the chapter.

The Role of Content/Standards Within the Core Curriculum Parallel

The current standards movement, as conceived by national education organizations within the various content areas, seeks to identify the same kinds of powerful knowledge emphasized within the Core Curriculum Parallel. The best of the subject area standards statements delineate a concise set of facts, concepts, principles, and skills that reveal the structure of a discipline. These standards statements extend the work of Bloom, Bruner, Phenix, and Taba by posing the question "What knowledge, understanding, and skill are essential for an adult to have about this discipline?" Most specialists who worked to develop these standards documents believe that (a) what students learn should be of service to them as adults and (b) standards should make current learning experiences easier to assimilate and retain. The Comprehensive Curriculum Framework supports alignment of textbook goals and state or local standards. On the other hand, educators who use the Core Curriculum Parallel will go a step further. They will move from mere alignment of content with text material to guiding a student search for meaning in content. These teachers will look at the content they must teach (and often beyond it) to find the essential facts, concepts, principles, and skills that give substance to the content. Figure 4.3 reviews and illustrates the key categories of knowledge.

The focusing questions of the Core Curriculum Parallel (Figure 4.1) directed us to use the key facts, concepts, principles, and skills of the discipline as anchors for

(Text continues on page 91)

Figure 4.2. Using the Key Curriculum Components to Develop a Core Curriculum Unit

Curriculum Components	*Modification Techniques*
Content/ Standards	• Identify the major disciplines of knowledge in the unit • Find the big ideas in each discipline by consulting an expert in the discipline, a national or state standards document, or a college textbook • Diagram standards to make a list of essential knowledge, concepts, principles, and skills of the discipline • Identify appropriate representative topics • Develop or remodel curriculum units to address key concepts, principles, and skills in the discipline through the use of representative topics • Expect and foster changes and increasing levels of cognitive sophistication as you and your students become more experienced
Assessment	• Preassess students for prior knowledge of major facts, concepts, principles, and skills within the topic or discipline • Develop rubrics that measure students' knowledge of concepts, principles, and skills • Consider concept maps as an assessment format • Pre- or post-assess to determine student growth in major facts, concepts, principles, and skills within the topic or discipline
Introductory Activities	• Provide students with concept maps • Develop and share advance organizers that support development of concepts and principles • Use focusing questions to help students assess their prior knowledge related to key concepts, principles, and skills • Develop initial learning experiences that show students what experts at the frontier of the discipline investigate • Provide an introduction that explains how the topic students are studying is representative of the discipline at large
Teaching Activities	• Use inquiry teaching methods with debriefing techniques • Develop or provide simulations or role-playing—opportunities that mimic the role of information analyst • Use a Concept Attainment Model, coupled with examples and nonexamples, to teach new concept categories • Use Wasserman's (1988) Play-Debrief-Replay method during examination of data, tables, examples, observations, or hands-on discovery • Use questioning and Socratic techniques to support the examination and classification of data, concept development, and identification of principles and rules • Teach inductively, beginning with examples, and foster the rules and principles that explain patterns and relationships

(Continued)

Figure 4.2. Continued

Curriculum Components	Modification Techniques
Learning Activities	• Find high school texts and college resources to identify the major concepts, skills, and principles within a field or discipline • Have students analyze and talk about examples, information, and data in small groups using a cooperative learning or guided discussion format • Have students use raw data, examples, events, and observations to detect patterns and draw conclusions • Ask students to suggest and test principles • Have students identify patterns and categories • Ask students to work as firsthand inquirers and analysts in the discipline • Have students focus on analytic skills, problem-solving skills, and skills of the discipline • Locate experiments, published simulations, and problem-solving activities that can be used during the unit • Provide opportunities for students to note characteristics and attributes, and search for patterns, sequences, and relationships
Resources	• Locate, reproduce, and distribute samples of research studies and investigations in the discipline or field • Provide biographies of historical and contemporary inquirers, inventors, and researchers in the field • Provide journals, blank charts, tables, and diagrams so that students can record their data, reflect on their learning experiences, and outline a schema that represents their understanding of the relationships between concepts and principles • Develop and share a format for developing hypotheses, designing studies, recording data, and formulating conclusions • Provide students with concept maps and advance organizers that preview the important concepts and principles explored in the unit • Provide graphic organizers to support cognitive and methodological skill acquisition • Develop clear directions and expectations for data analysis, observations, field studies, and independent study • Identify and locate numerous examples related to the concepts addressed in the unit • Provide access to Inspiration® software to develop concept maps
Products	• Ask students to create products that reflect their inquiry and analysis work • Assign concept maps to analyze the acquisition of concepts and principles • Ask students to make predictions, explain patterns, and demonstrate the relationship between raw data and primary source information and the core concepts and principles in the discipline • Ask students to demonstrate connections between unit activities and experiences and the concepts and principles in the discipline. Reflective essays, journal entries, charts, diagrams, and collages support this task • Provide graphic organizers that allow students to communicate their acquisition of concepts, principles, and skills

Extension Activities	• Be sure that extension activities stem from or relate back to the key concepts and principles that give meaning to the content • Ask the gifted education specialist or the media and technology specialist to support your search for adult role models of inquiry and research, primary source documents, field study opportunities, and real-world problems that relate to the core knowledge in the unit or discipline • Ask content area specialists and other teachers who are experts in inquiry-based teaching to team-teach, coach, or provide useful feedback on the progress and success of the lessons
Grouping Practices	• Work with large groups of students to overview the goals of the unit, to provide directions, and to share information about the discipline and representative topic • Work with large groups of students to facilitate acquisition of essential knowledge • Use pairs and small groups of students to support analysis of examples and information as students develop concepts and principles • Briefly conference with individual students to assess the degree to which they are able to relate examples and raw data to core concepts and principles • Observe individual students and provide feedback to support the development of analytic thinking • Debrief students in large group, using concept maps and diagrams, to ensure that the entire class can connect activities, data, and examples to core concepts and principles
Modifications Based on Learner Need, Including Ascending Intellectual Demand	• Increase or decrease your scaffolding to support concept attainment and cognitive processing • Use deductive or inductive questioning to support and scaffold students' understanding of major concepts and principles • Provide additional representative topics for comparison to reduce ambiguity or to add additional layers of complexity • Encourage a continuing commitment to intrinsic motivation and to the world of ideas • Ask students to examine ramifications, exceptions, or extensions of the basic concepts, principles, and skills • Provide students with additional raw data to examine • Use the Parallel's guidelines for Ascending Intellectual Demand in selecting resources and designing learning activities and products

curriculum planning because it is the facts, concepts, principles, and skills that answer the parallel's driving questions.

There are at least six ways to determine these elements in any segment of curriculum. First, and most desirable, is a district curriculum map that delineates essential facts (vs. a mass of facts of nonequivalent value), skills, overarching concepts,

Figure 4.3. Categories of Knowledge

Knowledge Category	Definition and Examples
Fact	A specific detail; verifiable information *Examples:* • *The capital of New York is Albany.* • *5 + 7 = 12* • *George Washington was the first president of the United States.*
Concept	A general idea or understanding, a generalized idea of a thing or a class of things; a category or classification *Examples:* • *Biome* • *Government* • *Landscape* • *Fiction* • *Integer*
Principle	A fundamental truth, law, rule, or doctrine that explains the relationship between two or more concepts *Examples:* • *Balance is an important factor in predicting the longevity of a biome.* • *Forms of government allow for varying amounts of individual freedom.* • *An artist's use of light changes the rendering of a landscape.* • *Conflicts arise between protagonists and antagonists.* • *Two positive numbers can be added in either order.*
Skill	Proficiency, an ability or a technique, a strategy, a method, or a tool *Examples:* • *Learning how to grid a plot of ground and make systematic observations* • *Learning how to analyze the plot of a story (e.g., rising and falling action)* • *Learning how to conduct a social action campaign* • *Learning how to compare and contrast* • *Learning how to calculate statistics*
Attitudes	Beliefs, dispositions, appreciations, and values *Examples:* • *An appreciation of the limits of the environment* • *A belief in the critical importance of individual democratic rights.* • *An appreciation of the use of light in Impressionist landscapes* • *A positive attitude toward reading* • *Intrinsic motivation for learning about real-world data*
Problem Solving	The ability to transfer and apply acquired knowledge to address a goal *Examples:* • *Identifying the percentage of open land left in a community or state* • *Developing a strategy to increase parent participation in PTA meetings* • *Creating a meaningful format for displaying a data set* • *Creating an original fiction anthology*

principles, and grade levels at which these elements will be introduced and extended.

Second, in the absence of such local documents, teachers can turn to high-quality standards documents that are often organized conceptually and presented according to key principles and that specify key methodological skills. In some instances, state standards documents achieve clarity and direction. When they do not, teachers can draw upon the high-quality standards developed by national professional organizations or standards documents published by states other than their own.

Third, there are books that provide excellent guidance in understanding what it means to teach conceptually and how to plan curriculum with that mindset. Among very helpful books currently available are *Concept-Based Curriculum and Instruction: Teaching Beyond the Facts* by H. Lynn Erickson (1998) and available from Corwin Press, *The Multiple Menu Model* by Joseph Renzulli and colleagues (Renzulli, Leppien, & Hayes, 2000) and available from Creative Learning Press, and *Understanding by Design* by Grant Wiggins and Jay McTighe (1998) and available through the Association for Supervision and Curriculum Development. A fourth very useful book—and one that provides a teacher's perspective on the task of designing meaning-based curriculum—is *Starting From Scratch* by Steven Levy (1996) and available from Heinemann. Although each of these books differs in its approach to curriculum design, each deals clearly and directly with what it looks like to move beyond even well-planned, information-based or skills-based teaching to meaning-rich teaching that reveals to learners the power and utility of the disciplines.

Fourth, college textbooks are often rich resources for unearthing the key concepts, driving principles, and practitioner skills in a discipline. At this level, texts nearly always move from organization by topic and a coverage orientation to looking at a discipline through the organizational framework of experts. Thus even a quick survey of the table of contents and headings in chapters in college texts can provide a sturdy starting point for identifying the authentic essentials upon which a topic or discipline is most effectively taught.

A fifth way to identify the elements of the disciplines is collaboration with experts in those disciplines. Community members who are practitioners in a discipline—or even Internet contacts who practice the disciplines at a high level—are not only invaluable in helping teachers understand what really matters in a discipline but are also excellent sources of information on authentic problems and products related to the discipline.

Finally, many teachers simply take the plunge into concept-based teaching by using available text and standards documents, their own knowledge of the subject in question, some common sense, and a bit of tolerance for ambiguity.

When teachers use these methods to locate the key information, concepts, principles, and skills in a discipline, they may discover that the topic of the original curriculum has to be revised to accommodate the concepts, principles, and skills to be incorporated within the unit. For example, in the past, a kindergarten class might have participated in a November social studies unit titled "Thanksgiving Day." As a result of the need to address core elements that give social studies focus, continuity, and purpose, the teacher may now look at the unit as focusing on "Harvest Traditions Around the World," or "The Legacy of Harvest Traditions."

A Case in Point

Let's take a look at Keara, a teacher who wants to structure her second grade social studies unit conceptually so that her students will see meaning in the unit and begin to think about social studies through the lens of concepts. As presented in the textbook, students will study about Kenya, Japan, Mexico, and Canada. However, the textbook gives no assistance in determining the key concepts, principles, and skills embedded in social studies. Keara has no standards documents. She goes to a bookshelf at home and pulls off a dusty copy of an old college anthropology text. In the table of contents, she quickly identifies five chapters that seem promising: The Nature of Culture, Kinship and Descent, Family and Household, The Arts, and Economic Systems. She skims those chapters.

In a modest amount of time, Keara jots down a list of concepts that clearly connect to her second grade study of four cultures, a list of principles that help make meaning of the study of culture, and a number of skills that are used by experts in the study of cultures. Figure 4.4 presents Keara's lists.

It seems evident that even this early "scavenger hunt" in a college text has positioned Keara to guide her students in understanding both why we study cultures and what we learn about ourselves and others in doing so and how experts study cultures. While Keara has just begun to reframe her unit conceptually, she has developed a foundation for her planning that is more authentic and richer in meaning than a fact-based or topic-based study of four cultures—even a study that carefully aligns content objectives and curriculum plans. She is now on her way to answering for herself and helping her students answer the focusing questions of the Core Curriculum Parallel (Figure 4.1).

Assessment Strategies and the Core Curriculum Parallel

In Chapter 3, we discussed the characteristics of exemplary assessment. To be effective, assessments must be aligned to the learning goals. Second, they should be honest and accurate measures of students' learning over time. Third, they must provide some kind of performance or product with which to evaluate student learning. These characteristics are as valid for high-quality Core Curriculum assessments as they are for any of the assessments designed for use with the other three curriculum models described in this book. However, the nature of the learning goals within the Core Curriculum Parallel requires special attention to the design of appropriate rubrics and assessment formats.

In curriculum designed with the Core Curriculum Parallel, learning goals will address core concepts, principles, and skills in a discipline or field of study. Therefore, assessments will also focus on student growth related to core concepts, principles, and skills.

Figure 4.4. Keara's Starting Point in Concept-Based Planning

Concepts	Principles	Skills and Methods of the Discipline
Culture	A culture consists of the shared	Observation
Society	knowledge, art, customs, habits,	Hypothesizing
Needs	values, beliefs, symbols, and	Comparing and Contrasting
Rules and Order	perceptions of its people.	Analyzing Data
Change	Culture is reflected in people's	Finding patterns
Adaptation	behaviors.	Drawing Conclusions
Values	Cultures are learned through	Classifying
Habits	language, experience, and	Seeing Relationships
Customs	behaviors.	Making Analogies
Symbols	A culture must satisfy the basic needs	Categorizing
Beliefs	of people.	Sequencing
Roles	Cultures have rules to provide an	
Tolerance	orderly existence.	
Interdependence	Members of a culture are dependent	
Symbols	on one another.	
Needs	Members of a culture have established	
	roles.	
	Cultures tolerate some variance	
	among individuals.	
	A culture must have the capacity to	
	change in order to adapt to change.	
	Cultures must strike a balance	
	between the needs of individuals	
	and the needs of society.	

To design an appropriate rubric to measure growth in concept attainment, the levels within the rubric must attend to ever increasing levels of knowledge acquisition. Care must be taken to ensure that the rubric does not emphasize the quantity or mechanics of the product (e.g., neatness, proper spelling, and number of bibliographic entries) over the quality of the knowledge. An illustration of this approach follows. You will note here a more meaning-oriented rubric than the rubric Lydia developed in Chapter 3 to assess her students' work.

A group of fifth grade students in a science class might be expected to acquire a conceptual understanding of the term "migration." A fitting pre- or postassessment strategy might be to ask students an open-ended question that probes their understanding of the concept. Using a five-level rubric, the depth of student understanding of the concept might be sequenced accordingly (see Figure 4.5).

Figure 4.5. A Rubric for Measuring Growth in Concept Attainment

	Beginning	*Developing*	*Competent*	*Proficient*	*Expert*
Level of Understanding	The learner communicates the term associated with the abstract concept.	The learner paraphrases the definition of the concept.	The learner provides examples and nonexamples of the concept.	The learner provides key attributes that distinguish the concept category.	The learner links the concept with other related concepts.
Example	Migration	"Migration is movement of living things for a real reason or purpose."	Examples: Butterflies Whales Salmon Nonexamples: When a subdivision is built Fires Accidents	Beneficial Change Large groups Movement Purposeful Causes Effects Universal	"People and animals migrate to improve their chances to meet their needs."

A rubric such as this one aligns closely with a standard or objective that stresses concept acquisition. It also allows teachers to measure change over time when used during both their pre- and postassessment.

If, on the other hand, the knowledge goal in a Core Curriculum unit addresses the acquisition of a principle or rule, the rubric shown in Figure 4.5 might vary slightly to assess student understanding of unit principles. Figure 4.6 illustrates a rubric for the science principle "Animals and insects migrate to fulfill basic needs."

In this example, students might be asked to explain the principle orally or in writing. Another option is to provide students with a word bank, consisting of key concepts from the unit, and ask the students to make a concept map or web that explains the connections between the concepts. Related examples and principles may also be included. Figure 4.7 provides a simple example of such a concept map activity.

If the content standards in a Core Curriculum Parallel unit stress the acquisition of a skill, the rubric and assessment strategies in the parallel call for a similar emphasis. An observation, product, or performance might, for example, be used as the assessment technique to determine level of student proficiency with a particular skill. Students in a science unit might be expected to learn how to detect a pattern. Their assessment might provide them with a specific set of data from which to work. Students might be asked to compare and contrast the data over time and identify emerging patterns in the data.

Figure 4.6. A Rubric for Measuring the Acquisition of Principles

	Beginning	*Developing*	*Competent*	*Proficient*	*Expert*
Level of Understanding	The learner defines and provides examples of the key concepts within a rule or principle.	The learner identifies a relationship between two or more concepts.	The learner explains the relationship as conditional, if/then cause/effect, part/whole, etc.	The learner provides novel examples of the principle or rule within a discipline or field of study.	The learner provides novel examples of the principle across disciplines or fields of study.
Example	Butterflies Whales Salmon	"Animals move around to get what they need."	"Animal migration is all about reasons and results."	"We studied whale migration in class but migration happens a lot in biology, for example, with butterflies and even people."	"Migration in animals is like the Westward Movement in history."

In sum, the need for valid and reliable pre- and postassessments is as vital within the Core Curriculum Parallel as it is within any kind of curriculum unit. The format for the assessment, however, varies a bit from the Comprehensive Curriculum Framework example. It varies in order to conform more readily to measuring changes in students' understanding and uses of concepts, principles, and skills that are the keys to helping students answer questions related to how knowledge is organized in the subject, what it means, how people use it, and so on. It's not so difficult, really. It's just a matter of making certain that just as a unit in the Core Curriculum Parallel will be focused to stress essential information, concepts, principles, and skills, so must assessments focus on the framework the unit stresses.

Introductory Activities in the Core Curriculum Parallel

Like all introductions, initial activities in the Core Curriculum should generate excitement and enthusiasm; provide for the preassessment of prior, related student knowledge; orient students to the learning goals; and provide students an opportunity to share previous experiences with the topic. However, in the Core Curriculum,

Figure 4.7. An Example of a Concept Map or Web

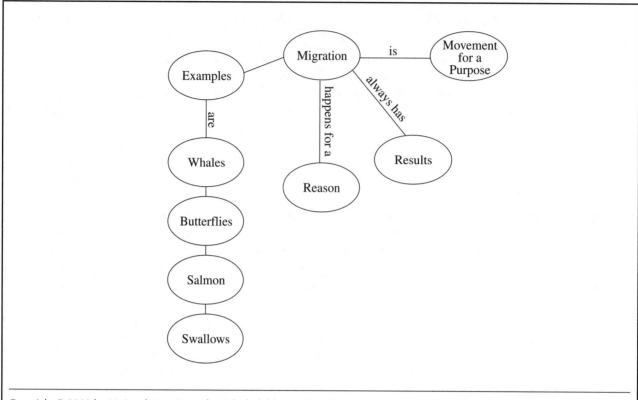

the introductory activities also function as a vehicle for helping students focus on the concepts, principles, and skills that are central to the Core Curriculum Parallel.

For many students, the role of inductive thinker and analyst, also common in the Core Curriculum, is both new and interesting. Nevertheless, it can also be puzzling and strange. To support student acquisition of this new role, teachers can use introductory activities to explain the kinds of thinking students will perform in order to come to a deep understanding of core knowledge. The teacher needs to assure students that it is perfectly acceptable for them to draw tentative conclusions, revise their thinking, and think out loud. The teacher should explain that it's important for students to think their way to understanding rather than only memorizing or paraphrasing someone else's thinking. Further, the teacher should review her role as a coach and support system for students' thinking, noting that she may answer their questions with a related question to help them focus their own thinking rather than giving them an answer.

Second, teachers of Core Curriculum make a special attempt to use introductory activities as an opportunity to explain to students the relationship between the representative topic they will study, the larger field of study, and the discipline as a whole. For example, in a third grade science study of the structure of plants and the function of plant systems, a teacher might use the study of fast-growing radish seeds and plants as the representative topic. During the introductory activities, the teacher displays a large set of five concentric circles that depict the relationship among radish plants, the field of botany, the discipline of biology, and the discipline of science. The teacher and students spend a brief amount of time discussing the relationships among the four terms in order to help students see how the topic they are studying relates to and represents the other three.

Third, teachers can develop a list of key facts, concepts, principles, and skills the students will learn about during the study. With a concept map or similar diagram, teachers and students can use lines, arrows, and oval shapes to build a map that will depict the relationships among facts, concepts, principles, the representative topic, and the field and/or discipline.

Readers will also recall, from Chapter 3, the importance of focusing questions in introductory activities. These questions help students reflect on their own knowledge related to the Core study. These questions are also useful in monitoring student learning over time, to identify areas of confusion, or to note concepts, principles, or skills that need additional study and support. Further, teachers can use the questions to explore the nature of the concepts, relationships among the concepts, principles, facts, and skills central to the Core study.

As with any high-quality curriculum, the use of guiding questions, concept maps, and advance organizers provides support for students from the early stages of their work. These tools allow students initial opportunities to examine the relationships among the representative topic they are about to study and the overarching concepts, principles, and skills of the discipline at large. The use of new, unusual, and even discrepant information or examples provides intrigue and compels students to attend to unit activities. The use of a can each of diet soda and regular soda dropped into a 20-gallon aquarium, for example, can provide a powerful introduction to the study of relative density.

Introductory learning activities are often overlooked or underused. The decision to hasten or eliminate these experiences can short-circuit student learning. Assuming a class of students with varied levels of experience with and knowledge about the subject at hand, the quality and comprehensiveness of introductory activities often predicts the degree to which all students can develop rich schemes of thought, analogies, and deep understanding of content. The shared conversations, examples, experiences, and questions posed during introductory activities create a bond among the family of learners. They also provide a shared anchor that the teacher can reference during the remainder of the study to foster acquisition of content.

Revising the Remaining Curriculum Components to Address the Goals of the Core Curriculum Parallel

The Core Curriculum Parallel has two primary goals: to acquaint students with the key information, concepts, principles, and skills of a discipline through the study of representative topics, and to foster this learning by helping students think their way to an understanding of this core knowledge. When students achieve these goals, they are able to answer the parallel's focusing questions (Figure 4.1) and thus to demonstrate understanding of the structure and function of the discipline in an authentic way.

To accomplish these goals, changes are required in the learning objectives and teaching and learning methods when planning curriculum with the Core Curriculum Parallel. These changes create a domino effect that also impacts the other curriculum components. The chapter has already discussed changes in content, assessment, and introductory activities. Reconfiguration of the other curricular elements for the Core Curriculum Parallel is discussed in the following sections.

Teaching Methods and the Core Curriculum Parallel

Figure 3.7 in Chapter 3 provides a list of teaching methods arranged along a continuum, with direct teaching activities near the top of the figure and strategies becoming more indirect as the figure continues. There are particular methods at both ends of the continuum that teachers can use to help students acquire core knowledge. Appropriate indirect teaching methods include cooperative or collaborative learning, Socratic questioning, discovery learning, inductive teaching, concept attainment, Play-Debrief-Replay, simulations, and problem-solving or problem-based learning. Appropriate direct teaching methods that foster core knowledge acquisition include lecture, deductive teaching, and coaching. The decision to use a direct or an indirect method will hinge on the amount of available instructional time, access to resources at students' independent reading levels, students' proficiency with various analytic thinking skills, and students' prior knowledge in the content area.

For example, a high school English teacher teaching the concept of narrative poetry inductively might decide to use a combination of inductive teaching and modified Socratic questioning. The teacher would ask students to construct their own definition of narrative poetry after reviewing exemplars from the genre. Students might read "Paul Revere's Ride," "Casey at the Bat," "Charge of the Light Brigade," and "The Highwayman" to compare and contrast key characteristics and attributes of narrative poems. Students would then use this information to develop a definition of the concept of narrative poetry. Later, they might also develop a set of principles that explain the significance of narrative poems within a historical setting. The teacher would combine this instructional method with the use of modified Socratic questioning to help students clarify their comparisons—or perhaps to clarify the thinking processes they used to develop the concepts and related principles.

In another setting, a teacher might elect to use a deductive or more direct teaching approach. When teaching deductively, a teacher helps students acquire core concepts and principles by first naming the concept or providing students with the principle. Next, the teacher explains the major attributes and characteristics that distinguish the concept or principle. Finally, the teacher provides students with new information or examples and asks them to find evidence within the examples that transfer the recently acquired concept or principle to the new context.

For example, a ninth grade earth science teacher might want to teach the concept of a spiral galaxy. The teacher would define a galaxy and explain the unique characteristics of a spiral galaxy as one composed of armlike stars that spiral around a center. Next, the teacher gives students several photographs of our galaxy and of the Andromeda galaxy as examples of spiral galaxies. Then, the teacher provides a series of photographs from the galaxy in the constellation Ursa Major and asks students to find characteristics and attributes of a spiral galaxy in this new example. Last, the teacher asks students to explain why the photographs depict a spiral galaxy.

Core Curriculum developers or teachers must be mindful of at least one very important caution. Without careful teacher monitoring, questioning, and probing it is far too easy for students to become lost in an array of facts, data, information, and tasks, without focusing on the core concepts and principles behind the information. When this occurs, students may become preoccupied with finding the "answers" to their teacher's questions and lose focus on the essential questions related to the structure of the discipline, key concepts, and principles. Through skillful use of Wassermann's (1988) Play-Debrief-Replay teaching method, expert Core Curriculum teachers periodically stop students' small group discussions and learning activities, bring the small groups together as a large group, and provide semistructured debriefing discussions designed to elicit patterns across data sets to help students draw conclusions, make hypotheses, and develop rules and principles. In this way, the teacher plays a leadership role in helping students focus on making meaning of what they are studying.

Learning Activities and the Core Curriculum Parallel

To be most effective, Core Curriculum teaching methods must be coupled with learning activities that provide numerous opportunities for students to think analytically and to draw conclusions inductively and deductively. Most of the analytic thinking skills and many of the critical thinking skills listed in Figure 3.8 of Chapter 3 strengthen this connection. Analytic skills worthy of particular emphasis in Core Curriculum units include comparing and contrasting, classifying, finding patterns, making analogies, seeing relationships, and showing cause and effect. Key critical thinking skills are deductive and inductive thinking and judging essential and incidental evidence; key executive thinking skills are formulating questions, developing hypotheses, summarizing, and generalizing.

Least effective in helping students make meaning of the discipline are activities that require students to memorize or paraphrase new information. Although some of the activities in any unit must call on students to learn or memorize information, in this parallel, activities that stress meaning making and discovery are in the foreground.

Grouping Practices and the Core Curriculum Parallel

In order to support the development of concepts and principles, students need to be coached and guided as they attempt to think their way through problems, questions, and investigations. The teacher's role within the Core Curriculum Parallel is one of coach, guide, and facilitator. The successful use of these teaching strategies requires in-depth content knowledge on the part of the teacher and a strong ability to follow and respond to differences in students' trains of thought and individual reasoning processes. The teacher's job is to help students find the answers and learn new concepts and principles by analyzing new information, identifying patterns and categories, and generating hypotheses, generalizations, relationships, and principles.

Students who work with Core Curriculum units must process their way through new information. When students experience problems or frustration with this role, teachers must be ready to step in with follow-up questions, hints, or examples that jump-start a stalled cognitive process. They must be able to shed sufficient light on a problem or concept to allow students to see their way through to a solution or generalization. A long-term observation of a teacher implementing a Core Curriculum unit reveals a continual use of open-ended questions, follow-up questions, clarifying questions, and reflective questioning strategies.

In addition, opportunities for students to work in pairs or small groups facilitate the analytic and reflective dialogue among learners that fosters concept attainment, the development of principles and generalizations, and the acquisition of methodological, cognitive, and inquiry skills.

Resources in the Core Curriculum Parallel

It's not hard to imagine that changes in learning goals, as well as in introductory teaching and learning activities would require concomitant changes in the choice of student and teacher resources. Rather than simply reading a section of the textbook and paraphrasing the author's perspective on causes of the Civil War, students working with the Core Curriculum use factual information, tables, graphs, maps, raw data, examples, events, and observations to detect patterns and draw inferences. Students not only study the conclusions of others, they analyze information and draw inferences on the basis of the analysis.

High school and college texts can provide core knowledge for the teacher about to implement Core Curriculum. Grade-level textbooks can also be used by students for information acquisition. However, learners also need access to tools, primary sources, examples, tables, charts, graphs, evidence, and data. They need to engage in observations, dialogue, and firsthand analysis. Depending on students' age and experience, graphic organizers and templates can provide support for the novice thinker, and frequent debriefing sessions and the use of Socratic questioning can speed the inquiry and discovery process.

Teachers of a Core Curriculum Parallel unit also have special resource needs. Ideas for discovery learning, document analysis, simulations, and problem-based learning experiences don't just pop out of the air. Access to high-quality commercial simulations, such as those published by MESA, Tom Snyder, Foss, GEMS, Interact, and Kendall-Hunt (as well as many other excellent publishers), provide a wealth of ideas. Web-based simulations or journal descriptions of simulations other teachers have designed can be equally helpful. For the teacher who has an interest in curriculum development, there are dozens of books that describe the process for developing and writing such simulations and problem-based learning activities in social studies, science, math, health, and art.

Products in the Core Curriculum Parallel

The choice to use the Core Curriculum Parallel also impacts the nature of student products—both short-term products and longer term, or culminating, products. Concept maps, hypotheses, theories, expository essays, research reports, journal reflections, charts, diagrams, and tables can reflect the thinking of student inquirers and provide a vehicle for learners to share their knowledge about overarching concepts and principles that result from the study of the representative topic as well as their expanding skill as analytic thinkers.

As is the case with other components of a Core Curriculum Parallel unit, the focus of a product in this parallel is helping students come to understand the organization and nature of the discipline, make sense of its organizing framework, and use its key concepts, principles, and skills. Both the product assignments and plans for assessing products should focus on student understanding and application of these fundamental building blocks of meaning.

If students in Keara's class were to observe several examples of Japanese customs and home life in class over a two-day period, their product might be to develop an inductive conclusion or principle to explain the causes and effects of these traditions and habits. If students in a Grade 6 statistics unit flip a penny 100 times to gather probability data, their related, short-term product might be a table of results. More important than the table, however, would be a written explanation of the inductive conclusion they drew about the relationship between the number of data sets observed and the changes in probability. The two products—tables and conclusions—can also be used as a seamless assessment to measure the extent to which students understand basic concepts and principles about probability and sample size.

Whether daily (short term) or culminating (long term), products created in Core Curriculum should support development and communication of core knowledge. As such, they must call on students to understand, convey, illustrate, and use the key information, concepts, principles, and skills of the topic.

Extension Activities in the Core Curriculum Parallel

Within the Core Curriculum, extension activities can be used effectively to provide opportunities to learn additional information, examples, concepts, principles, skills, and applications not addressed in the basic Core Curriculum plan. This allows for close alignment of extension opportunities with content goals but still allows student to pursue their particular questions or interests. Figure 4.8 provides examples of extension activities for an eighth grade health unit on the concept of violence in which the extension activities closely align with the unit's goals. The figure describes

Figure 4.8. Illustrations of Extension Activities Aligned With Core Curriculum Goals

Subject Area: *HEALTH* Grade: *8* Concept: *VIOLENCE* Disciplines: *Psychology, Sociology*		
Knowledge Categories	Essential Knowledge	Potential Extensions
Facts	• Risk factors associated with violence • Situations that lead to fights	Myths versus facts about the causes and frequency of violence
Concepts	• Victim • Violence • Assailant • Mediation • Resolution • Escalation • Hostility • Free-floating anger	Learn more about: • Confrontation • Negotiation • Gangs • Fight or flight • Instigator • De-escalation • Micro-insults • Risk factors
Principles	• Violence is often perpetrated by people who have had personal contact with the victim • Poverty is more highly correlated with violence than is ethnicity	• The relationship between access to various weapons, especially guns, is correlated to incidence of violent crimes • Frustration and hopelessness may increase violence
Skills	• Conflict resolution skills • Conflict mediation strategies	• Developing advice for students about how to deal with a bully • Investigating nonviolence in popular music
Applications	• Logging violence on television • Interviewing people about their experiences with violence	• Analyzing violence in popular music • Analyzing domestic violence statistics in your town

the unit's essential knowledge in five areas of knowledge. The third column of the figure illustrates some ways in which the key categories of knowledge can be extended as student interest evolves. Contemporary textbooks often provide a wealth of suggestions for extension activities in teacher's guides and student texts.

While time constraints make it impossible to do everything that would be interesting and helpful to student learning within a particular segment of study, it is still important to allow students opportunities to pursue relevant, interesting, and motivating knowledge as an extension of their core study. By helping students develop extension activities, investigations, or products that reinforce and extend the key concepts, principles and skills of the core curriculum, teachers can attend to both student curiosity and content goals.

Modification for Learner Need and Ascending Intellectual Demand in the Core Curriculum Parallel

It is the contention of this book that concept-based teaching and analytic learning opportunities should not be restricted to a select group of students. The roots of this parallel stem from general education and the fervent wish of scholars and researchers in the disciplines to instill an intrinsic appreciation for the world of ideas in all learners. It is the belief of many experts in the disciplines that the best way to achieve this ideal is through frequent student exposure to a curriculum that addresses the structure of a discipline by having students interact with examples, factual information, evidence, and the analytic and inductive process.

It seems evident that this approach to curriculum is already richer and more substantial than is curriculum designed with predominant emphasis on mastery of facts and skills. The Core Curriculum Parallel, correctly used, results in students wrestling with abstract and complex ideas, working at high levels of thought, and becoming more independent as thinkers and learners. Thus many students would find the Core Curriculum quite challenging, particularly as they work through the transition from a more teacher-directed and prescriptive classroom.

In most classrooms, in fact, there are students who require teacher support or scaffolding to read texts or supplementary materials, follow directions, find appropriate resources, use time effectively, and so on. For these students to benefit from the Core Curriculum—or the curriculum designed by another approach—teachers must modify materials, provide additional opportunities for direct instruction and hands-on learning, give support in following directions, and so on.

In most classrooms, there are also students whose level of advancement, interest, and capacity in a particular subject suggests a need to delve more deeply into the subject and to work at levels of ascending demand or challenge so that they continue movement toward expertise in that subject. It is this continual movement toward expertise that is addressed in the concept of "ascending intellectual demand" presented in this book. This concept will be the focus of sections in the book on modifications based on learner need. This emphasis is not intended to minimize the necessity of modifications required by most students at some points in their schooling, and by some students at most points in their schooling, to ensure growth toward competence in basic understandings and skills. Such approaches to modification of instruction for students who struggle with school have been examined and described effectively in many other publications. A goal of this book is to support teachers in understanding how to extend student capacity as it evolves beyond competence. For that reason, the book describes and emphasizes the concept of "ascending intellectual demand" as a means of guiding teachers who want to know more about extending student capacity beyond general expectations—even in the face of a rich and complex curriculum.

Most human endeavors reflect varying levels of expertise, and scholars have studied and written about the nature of expertise in most of those endeavors. We quickly get a sense of the difference between a young driver with a learner's permit and a NASCAR racing champion. We see the difference between someone who dons ice skates and takes to the rink for the first time and an Olympic medalist in ice skating. In our own careers, we understand the difference in confidence and competence between a brand-new teacher and one who has polished his or her craft for two decades. It is our contention that we benefit from thinking about our learners along a growth continuum not unlike that of the driver, skater, or teacher.

Figure 4.9 notes some common traits and skills of expertise distilled from examination of experts in a range of fields. This information is helpful because it provides some direction about the sorts of advanced attributes toward which teachers could be guiding their students. The figure should illustrate the fact that rich curricula, such as that suggested by the Core Curriculum Parallel, provide all students better opportunity to progress along a continuum toward expertise than do even well-aligned curricula focused primarily on acquisition of information.

Achieving "ascending intellectual demand" relies on the growing capacity of the teacher to (a) understand the continuum of developing knowledge, understanding, skills, and attitude in the subject in order to have a sense of where students are in their development as well as to know appropriate next steps in growth for each student and (b) design learning opportunities and environments that continually encourage students to take the next steps in learning and to support them in doing so.

Figure 4.10 proposes some ways in which teachers may prompt students to work at ascending levels of intellectual demand in the Core Curriculum. In addition to these approaches to assisting students to move toward expertise, it is also important for teachers to take into account in their instructional plans both students' interests and their preferred modes of learning.

Using the Goals of the Core Curriculum Parallel for Lydia Janis's Civil War Unit

Determining Content

A year has passed since Lydia first revised her fifth grade textbook unit on the Civil War unit to address the components and exemplary characteristics described in the Comprehensive Curriculum Framework. As you recall from Chapter 3, her initial attempts at revision led to improvements in the introductory activities, the development of assessments and rubrics better aligned to the textbook objectives, and the creation of graphic organizers that supported improvements in students' ability to read and comprehend social studies content as presented within the structure of a textbook. When we left Lydia, we learned that she reconciled national and

Figure 4.9. Some Traits and Skills of Experts

Traits/Attitudes of the Expert	*Skills of the Expert*
• High curiosity, reflection, concentration • Understands domain at a deep level • Uses present knowledge to plan for future directions in learning • Raises questions about reasons for and use of knowledge • Spends time to lay foundation, understand contexts and problems • Seeks out multiple resources and knows how to use them • Demonstrates high level of skill that looks effortless • Can mentally represent a problem and its parameters • Transforms content to use in new areas • Reflective, evaluative behavior • Makes great number of connections and more complex connections • Sensitive to task demands when solving problems • Has confidence in ability to solve problems • Examines impact of decisions on self, others, and society • Self-monitoring • Able to step outside personal experience • Insightful • Open-minded • Tolerates risk and uncertainty • Assumes responsibility for own learning • Driven to work hard • Inspires self to work • Disciplined approach to work • Continues to push for improvement • Incorporates struggle and failure in the journey to learn • Chooses to learn from experience • Seeks meaningful practice and critique • Has a commitment to excellence • Leads others to productive accomplishment • Envisions new possibilities	• Organizes knowledge for meaning and accessibility • Maintains an internal organization and has a classification system • Represents problems in a qualitatively deeper way • Transfers content and skills from one context to use in another • Sees differences between typical and novel instances • Has fast, accurate pattern recognition • Reflects on adequacy of own thinking processes • Anticipates sequences in learning • Poses insightful questions about content and problems • Can recount and evaluate events and their impact • Anticipates problems • Uses efficient methods of reflection and problem solving • Uses efficient pattern recognition to apply prior knowledge to new situations • Develops systems and habits for effective, efficient learning • Searches for subtle examples and information • Gleans pertinent information from seemingly extraneous data • Has a heuristic rather than a formulaic approach to solving problems • Works at high level of abstract, analytical, and creative thinking • Works at level of automaticity • Flexibly adapts parameters to facilitate purposes • Engages others in reflective, insightful dialogue • Creates novel products and applications

Figure 4.10. Some Paths to Ascending Intellectual Demand in the Core Curriculum

- Call on students to use more advanced reading, resource, and research materials
- Assist students in determining and understanding multiple perspectives on issues and problems
- Adjust the pace of teaching and learning to account for rapid speed of learning or to permit additional depth of inquiry
- Develop tasks and products that call on students to work at greater levels of depth, breadth, complexity, or abstraction
- Have students apply what they are learning to contexts that are unfamiliar or are quite dissimilar from applications explored in class
- Design tasks and products that are more open-ended or ambiguous in nature and/or that call on students to exercise greater levels of independence in thought and scholarly behavior as learners and producers
- Develop rubrics for tasks and products that delineate levels of quality that include expert-level indicators
- Encourage collaborations between students and adult experts in an area of shared interest
- Design tasks that require continuing student reflection on the significance of ideas and information and cause students to generate new and useful methods and procedures to represent ideas and solutions
- Include directions and procedures that ask students to establish criteria for high-quality work, assess their progress in working toward those criteria, and seek and use feedback that improves their quality of efforts and methods of working
- Ask students to reflect on the personal and societal implications of solutions they propose to problems

state social studies standards with her textbook objectives by simply "marking off" the standards she believed were addressed in the textbook unit.

Between her last unit revision and this year, Lydia had time to read and learn more about standards and their purposes. She understands their role in ensuring equity and opportunity to learn for all students. She also learned that the developers of the standards documents took special care to identify the major facts, concepts, principles, and skills inherent in each subject area and discipline so that students could spend more time studying the key concepts and principles in any given field. This new knowledge led to some ongoing reflection for Lydia. She realized that the standards documents were indeed identifying what was "core" to each subject area and discipline. She began to wonder to what extent her textbook objectives really addressed the same kinds of powerful knowledge inherent in those standards documents.

Once again, Lydia turned to her teacher's manual and found the page that listed the objectives for the Civil War (see Figure 4.11). Working in the Core Curriculum Parallel, she needed to spend time actually analyzing the kinds of knowledge inherent in each objective statement. To do that, she would identify the content within

Figure 4.11. Lydia's Textbook Objectives for the Civil War Unit

1. Analyze the differences between the North and South (fact)
2. Describe how some enslaved people fought against slavery (fact)
3. Identify the difficulties faced by free African Americans (fact)
4. Identify leading abolitionists and describe their fight against slavery (fact)
5. Explain how the movement for women's rights began (fact)
6. Describe the compromises over slavery that temporarily prevented the South's secession (fact)
7. Analyze the reasons that the South seceded (fact)
8. Describe how the Civil War began (fact)
9. Compare and contrast the strengths of each side (fact)
10. Explain how technology changed the way wars were fought (fact/concept/principle?)
11. Analyze the effect of the Emancipation Proclamation on both the North and the South (fact)
12. Describe how women on both sides supported the war effort (fact)
13. Evaluate the effects of the war on the North and South (fact/principle?)
14. Describe Sherman's March (fact)
15. Describe Lee's surrender at Appomattox (fact)

each objective statement and categorize it as fact, concept, principle, skill, disposition, or application. She used the state standards document (Figure 4.12) for this purpose. Her results are printed in parentheses next to each objective listed in Figure 4.11.

Lydia also noted 15 learning objectives listed within the two chapters of the textbook. Most of the objectives required students only to identify and describe facts. In addition, Lydia was struck by the discreteness of the 15 objectives. Few principles

Figure 4.12. Categories of Knowledge

Knowledge Category	Definition and Examples
Fact	A specific detail; verifiable information
	Examples: • *The capital of New York is Albany.* • *5 + 7 = 12* • *George Washington was the first president of the United States.*
Concept	A general idea or understanding, a generalized idea of a thing or a class of things; a category or classification
	Examples: • *Planet* • *Biome* • *Capital* • *Narrative poem* • *Vowel*

(Continued)

Figure 4.12. Continued

Knowledge Category	Definition and Examples
Principle	A fundamental truth, law, rule, or doctrine that explains the relationship between two or more concepts *Examples:* • *Planets revolve around a star.* • *Forms of government allow for varying amounts of individual freedom.* • *Emotions often govern human behavior.* • *People always have more wants than needs.* • *Two positive numbers can be added in either order.*
Skills	Proficiency, ability or technique, strategy, method, or tool *Examples:* • *Learning how to use a telescope* • *Learning how to calculate statistics* • *Learning how to conduct an interview* • *Learning how to compare and contrast* • *Learning how to apply glaze to a piece of greenware*
Attitudes	Beliefs, dispositions, appreciations, values, perspectives, and empathy *Examples:* • *An appreciation for the magnitude of the universe* • *A belief in the critical importance of individual democratic rights* • *An understanding of "road rage"* • *A positive attitude toward reading* • *Intrinsic motivation for learning*
Application and Problem Solving	The ability to use knowledge to address a goal that may not be immediately understandable Examples: • *Using knowledge about the development of the U.S. Constitution and the role of compromise and consensus to create support for current legislation.* • *Using the knowledge gained in a unit of preventing violence to study violence statistics in the local community.* • *Developing a strategy to increase parent participation in PTA meetings* • *Creating effective solutions for schoolwide bullying* • *Creating an original poetry anthology*

Figure 4.13. Social Studies Performance Standards From Lydia's Standards Document

Demonstrate an in-depth understanding of major events and trends in U.S. history (history)

1. Analyze data in order to see persons and events in their historical context; understand causal factors and appreciate change over time (history)
2. Examine current concepts, issues, events, and themes from historical perspectives and identify conflicting ideas from competing narratives or interpretations of historical events (history);
3. Explain reasons for conflict and the ways conflicts have been resolved (history)
4. Explain how economic factors influenced historical events in the United States (history)
5. Display empathy for people who have lived in the past (history)
6. Describe and analyze, using historical data and understandings, the options which are available to parties involved in contemporary conflicts or decision making (history)
7. Identify and evaluate various perspectives associated with places and regions (geography)
8. Evaluate situations involving conflicts between citizen's rights and propose solutions to these conflicts (government)
9. Use maps, globes, models, graphs, charts, and databases to analyze distributions and patterns (geography)
10. Identify governmental activities that affect the local, state, national, and international economy (economics)
11. Explain how specialization leads to more efficient use of economic resources and economic growth (economics)

were provided to help students integrate and transfer the vast amount of historical information about conflict and resolution to other cultures and time periods.

On the other hand, the state standards document (Figure 4.13) emphasized concepts, principles, dispositions, and skills. Eleven standards from this document had been selected by Lydia's school district for emphasis within the Civil War unit. These standards, taken from *The Framework: K-12 Curricular Goals and Standards* (Connecticut State Department of Education, 1998a), included the goals listed in Figure 4.13.

As she read this list, Lydia concluded that the standards document did capture the key understandings that students should develop about this period in United States history. She had to make a decision: Which set of goals would dictate student learning: those in the textbook, the standards document, or both? To make this unit meaningful for her students, she decided to reframe the unit around the more powerful standards described in her state document. The students would acquire the factual knowledge about the Civil War embedded in the two textbook chapters. However, this knowledge would be used as a bridge to develop the more long lasting concepts, principles, and skills associated with historical thinking and themes. To do this, she wouldn't have to abandon the text and its lesson plans, but she would have to replace the textbook objectives with standards.

Understanding the Standards

Making a conscious decision to teach a unit of study by addressing core knowledge is the first big step in unit development or lesson remodeling. However, teachers also need an opportunity to come to a deep understanding of the concepts, principles, and skills that provide the structure for a discipline. There are at least three strategies that educators and curriculum developers can use to become more knowledgeable about these big ideas.

One strategy for increasing our familiarity with the big ideas in a discipline involves a simple listing, underlining, or categorizing procedure. Consider the fourth standard in Lydia's state document, reprinted below:

Explain reasons for conflict and the ways conflicts have been resolved.

This standard was designed to describe one vital aspect of the study of history. It represents core knowledge in the field of history. When Lydia examined the standards statement, she carefully underlined and listed of the key ideas embedded in the sentence. Her list looked like this:

▷ Reasons (methodological skill—cause and effect)

▷ Conflict (concept)

▷ Resolution (concept)

▷ Explanations (principle)

On further analysis, she categorized each of the terms and phrases within each of her standards statements. Figure 4.12 may be helpful in categorizing a phrase or item within one of the six categories of knowledge. In the example above, one possibility might be to categorize "reasons" as a cognitive thinking skill associated with the inquiry process an historian undertakes. In a similar manner, both "conflict" and "resolution" could be categorized as major concepts within the field of history. If one were to identify a relationship between the two concepts, conflict and resolution, and the cognitive process of identifying causes and effects, it might be possible to develop teachable principles such as these:

1. All conflicts have causes
2. The key to resolving conflicts is a comprehensive understanding of related causes and effects.

If we extend this process and categorize all of the standards for the Civil War unit listed in Figure 4.13, we create an opportunity that fosters a deeper understanding of the nature of complex, multifaceted standards statements. Figure 4.14 depicts this process for categorizing the 12 standards in Lydia's revised unit. Figure 4.15 demonstrates how this process can be generalized to the first two standards in Figure 4.14. The words in parentheses indicate the specific aspects of the Civil War that will be aligned with the general standards statements.

Lydia knew that in the past she had concentrated her teaching around the events related to the Civil War. She had addressed these events in chronological fashion, moving from the causes of the Civil War to the events and people involved in the battles and the war. Equipped with new knowledge about the importance of big ideas and concept-based teaching, Lydia revised the sequence and content of her lesson plans and approached the four-week unit by first having students study the difference among **states, a federation, and a nation.** Next, she planned to introduce a study of the **livelihoods and economies** of various people and groups (e.g., factory workers, slaves, factory owners, plantation owners, farmers, women, and children) in the North and the South. She followed this with an examination of slavery: its conditions, roots, and consequences. Next, she planned to have students learn about the various perspectives within the emerging nation **about state and civil rights issues.** Then, students would examine the concepts and principles related to

Figure 4.14. Categorizing the Knowledge Categories Within Standards Statements

Standard	Facts	Concepts	Principles	Dispositions	Skills	Application
1	X	X	X		X	
2	X		X	X	X	
3	X	X	X		X	X
4	X	X	X		X	
5	X	X	X	X		
6	X	X	X	X		
7	X	X	X		X	X
8	X	X	X	X		
9	X	X	X		X	X
10	X	X	X		X	
11	X	X	X		X	

Figure 4.15. Identifying the Knowledge Categories in Complex Standards Statements

Standard	Facts	Concepts	Principles	Dispositions	Skills	Application
1	Acquire information about major events (that led to the Civil War)	Understand the concept of trends (by studying events related to the Civil War over time)	Understand that trends emerge from a search for patterns		Analyzing data to identify trends Finding patterns (in social studies data and information)	
2	Acquire information about famous people, important events, and dates (related to the Civil War, e.g., Davis, Lee, Brown, Sherman, Lincoln, Harper's Ferry, Appomattox, Missouri Compromise, Emancipation Proclamation, and Gettysburg Address)		Develop generaliza-tions about causes and effects (of the Civil War) and changes over time	Appreciate historical perspectives (on the Civil War, states' rights, and slavery) Appreciate the historical context (of existing economic conditions in the North and South)	Analyzing data sequentially Identifying cause and effect	

perspectives, viewpoints, balance, conflicts, compromise, consensus, and resolution by studying specific examples, documents, people, and events in the 1860s. Students would learn about the familiar people and events related to the Civil War but within the larger context of the disciplines of history, geography, economics, and government.

Planning Assessment Strategies

Lydia was comfortable with the use of preassessments, ongoing assessments, and rubrics to measure her students' learning progress. She knew she would have to use similar procedures to measure student learning in this unit. She identified several of the major concepts related to the Civil War (states' rights, conflict, perspective, slavery, federation, nationalism, compromise, consensus, economy) and principles related to the Civil War. She developed a word bank of the concepts and designed a pre- and postassessment that asked students to create a concept map, to provide examples of the concepts in the word bank, to draw lines between related concepts and explain the resulting principle, and to give definitions and examples of each concept. She used rubrics similar to the one reprinted in Figure 4.16 to measure students' conceptual learning over time.

On the other hand, when the knowledge goal in a Core Curriculum unit addressed the acquisition of a principle or rule, Lydia used a rubric similar to the one shown in Figure 4.17. In this example, Lydia's students might be asked to explain, orally or in writing, the principle related to the causes of civil wars. Another option would be to provide students with the same kind of word bank used in the first example and ask them to make a map or web that explains the connections among the concepts.

When the core knowledge was focused on a skill instead of a concept or principle, however, Lydia changed her assessment strategy and used an observation, product, or performance. When the skill was cognitive, her assessment strategy asked students for a written reflection on their cognitive process in work that used the specified kind of thinking, or she used an observable think-aloud performance. For example, when Lydia altered her fifth grade Civil War unit to reflect the core knowledge in the discipline of history, she expected her students to use historical thinking skills. Specifically, she might ask them to demonstrate their ability to use multiple evidence sources in order to make a warranted historical claim or argument.

To assess growth in that ability and evaluate the extent to which individual students can create a strong argument, Lydia created a skills-based checklist of criteria similar to the one reprinted in Figure 4.18. Each item on the checklist was rated on a 1-3 or 1-5 scale, so that growth between the preassessment and the postassessment could be easily analyzed.

The need for valid and reliable pre- and postassessments is as vital within the Core Curriculum Parallel as it is within any kind of curriculum unit. The format for the assessment, however, varies in order to conform more readily to measuring changes in students' acquisition of concepts, principles, and cognitive skills within a discipline. Both the assessment strategy and the assessment criteria vary slightly to accommodate this special purpose.

Figure 4.16. A Rubric for Measuring Growth in the Attainment of the Concept "Civil"

	Beginning	Developing	Competent	Proficient	Expert
Level of Understanding	The learner can communicate the term associated with the abstract concept.	The learner can paraphrase the definition of the concept.	The learner can provide examples and nonexamples of the concept.	The learner can provide key attributes that distinguish the concept category.	The learner can link the concept with other related concepts.
Example	Civil	"Civil means something to do with the citizens of a place. A civil war is a war fought inside a country and among its citizens."	Examples: • I am a citizen of the United States. • I am not a citizen of Russia. • World War II was not a civil war. • Ireland is having a civil war now.	• Citizens • Members • State • Nation • Law • Rights • Laws • Public • Internal	"People have civil wars when they can't resolve their conflicts or achieve their rights peaceably."

Planning Introductory Activities

Next, Lydia considered how she might alter the introductory activities for the unit to fit the parameters of the Core Curriculum Parallel. She knew she needed to develop several aspects of an introduction that were missing from the original unit. She wanted to preassess her students on their prior knowledge about the facts, concepts, and principles related to the Civil War. She also knew that her students didn't necessarily connect the study of the Civil War with the study of history, geography, economics, or government, so she needed to show them how this topic was related to those important disciplines within the social sciences. She wanted to prepare them for their role as thinkers and analyzers of documents, examples, data, and events. She also wanted them to understand what concepts and principles were all about. Finally, she wanted them to have an opportunity to tell her what they wanted to learn about the Civil War so that she could begin planning related extension activities.

In order to show her students how the Civil War related to the four disciplines of history, government, economics, and geography, Lydia prepared a flow chart. She

Figure 4.17. A Rubric for Measuring the Acquisition of Principles and Rules

	Beginning	*Developing*	*Competent*	*Proficient*	*Expert*
Levels of Understanding	The learner can define and provide examples or a synthesis of the essential information upon which a principle is based.	The learner can identify a topical or temporal relationship among concepts and essential information.	The learner can extend the principle or rule to novel examples within the discipline or field of study.	The learner can articulate a general conceptual relationship as conditional, if/then cause/effect, part/whole, etc.	The learner can extend the principle across disciplines or fields of study.
Example	"The Civil War was a war between the northern and southern states in the United States in the 1860s."	"The Civil War was fought because of disagreements about slavery, economics, and states' rights."	"There are civil wars going on right now in Yugoslavia, Ireland, and Mexico. They are caused by the some of the same kinds of things that caused our Civil War."	"Civil wars are caused by citizens' inability to find a way to resolve their differences ·about rights and laws peacefully."	"Empathy, compromise, and consensus can be used to resolve conflicts peacefully because they honor individual perspectives and values."

listed the four disciplines on the chart and under each discipline listed some of the major concepts in each discipline that students would study in order to understand the "big ideas" about the Civil War. She prepared open-ended discussion questions to generate students' conversations about their interests, their prior experience with these concepts, and the Civil War in particular. She also developed and printed multiple copies of her preassessment. Finally, Lydia visited the Library of Congress Web site and downloaded several copies of some Matthew Brady photographs of the Civil War. She made her selection carefully because she wanted to choose a small set of photographs that could be used to detect a pattern and a relationship—just the kind of thinking she would expect students to use as they unearthed the concepts, principles, and core knowledge related to this topic. Lydia used these photographs and the accompanying analysis activity as the culmination of her introductory activities.

Figure 4.18. Criteria for Judging the Strength of an Argument

- Clearly states the claim or argument
- Provides sufficient evidence related to the claim or argument
- Selects credible evidence sources
- Consults multiple sources
- Selects relevant evidence
- Clearly explains all assumptions
- Provides a logical argument
- Refutes alternative claims or arguments

Selecting Teaching and Learning Activities, Grouping Strategies, Resources, and Products

Because of the need in the Core Curriculum Parallel for students to understand the key concepts and principles of a discipline, Lydia's predominant teaching methods were inductive. She used concept-based teaching, open-ended questioning strategies, coaching, Socratic questioning, and scaffolding to help students analyze information about events, individuals, and settings related to the concepts that she used to structure her four-week unit. As students examined documents, photographs, evidence, and information, she continually posed questions: "What does this mean to you? How is this the same or different from the things we have just studied? Which pieces of information fit together as a category? Can you give me other examples of this concept? Do you see a pattern emerging? What do you think caused this? What rule or principle can you make now that you have reviewed this information? What do you think will happen next? Why did this happen? Is there more than one reason? Will there be more than one effect? How do you know your answer is right? Can you show me evidence to prove you conclusion is valid? What other information do you need to be sure? Do the other students see it the same way you do? Why or why not?"

During one point in the unit, when students were examining varying perspectives on people's rights compared with the rights of states, she allocated two days for them to re-create the Lincoln Douglas debates and the Dred Scott decisions. These role-play activities and simulations were followed by small group reflection opportunities and large group debriefing sessions in order to flesh out the related concepts and principles. The students enjoyed the departure from their normal routine and became extremely motivated about finding and citing evidence to "prove" their point of view.

If a visitor to the classroom had been asked to describe Lydia's behavior and role during this unit, he or she would more than likely remark that she "Answered all of the students' questions with more questions" or that she "Gave them information and asked them to think hard about what it really meant." Also the visitor would probably have noticed that Lydia spent the majority of her time giving students something to think about, helping them think their way through it and decide what it meant in the broader scope of history, geography, economics, and government.

However, on occasion, Lydia would also teach deductively, by explaining the nature of a concept and providing information about its key attributes, characteristics, and examples. This was most often the case when students were dealing with factual information, concepts, or skills that were novel or difficult for them to comprehend, such as the concept of suffrage or people's reaction to the Harper's Ferry incident.

If the introductory activities are successful, students should come to an understanding about their role in a Core Curriculum unit. In the case of Lydia's Civil War unit, her students understood that they were going to be given data, tables, charts, graphs, information about events and actions, photographs, and documents, and that they would be expected to work together to develop an understanding of the underlying concepts or principles. The focusing questions Lydia developed and shared during the introduction scaffolded their analysis of video footage they viewed, the Emancipation Proclamation, and additional Matthew Brady photographs. Students reviewed abridged diaries of women, slaves, soldiers, and the newspaper articles of the time. They were on a constant search for concepts, categories, patterns, relationships, causes, effects, and principles. Some of Lydia's focusing questions to support student learning about the concepts and principles that connect the Civil War with the discipline of economics included the following:

> ▷ What are the factors that explain economic conditions?
>
> ▷ How do resources, goods, and services interact?
>
> ▷ How do resources, goods, and services affect wants and needs?
>
> ▷ How do resources, goods, and services affect supply and demand?
>
> ▷ How does supply and demand effect economic well-being?
>
> ▷ What are the special characteristics of Northern economic conditions? What were Southern economic conditions?
>
> ▷ How did these economic conditions affect the Civil War?

The nature of these focusing questions goes to the very heart of the discipline. They vary greatly from those printed in Lydia's original textbook unit and printed on the next page:

> ▷ What was the Fugitive Slave Law?
>
> ▷ How did Frederick Douglass and Harriet Tubman fight against slavery?
>
> ▷ What events help turn the war in favor of the Union?
>
> ▷ Why did Lincoln announce the Emancipation Proclamation after the Battle of Antietam?

The use of Socratic teaching methods, focusing questions, and simulations provided support for the students' analytic inquiry. Lydia's choice of resources and materials provided students with opportunities to examine the relationships among the representative topic they studied, the related evidence and information gleaned from political cartoons, newspaper accounts, diaries, and their textbooks, and the overarching concepts and principles within the related disciplines. The use of large group and small group sessions supported students' analysis and concept attainment through the use of discussions, shared inquiry, think-pair-share activities, and debriefings.

Last, Lydia's use of short-term or daily products such as document analysis worksheets, graphic organizers, concept maps, and reflective journals provided ongoing assessments to help her monitor and adjust her instructional support to ensure students' success with analytic information processing. For example, Lydia planned to have students meet in small groups to analyze perspectives on slavery by reviewing "Cannibals All! Or, Slaves Without Masters," written in 1857 by George Fitzhugh, and "My Bondage and My Freedom," written in 1852 by Frederick Douglass. Lydia knew the documents would be tough going for fifth graders. Therefore, she prepared advance organizers that alerted students to unfamiliar terms in the passages: She gave them yellow markers to mark the important phrases, numbered each line of the documents so students could follow them more easily, and provided focusing questions to guide student thinking. These instructional aids fostered students' inquiry and enabled them to use authentic documents from the time period to draw their own conclusions.

Lydia also developed a culminating product for her students to help them focus on the key information, concepts, and principles in the Civil War unit. Students could work alone or in groups of two, three, or four to develop a visual plan for a Civil War quilt. Directions for the quilt product, as well as criteria she and the students would use to support successful work, made it clear that the goal of the product was a demonstration of student understanding of what was important during the time period and why it was important. Specifically, quilt squares had to depict (1) key people and events of the Civil War period, (2) livelihoods, cultures, and economies of various groups in the North and South, (3) roots and consequences of slavery, (4) how varied viewpoints and perspectives led to conflict, (5) how these varied viewpoints were dealt with through conflict resolution and compromise, and (6) other conclusions they had drawn about what is most significant to understand from the Civil War period. These requirements for the culminating product ensured that students would review and focus on both essential information about the time period and key concepts and principles they had studied. To strengthen the focus, and to call on key skills students had developed during the unit, the culminating product assignment also asked them to do some reflective writing to go along with the quilt design. Specifically, each student had to individually interpret the quilt on which they worked by addressing how the quilt depicted the six requirements. They also had to provide evidence that their conclusions were well supported in information they had studied. This process caused them to reflect on their inquiry as they draw on key skills in their unit, including analysis, cause and effect, providing evidence, generalizing, and seeing relationships. The assessment rubrics illustrated in Figures 4.16 through 4.18 provided Lydia with a starting point for developing criteria to determine student growth as reflected in the culminating product.

Choosing Extension Activities

Lydia wanted her extension activities to support students' interests in subtopics and related concepts aligned with the Civil War. Her open-ended questions during the unit's introduction identified students with interests in several topics connected to core information, concepts, principles, skills, and applications related to this Core Curriculum unit. Some students preferred to gather more information about the Battle at Gettysburg because they had traveled there during summer vacations. Other students wanted to read more about Abraham Lincoln and Jefferson Davis because they had seen their statues on vacation trips. One group of students wanted to read more about slavery during the Civil War period—some in novels and others in nonfiction. The majority of students, however, wanted an opportunity to examine more of Brady's photographs or to watch Ken Burns's videos on the Civil War.

Armed with this knowledge, Lydia labeled social studies time on three Thursdays as Specialty Days. During this time, students developed study questions related to their interests in the Civil War, used library research skills to find information regarding their questions, reviewed the information, developed their findings, and participated in a small group sharing experience. Important in the whole process were Lydia's debriefing questions. She continually asked students to reflect on what they had chosen to study and related it back to the core knowledge, concepts, principles, and skills they had studied together. She also provided guiding questions to help students maintain this focus as they shared their work with one another.

Lydia found that the extension opportunity promoted ownership in the unit among her students. The interest-based investigations also yielded contributions for students to make to the Civil War unit as the extension activities and unit as a whole evolved simultaneously.

Modifying Plans Based on Learner Need, Including Ascending Intellectual Demand

Lydia realized that despite all of her preplanning to improve the quality of the Civil War unit, there were students who would need a modified approach to the unit of study based on their level of sophistication with materials and content. For students with learning difficulties, she chose different print documents, song lyrics, and sections from children's historical fiction to support the analytic reading of students who would have a difficult time using the selections cited above. Some of the students also used the Ken Burns videos on the Civil War to lend further support for understanding text material. In addition, she worked with students needing additional help in small groups and during conferences to scaffold their concept-based learning and analysis of the documents. Finally, students with difficulty in written language had the option of tape-recording the analysis for their culminating products and working with the teacher to prepare for the tape recording.

For her more advanced readers and thinkers, Lydia understood that she would need to guide them to work at a more intense level of intellectual demand in order to ensure their growth and challenge during the unit. For these students, Lydia searched for more sophisticated print documents. She found excerpts from *Uncle Tom's Cabin*, the Emancipation Proclamation, and the Fourteenth Amendment to the Constitution for them to read during related learning activities. However, the most challenging option appeared when she discovered a Civil War-related Supreme Court decision, *Ex parte Milligan*, regarding three men in Indiana who were found guilty by a military court of conspiring with the Confederate States of America to set up a Northwestern Confederacy. Later, they were sentenced to be hanged. Lydia planned to ask her advanced learners and readers to review Lincoln's martial law proclamation in 1862, the arrest and conviction of the three defendants, the Supreme Court appeal and brief, and the Justices' opinions. Students would search for evidence in the brief regarding the suspension of the defendants' civil rights of habeas corpus and the Supreme Court's reversal of the lower court's conviction. She would have the students work with this case when other students needed additional time for readings, reteaching, or guided small group discussions in order to be comfortable with the key information, concepts, principles, and skills that formed the core of the unit.

The advanced students were ready for a real challenge. The complexity of materials and the abstract nature of the concepts behind the ruling would provide that opportunity. Further, this exploration would call on these students to use scholarly behavior, reflect on the significance and societal implications of ideas, examine an issue from multiple perspectives, and link what they are learning in the unit with unfamiliar contexts. With proper support from Lydia and their peers, her advanced students could achieve a deep understanding of the role of the Bill of Rights, the Constitution, and the Supreme Court in ensuring and protecting the civil rights of all citizens. Once again, she would blend information and insights from these students into whole-class discussions on a range of topics.

Looking Back and Ahead

The essence of the Core Curriculum Parallel is well expressed in the words of children's author Margaret Wise Brown, who in 1949 wrote and illustrated a picture book titled *The Important Book*. Each page of the book illustrates a common object such as a daisy or a spoon. Writing follows the pattern of listing several noteworthy traits of the object, then emphasizing the most essential one by ending with the line "But the important thing about _____ is that it _____." That's much like the goal of the Core Curriculum Parallel as it seeks to help students understand the essential nature of what they are studying.

As we attempt to provide students with a comprehensive K-12 curriculum that spans a multitude of topics and subject areas, we must also keep in mind our long-term purposes for teaching and learning. It is vital we remember that amid all of the details, facts, activities, and assignments, the important thing about school is that it provides students with the understandings and skills they can use all of the rest of their lives. Effective use of the Core Curriculum Parallel ensures that students can truly find the forest for the trees.

The Core Curriculum Parallel also sets the stage for meaning in the other three parallels of the Parallel Curriculum Model. The Curriculum of Connections asks students to look at key information, concepts, principles, and skills across contexts. The Curriculum of Practice asks students to think about and use key information, concepts, principles, and skills as a practitioner uses them. The Curriculum of Identity asks students to reflect on ways in which practitioners in a discipline use key information, concepts, principles, and skills to contribute to and learn from their work—and then to reflect as students on what they learn about themselves by comparing themselves with those practitioners. In each instance, the "core" of meaning in the exploration pivots on the essential structure of the content and discipline the student is studying.

5

The Curriculum
of Connections Parallel

One of the first things a visitor to the University of Virginia campus notices is its amazing horticultural beauty and remarkable architecture. A stroll through the center of campus offers a glimpse of history and an opportunity to view learning through the eyes of the university's founder, Thomas Jefferson.

One day last summer, two of the authors were fortunate to be treated to a historical tour of the center of campus by a caretaker who beamed with pride as he related stories about the design and layout of the campus. A portion of that guided tour is worth relating, for it serves as a fitting segue to our next curriculum parallel, the Curriculum of Connections.

The mall, as it is called, is a long, wide, open expanse of rolling lawn, surrounded on three sides with buildings. On both the east and the west sides of the great lawn sit single, elongated rows of five two-story brick buildings. Connected by walkways and columnar porticos, the two rows of buildings originally housed the classrooms and living quarters of the professors and deans of each of the 10 colleges served by the university.

The caretaker explained to us that Jefferson designed the university mall and its buildings as a metaphor to symbolize knowledge and learning. The two rows of buildings represent the two branches of knowledge, the arts and the sciences. The five buildings on each side of the lawn represent the five disciplines within each of the two branches of knowledge. The five buildings to the west of the lawn originally accommodated the five schools of the arts: philosophy, language, literature, the performing arts, and the visual arts. The five buildings to the east of the lawn housed the schools of science: math, earth science, physical science, life science, and the social sciences. Both sets of buildings were joined to the north by the Rotunda, a domed building that served as university offices, meeting rooms, and the library (see Figure 5.1).

What a profound story for an amateur historian to share with two strangers! We left with little doubt that his words would linger with both of us, far into the future.

Figure 5.1. The Branches and Fields of Knowledge

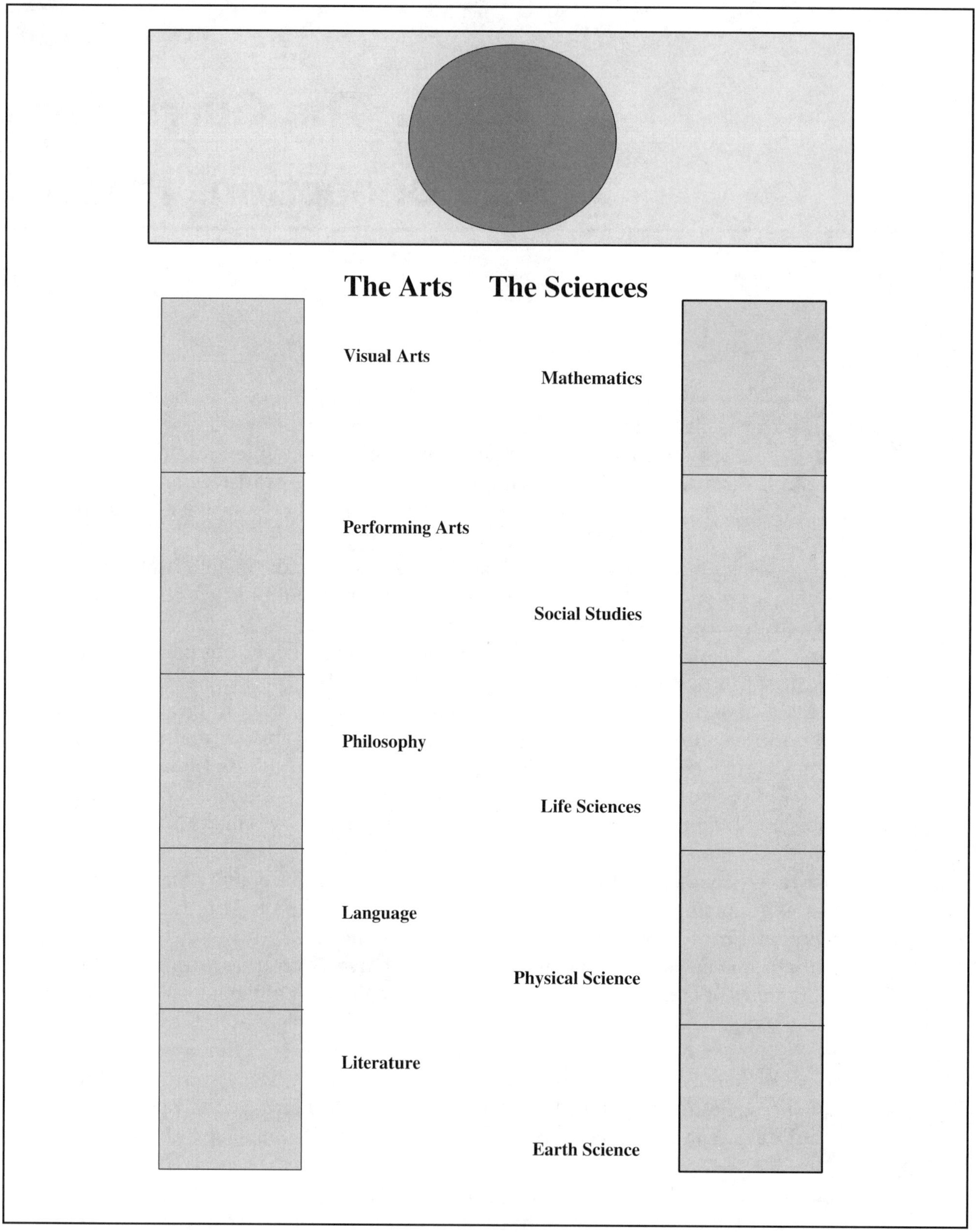

The Arts   The Sciences

Visual Arts

Mathematics

Performing Arts

Social Studies

Philosophy

Life Sciences

Language

Physical Science

Literature

Earth Science

Perhaps that was Jefferson's wish as well, to provide a powerful message that inspired young learners and college students to continue to seek wisdom by making connections across disciplines, time, events, and topics for the rest of their lives.

This chapter explains the second in a set of four parallel approaches to curriculum design—the Curriculum of Connections. Like the other three curriculum parallels, The Curriculum of Connections Parallel uses the key components within the Comprehensive Curriculum Framework to design powerful and effective learning experiences for students. It also strives to improve the impact of curriculum and instruction by helping students build connections. However, the connections forged within this parallel are separate and distinct from the kinds of connections students make as they participate in the Core Curriculum, the Curriculum of Practice, or the Curriculum of Identity.

This chapter explores those differences and provides descriptions of the various ways in which the key curriculum components can be modified to fit the special functions of the Curriculum of Connections. In addition, the reader will find examples, charts, and tables designed to support the curriculum writing or curriculum remodeling process.

What Is the Curriculum of Connections?

The Curriculum of Connections is a format for designing teaching and learning activities, lesson plans, or curriculum units that focus on the discovery of relationships, associations, and ideas across various aspects of knowledge and information. The ability to grasp multiple and layered connections is acquired as a result of a learning and maturation process that gradually yields analogous relationships, thereby enlarging one's perspective, cognition, and awareness.

A learner can discover connections by examining data, facts, and concepts within a topic or discipline. Lessons and units designed around the Curriculum of Connections, however, are more likely to emphasize the search for overarching connections, those that can be developed across events, time, places, topics, principles, and disciplines. The Curriculum of Connections bears a strong resemblance to the Core Curriculum in that it examines the concepts and principles within a discipline. Nonetheless, the purpose for making connections in this parallel is to identify or use macroconcepts (overarching concepts that connect many disciplines and topics), themes, principles, generalizations, processes, or dispositions across disciplines and novel problems. The Curriculum of Connections Parallel provides opportunities for learning by supporting students as they use analogous or comparative thinking among equivalent classes, relationships, and systems in the same or varied disciplines to discover connections through reflection.

In much the same way that an infant or a pet peers into a full-length mirror and initially believes that it sees a new, enticing, and unusual playmate, the Curriculum of Connections brings together two or more seemingly different, but intriguing, ideas for students to examine. When successful, the analysis and examination of these apparently distinct entities results in a deeper understanding of equivalence through the use of insight and the recognition of symmetry and congruence.

The Curriculum of Connections asks students to take on the role of detective. As students proceed through a lesson or unit of study, they develop or use a set of basic rules about how things look, work, and relate to each other in a specific circumstance or venue. Then, they actively search for the ways in which these same characteristics, concepts, processes, dispositions, rules, and principles apply in new contexts. This deductive search for meaningful connections and analogies helps students achieve deeper understanding and draw conclusions about new and unfamiliar sets of information—and, in fact, about life itself.

Students can identify connections by using previously learned characteristics, concepts, and rules to examine two or more people, events, products, topics, time periods, cultures, or disciplines. The generalizations that result from this search help learners appreciate the fact that we can "see the world in a grain of sand" and that there truly are fewer than "six degrees of separation" between any one topic, person, or event, and other topics or people across time and cultures. The essence of this curriculum parallel is its emphasis on the development of connections: personal, topical, temporal, intradisciplinary, or interdisciplinary.

Focusing Questions in the Curriculum of Connections

Each of the four curriculum parallels structures its format and purposes around the key questions it helps students answer. The *Core* Curriculum Parallel asks students to consider three overarching questions: What is the structure of this discipline? What are the key concepts and principles in this discipline? How can I develop an understanding of the concepts and principles as a result of studying this topic?

By contrast, the Curriculum of *Connections* extends these understandings and poses three additional overarching questions: How are the key concepts and principles in this topic or discipline related to the key concepts and principles in other topics or disciplines? How might I use what I already know about the key concepts and principles in a topic or discipline to acquire a deeper understanding of those same concepts and principles in other topics and/or disciplines? How might I use interdisciplinary concepts, themes, and processes to solve novel problems? Figure 5.2 lists "smaller" questions on which students will need to focus in order to formulate answers to the three over-arching questions.

To support the development of a curriculum of connections teachers must pose to themselves three questions: What are the major concepts and principles in the discipline that are related to the topic or unit that is my focal point? What other topics or problems in this discipline or other disciplines address these same concepts and principles? How might I develop a connection between the topic or unit that is my focal point and other topics or problems to encourage a deeper understanding of the concepts and principles that connect them?

Figure 5.2. Some Focusing Questions for Students in the Curriculum of Connections

What key concepts and principles have I learned?

In what other contexts can I use what I have learned?

How do the ideas and skills I have learned work in other contexts?

How do I use the ideas and skills to develop insights or solve problems?

How do different settings cause me to change or reinforce my earlier understandings?

How do I adjust my way of thinking and working when I encounter new contexts?

How do I know if my adjustments are effective?

How does looking at one thing help me understand another?

Why do different people have different perspectives on the same issue?

How are perspectives shaped by time, place, culture, events, and circumstances?

In what ways is it beneficial for me to examine varied perspectives on a problem or issue?

How do I assess the relative strengths and weaknesses of differing viewpoints?

What connections do I see between what I am studying and my own life and times?

The Purpose of a Curriculum of Connections: Why Should a Teacher Emphasize Connections and Relationships?

The Curriculum of Connections emphasizes relationships, patterns, and ideas for several reasons. First, the ability to recognize connections and relationships both broadens and deepens one's understanding of and appreciation for the interconnectedness of knowledge. At its most sophisticated level, the ability to see connections offers a worldview that perceives all topics and disciplines as sharing integrated facets or as aggregates, sharing common and analogous attributes, purposes, or functions. In turn, an appreciation for analogous thinking fosters a habitual search and appreciation for the many ways in which units are parts of classes, classes are part of a system, and that systems share common functions, attributes, and principles. It is this appreciation of universality and timelessness that distinguishes wisdom from content expertise. With wisdom comes the ability to search for, perceive, and appreciate, for example, the aesthetics of science and the science of pottery.

The acquisition of an integrated perspective was never more apparent than in the words of a graduate student—a carpenter by trade—who returned to college to pursue a second career as a teacher. During his first graduate class, his fellow students, all practicing teachers, became involved in an animated conversation about teaching and learning activities in various subject areas. After listening to them in silence for 15 minutes, he finally remarked in a quiet but firm voice, "You teachers really slay me—all this talk about math versus reading, music versus science—everything's a separate subject area to you. You know, when I build a set of stairs for a customer, I never stop and think, 'Now I'm doing science, now I'm doing math, now I'm using psychology.' I just see it all as part of the same thing."

The ability to perceive and search for connections also decreases "nearsightedness" or episodic thinking, and the accumulation of isolated, disconnected information and details. In fact, an accumulating body of research suggests that the ability to create connections among concepts, principles, events, and disciplines actually supports increases in long-term memory, enhances retrieval, and develops a "high road" transfer of acquired knowledge to novel and complex situations and ill-structured problem solving.

The ability to see these connections, and a disposition to look for commonalties and connections, actually diminishes a learner's sense of confusion and frustration when confronted with new data or information. Looking for familiar themes and concepts in strange situations also decreases the amount of time needed for a learner to understand new content, improves efficiency and precision, and enhances a learner's self-efficacy for independent learning.

A purposeful search for connections also improves insight and creativity through metaphoric thinking and analogy making. When confronted with a problematic situation, astute connection makers continually ask themselves, What does this remind me of? How can I connect and use what I already know to solve this problem?

The "Eureka!" sensation and the feeling of "Aha!" usually follow a lengthy incubation period that revolves around a difficult problem or a confusing situation. The willingness to tolerate the ambiguity that accompanies uncertainty and indecision allows us to search our minds, purposefully or unconsciously, for metaphors, connections, and analogous situations stored in our long-term memories. When discovered and retrieved, these connections and analogies can be generalized, transferred, and applied to a novel problem in order to solve it in an effective and creative manner. A prolonged search for the proper analogy also prevents us from leaping to action or judgment and reduces the likelihood of implementing ineffective solutions or drawing inappropriate conclusions.

Last, and possibly most important, the ability to see connections also supports a person's ability to view ideas or events from multiple perspectives. This, in turn, enhances empathy, open-mindedness, and nonjudgmental thinking while decreasing stereotypical thinking and bias.

The Curriculum of Connections:
When Should I Use This Parallel?

Despite the importance of these varied purposes and benefits for the Curriculum of Connections, we must appreciate the fact that no curriculum approach is appropriate for all situations. It is as ineffective to "force fit" this parallel into every unit of instruction as it is to make it fit the needs of every learner and every teacher in the same way and time. Personal content knowledge, grade-level expectations, the availability of resources, and opportunities to work with teachers from other disciplines predicts the likelihood of deep understanding and efficacy as well as initial implementation and long-term use.

The journey to professional expertise is a long one, and many teachers may discover and apply these connections only after lengthy study and reflection in multiple content areas. We can, however, support the likelihood that more teachers will be able to develop these connections and identify interdisciplinary generalizations and macroconcepts through interdisciplinary collaboration with colleagues and exposure to advanced content in various disciplines.

Although not every teacher or student may be prepared to find themes, concepts, principles, and universal connections independently, most teachers and students can be supported and coached to enhance their ability to think and reflect in this manner. Separate sections of this chapter illustrate various techniques that can be used by teachers and teachers' coaches to scaffold this kind of thinking for both youngsters and adults.

The Characteristics of the Curriculum
Components Within the Curriculum of Connections

If an educator analyzed a lesson or a unit designed by using the Comprehensive Curriculum Framework and compared it to a lesson or unit that emphasizes connections and relationships, the key components (i.e., content/standards, assessments, introduction, teaching activities, learning activities, grouping strategies, modification based on learner need, resources, products, and extension activities) would be evident in both examples. The characteristics and format of these components would, however, exhibit subtle differences in order to promote the understanding of principles and macroconcepts that connect topics within or across disciplines. This section describes those differences across the key curriculum components that are part of the Comprehensive Curriculum Framework.

Figure 5.3 provides a graphic organizer that lists the key curriculum components as they might appear within the Curriculum of Connections in the left column. Techniques for developing each component are listed in the right column.

(Text continued on page 136)

Figure 5.3. Using the Key Curriculum Components in the Curriculum of Connections

Curriculum Components	Reconfiguration Techniques
Content/ Standards	• Identify the units or topics you are assigned to teach. • Identify the discipline(s) with which these topics are associated. • Make a list of the major facts, concepts, principles, dispositions, and skills to be addressed in each unit of study. • Consider the kinds of information students will learn—places, events, people, things, or characteristics. Identify analogous items in other topics, locations, time periods, fields, or disciplines. • Consider the concepts that students will learn in this unit. Identify the use of similar concepts in other topics, fields, or disciplines. • Consider the principles that students will learn in this unit. Identify analogous principles that explain relationships within other topics, fields, or disciplines. • Consider the dispositions that students will address in this unit. Identify analogous dispositions, in other situations, career areas, fields, or disciplines. • Consider the skills that students will learn in this unit. Identify analogous skills needed to think, learn, investigate, or produce in other topic areas, fields, or disciplines. • Consider working with colleagues who teach different subject areas to the same students. Discuss how you might connect two or more units of instruction through a focus on common concepts, principles, skills, and dispositions.
Introductory Activities	• Provide students with concept maps. • Develop and share advance organizers that list the major concepts, principles, skills, and dispositions they will acquire in this unit. • Introduce the ideas of macroconcepts, generalizations, and themes. • Share a familiar Aesop's fable with students or ask them to identify and list common axioms, adages, or proverbs. Ask students to discuss and identify the purpose for proverbs and axioms. Explain that this unit of instruction will have a similar purpose. • Provide students with three parts of an analogy or a portion of a simile. Ask them to complete the missing portions. Discuss why or how they use analogies or similes in their daily lives. • Make a list of the many ways that analogies, metaphors, and similes support new learning, decrease confusion, or enhance problem solving. Explain that the purpose of this unit will be to build the same kinds of bridges and connections for students. • Develop and share focusing questions that bridge two or more concepts, skills, principles, or dispositions across topics and disciplines. • Introduce the overarching theme, generalization, or macroconcept at the onset of the integrated unit. Remind students that they will continually search for connections between the specifics they are studying in one discipline and these multidisciplinary themes and macroconcepts. • Prepare a list of the concepts, skills, principles, and dispositions students will learn during this unit. Next to each, print a symbol of a bridge, connection, umbrella, and so on. Tell students that throughout the integrated unit they will continually search for the words or terms they can use to describe the macroconcepts, dispositions, processes, generalizations, or themes that apply to similar classes or relations across multiple disciplines or topics. • Introduce an intriguing problem or puzzle in a topic or discipline distant from the unit or discipline students are about to begin studying. Tell students that careful reflection during the course of this unit should help them discover macroconcepts, themes, generalizations, or analogies that will, in turn, help them solve the cross-discipline puzzle or problem by the end of the unit.

Assessments	• Supply students with word banks that list major concepts and ask them to create concept maps that link related concepts and principles in one topic with those in another topic or discipline.
	• Develop rubrics that address growth in the understanding of macroconcepts, processes, and generalizations across topics and disciplines.
	• Provide preassessments to identify students' prior experiences with the discipline and the concepts and principles they have attained to date. Build on this knowledge in the upcoming unit through the use of synectics and metaphoric thinking.
Teaching Methods	• Use the synectics teaching model to help students build a bridge between the concepts, principles, and dispositions in one unit and analogous concepts, principles, skills, and dispositions in another model.
	• Share or help students create metaphors to build bridges between topics and disciplines.
	• Use Socratic questioning and deductive logic as scaffolds to help students make connections between abstract units, classes, relations, and systems.
	• Provide opportunities for students to work in cooperative groups as they make analogies between topics, events, and disciplines.
	• Use examples and nonexamples within the Concept Attainment Model to help students develop macroconcepts and themes.
	• Improvise on Wassermann's (1988) Play-Debrief-Replay teaching methods. Help students acquire and reflect on learned concepts and principles, and then replay the use of the same concepts and principles with another venue. Follow with another debriefing and reflection opportunity.
	• Use intra- or interdisciplinary problem-solving simulations or scenarios to support the development of macroconcepts.
Learning Activities	• Develop learning activities related to content acquisition that require students to identify connections, acquire macroconcepts, make cross-discipline generalizations, and use themes to solve integrated problems. Involve students in the use of the following thinking skills:
	Comparing and contrasting
	Deductive and inductive thinking
	Making analogies
	Creative problem solving
	Making generalizations
	Hierarchical classification
	Seeing patterns and relationships
	Developing insights
	Systems thinking

(Continued)

Figure 5.3. Continued

Curriculum Components	Reconfiguration Techniques
Resources	• Provide students with concept maps and advance organizers that preview the important concepts and principles explored in the unit.
	• Find high school texts and college resources to identify the major concepts, skills, and principles within related fields and disciplines.
	• Provide graphic organizers to support analogy making, creative problem solving, and classification.
	• Identify and locate numerous interdisciplinary examples related to the concepts, principles, skills, and dispositions being addressed in the unit.
	• Find photographs, journals, data, primary source documents, newspaper articles, historical accounts, magazine articles, Web sites, paintings, and so on that address the same concept in various disciplines.
	• Locate an interdisciplinary problem or simulation related to the unit's learning goals.
	• Provide biographies of historical and contemporary inquirers, inventors, and researchers in various disciplines who used the same concepts or processes.
Products	• Ask students to create graphic displays that explain the patterns they have identified across topics, events, people, or disciplines.
	• Create an imaginary forum, similar to Steve Allen's old television show "Meeting of the Minds," in which students take on the role of various historical figures across time as they discuss a contemporary or historical problem or issue (Bourman, 1996).
	• Assign concept maps to analyze the acquisition of macroconcepts and integrated principles.
	• Ask students to demonstrate the relationship between the core concepts and principles in one topic, discipline, or event, and those in another field or time period.
	• Ask students to demonstrate their knowledge of integrated connections through the use of reflective essays, journal entries, charts, diagrams, analogies, and collages.
	• Provide graphic organizers or double-entry journals that enable students to communicate their acquisition of macroconcepts and generalizations.
	• Ask students to create a synectics diagram to demonstrate the use of metaphoric thinking to solve an interdisciplinary problem.

Extension Activities	• Ask the gifted education specialist to provide the connections unit to interested students as an extension of the regular course of study. • Ask the technology teacher to help you identify Web-site links to other topics, time periods, or individuals. • Ask the librarian to help you identify biographies of philosophers and books about philosophical thought to share with students. • Team with a teacher of another subject area to provide concurrent integrated units of study that culminate in an interdisciplinary problem-solving activity. • Provide interested students with an opportunity to study philosophy, wisdom, or epistomology. • Team with another content area specialist and identify macroconcepts, themes, dispositions, and interdisciplinary processes that can be incorporated within two or more consecutively taught units of instruction. • Teach students the process of hierarchical classification or systems thinking. • Teach students how to use the synectics model for making analogies or for problem solving. • Develop a simulated or real-world problem that students can solve by applying the concepts, principles, skills, and dispositions of one field to another topic or discipline. • Provide opportunities for students to interview and visit with artists, researchers, college professors, philosophers, and interdisciplinary problem-solving teams to discuss how they use knowledge in other fields and disciplines in their daily work and problem solving. • Ask content area specialists and other teachers who are experts in the concepts, principles, dispositions, and processes within one field or discipline to co-plan, team teach, coach, or provide useful feedback on the progress and success of the lessons.
Grouping Practices	• Work with large groups of students to overview the goals of the unit, to provide directions, and to share information about macroconcepts, generalizations, and processes. • Use pairs and small groups of students to support pattern finding and the development of macroconcepts and themes. • Briefly conference with individual students to assess the degree to which they are able to relate interdisciplinary examples and real-world problems to core concepts and principles. • Observe individual students and provide feedback to support the development of cognitive skills. • Debrief students in large groups, using maps and diagrams, to ensure that the entire class can connect macroconcepts, generalizations, and processes to core concepts and principles.
Modification Based on Learner Need, Including Ascending Intellectual Demand	• Increase or decrease teacher scaffolding to support the development of macroconcepts, interdisciplinary processes and dispositions, themes, and systems thinking. • Provide additional representative topics for comparison to reduce ambiguity or to add additional layers of complexity. Keep these topics within the same discipline to decrease cognitive difficulty or expand to other disciples to increase intellectual demand. • Use less obvious topics or disciplines for comparison with students with more sophisticated levels of deductive thinking. Encourage a continuing commitment to intrinsic motivation and to the world of ideas. • Use the Parallel's guidelines for Ascending Intellectual Demand in selecting resources and designing learning activities and products.

Choosing Appropriate Content and Learning Objectives to Support a Curriculum of Connections

Of the key components in the Comprehensive Curriculum Framework, the content and standards component probably changes the most to address the goals of the Curriculum of Connections Parallel. The differences are subtle, however, because an examination of the content objectives and standards would still reveal a concentration on concepts and principles. What would be different is the extent to which the content objectives address concepts and principles that cross topics, events, time periods, and disciplines.

Figure 5.4 demonstrates the nature of the concepts, processes, skills, principles, applications, and dispositions addressed in the Curriculum of Connections. A contrast between this table and a similar discipline-based set of knowledge categories in Figure 4.2 in the Core Curriculum chapter reveals the integrated and interdisciplinary nature of the knowledge highlighted in the Curriculum of Connections.

Once teachers and curriculum developers come to a clear understanding of the connected nature of knowledge, the search for integrating topics, concepts, and principles begins. During the initial stages of planning teachers clarify the names of the units or the topics they are assigned to teach in a specific content area. Next, teachers identify the appropriate discipline(s) associated with these topics and the major pieces of information, concepts, principles, dispositions, and skills that need to be addressed in each unit of study. To this point, the planning process for the Curriculum of Connections Parallel closely resembles the development process for the Core Curriculum Parallel.

However, after identifying the essential information, concepts, skills, dispositions, and skills related to a single topic, the teacher continues to search for analogous knowledge, topics, events, or people across time periods, cultures, or disciplines. Figure 5.5 demonstrates one aspect of this kind of thinking. Each column of Figure 5.5 lists several concepts related to a given subject area. The last column lists terms commonly referred to as macroconcepts. Macroconcepts are concepts that are essential to the structure of more than one discipline, although the terms for the concept may be slightly different from one discipline to the next.

The search for analogous concepts in multiple disciplines is evident in the use of the term "immigration" in social studies, "migration" in science, and "influence" in art. A Curriculum of Connections unit that seeks to illustrate and examine the same concept over multiple disciplines might ask students to study the causes and effects of movement, progression, migration, and immigration. For example, by concurrently exploring the movement and migration of people, animals, and art across cultures, geographic regions, biomes, or time periods, students come to a deeper understanding of the impact of movement on change and progress. Once these two macroconcepts are linked together in the students' minds, they can begin to explore the overarching, interdisciplinary generalization that explains the relationship between movement and progress, or movement and change, across time, cultures, and disciplines.

Figure 5.4. Categories of Knowledge Emphasized in the Curriculum of Connections

Knowledge Category	*Definition and Examples*
Macroconcepts	A general idea or understanding, a generalized idea of a thing or a class of things; a category or classification that extends across disciplines
	Examples:
	• *Form*
	• *Function*
	• *Systems*
	• *Change*
	• *Patterns*
	• *Conflict*
	• *Perspective*
	• *Adaptation*
Generalizations and Themes	A fundamental theme or generalization explains the relationship between two or more concepts in two or more disciplines
	Examples:
	• *Form follows function.*
	• *Change takes time.*
	• *Change is painful.*
	• *Measure twice, cut once.*
	• *Pennywise and pound foolish.*
Interdisciplinary Processes	Proficiencies, abilities or techniques, strategies, methods, or tools that have multiple, interdisciplinary applications
	Examples:
	• *Learning how to identify patterns*
	• *Learning how to make deductive inferences*
	• *Learning how to observe*
	• *Learning how to make a plan*
	• *Learning how to solve a problem*
	• *Learning how to research and communicate*
Interdisciplinary Dispositions	Beliefs, dispositions, appreciations, or values that transcend cultures, time, and disciplines
	Examples:
	• *An appreciation for patience*
	• *A belief in the critical importance of empathy*
	• *An understanding of perspective*
	• *A positive attitude toward curiosity*
	• *Intrinsic motivation for learning*

(Continued)

Figure 5.4. Continued

Integrated Problem Solving	The ability to use knowledge from more than one discipline to understand a problem and find a creative solution to it
	Examples:
	• *Using observations of chimpanzees that use reeds to extract ants from an anthill to develop a theory about the tool building practices of early man*
	• *Inventing Pringles® by thinking about the difference between raking dry and wet autumn leaves*

When a teacher decides to create a Curriculum of Connections, the search for common concepts, or macroconcepts, across disciplines or topics is the first step in the planning process. Figure 5.6 illustrates a teacher's use of a graphic organizer to support the search for discipline-based concepts, related concepts in other disciplines, and macroconcepts. The initial unit in social studies addressed the topic of early 19th-century immigration in the United States. The teacher listed the essential topic-based concepts in the first column. A search for related concepts in other disciplines proved fruitful in art and science but much more forced, artificial, and strained in physical education and the language arts. Rather than trying to make a connection to multiple disciplines just for the sake of making connections, the teacher's initial search for related concepts suggests that social studies, art, and science are indeed the best links for developing macroconcepts and integrated themes or generalizations.

Next, the teacher considered the principle that students will learn in this discipline-based unit when they search for relationships among the concepts. This principle is also listed in Figure 5.6. The results of a search for an analogous principle in the social sciences and an interdisciplinary generalization or theme are listed as well.

In a similar fashion, teachers might search for analogous skills, dispositions, or problems across topics, disciplines, events, times, and so forth. Once again, teachers would make a list of the skills, dispositions, or problems within the topic or discipline to be studied. By identifying comparable skills, dispositions, or problems in another topic, discipline, event, time period, and so forth, teachers would then be ready to generate authentic rather than forced or contrived connections for integration.

Figure 5.5. A Comparison of Discipline-Based Concepts With Interdisciplinary Macroconcepts

Social Studies Concepts	Science Concepts	Art Concepts	Music Concepts
transportation	evaporation	shadow	scales
government	circulation	light	notation
tributary	fertilization	perspective	rhythm
war	temperature	depth	beat
battle	gravity	hue	percussion
treaty	magnetism	tint	woodwind
commerce	energy	composition	harmony
leader	work	texture	echo
services	matter	line	jazz
goods	homeostasis	dimensionality	timbre
resources	sound	symmetry	resonance
culture	waves	portrait	range
immigration	resonance	media	baritone
poverty	plasticity	abstract	projection
navy	scientific method	gradiant	phrasing
explorer	evidence	aesthetic	mood
delta	migration	landscape	pitch
caste	tropism	realism	volume
migration	movement	influence	melody
longitude	pressure	balance	conductor

Language Arts Concepts	Health and Physical Education Concepts	Math Concepts	Interdisciplinary Macroconcepts
vowel	touchdown	multiplication	form
stereotype	goal	sum	function
claim	heat stroke	integer	systems
persuasion	dribble	prime number	structure
hero	drug	ratio	change
conflict	linesman	angles	communities
folktale	cancer	mode	constancy
resolution	fluid	denominations	symbolism
poetry	sprint	symbols	relationships
alliteration	fullback	ray	properties
symbols	sunscreen	perimeter	measurement
syllable	referee	correlation	classes
noun	offense	standard deviation	patterns
preposition	antioxidant	central tendency	observation
personification	warm-up	order of operations	cycles
skim	point guard	graph	variables
point of view	protein	pie chart	factors
cause and effect	emergency	random	criticism
archetype	accident	symmetry	movement
main idea	conditioning	chaos	perspective

Figure 5.6 Identifying Macroconcepts

Subject Area and Unit Name: Social Studies— Immigration to the United States at the Beginning of the 20th Century							
Social Studies Concepts	Related Math Concepts	Related Science Concepts	Related Language Arts Concepts	Related Music Concepts	Related Art Concepts	Related Physical Education Concepts	Interdisciplinary Macroconcepts
culture		species biome system habitat niche	genre	form	style		FORM
transportation immigration emigration		circulation migration transfer	segues storytelling		school influence	movement	MOVEMENT PROGRESSION CHANGE
resources needs	variables	survival energy	folktales		subject media		

Topic-Based Relationship: Immigrants used various means of transportation to move from their homes and cultures to the United States in order to seek abundant resources and opportunities to improve their living conditions.

Discipline-Based Principle: Throughout time, some individuals and subgroups within a culture have used available means of transportation to explore or resettle in other locations and regions in order to find or use new or additional resources or opportunities.

Interdisciplinary Generalization or Theme: Living things, human products, and technology adapt, improve, or make progress as a result of movement.

Keara's Cultures Curriculum

Using a similar process of seeking connections by looking for common concepts, Keara could revise her cultures unit to be a Curriculum of Connections unit. She would focus on the same set of concepts, printed on page 141, within a unit that compared and contrasted these elements across various cultures.

All of these concepts are related to ethnography. Keara's use of a compare and contrast focus could turn a unit that formerly centered on one culture into a systematic study of multiple cultures, resulting in the development of cross-cultural generalizations similar to those identified by ethnographers as a result of their case study or longitudinal research projects. Some examples of such interdisciplinary generalizations are listed on page 141.

In a similar fashion, teachers might search for analogous skills, dispositions, or problems across topics, disciplines, events, times, and so forth. Once again, teachers would make a list of the skills, dispositions, or problems within the topic or discipline to be studied. By identifying comparable skills, dispositions, or problems in another topic, discipline, event, time period, and so forth, teachers would then be ready to generate authentic rather than forced or contrived connections for integration.

> Anthropologist
> Ethnographer
> Culture
> Society
> Needs
> Rules and Order
> Change
> Adaptation
> Values
> Habits

> Customs
> Symbols
> Subcultures
> Shared Beliefs
> Balance
> Roles
> Tolerance
> Individual Interests
> Dependence

Remodeling Examples

The strategy just discussed to generate significant connections is often not used. Three more typical strategies to find connected content, concepts, principles, or problems come to mind. They are more common approaches to seeking connections—and less effective in generating connections essential to the nature and pur-

> Culture consists of shared knowledge, art, customs, habits, values, beliefs, symbols, and world perspectives.

> Culture is reflected in people's behaviors.

> Cultures are learned through language, experience, and behaviors.

> People create cultures to deal with problems and matters that concern them.

> A culture must satisfy basic biological, instrumental, and aesthetic needs.

> Cultures have rules to provide an orderly existence.

> Members of a culture are dependent on each other.

> Members of each culture have established roles.

> Cultures tolerate some variance among individuals.

> A culture must have the capacity to change in order to adapt to new circumstances.

> Cultures must strike a balance between the needs of individuals and the needs of the group in order to survive and prosper.

pose of the disciplines. Contrast the strategy just discussed with the three scenarios presented next. Determine which of the four techniques have the most promise for making authentic connections across topics, disciplines, cultures, times, events, places, and so on.

Scenario 1: We Read About It

When Michelle first heard about the Curriculum of Connections, she said that she already used that approach to design lessons—she'd just never called it that before. She said that in her district they call it thematic teaching. The high school teachers called it interdisciplinary teaching. Michelle offered an example. "In November, when we're supposed to talk about the Pilgrims with the kids during the social studies unit, I saved a lot of time by connecting it all together and choosing a great picture book about Thanksgiving and the Pilgrims to read aloud to my kindergartners during circle time. That way it's all related—social studies and reading."

Scenario 2: Webbing It

Margaret added, "I do it a little differently, but I still know what you mean. You see, in my school we're supposed to do social studies and science for a half an hour every day. Well, with all the emphasis on reading, writing, and math, there just isn't enough time to pack it all in. So, when I'm about to start a new social studies or science unit I just make a web, with the social studies or science topic in the center. Then, I think about all the activities I could have the kids do to connect the social studies or science unit to the other subject areas. Here's an example of what I mean. It sure saves a lot of time, and the kids love all the activities."

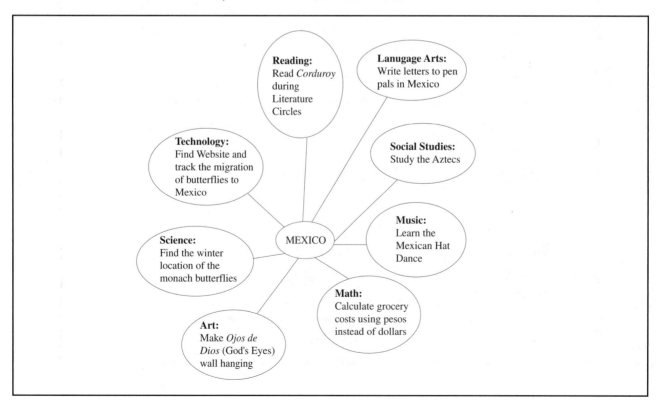

Scenario 3: Integrating Subjects

Montie, a sixth grade teacher, offered another perspective on webbing. "We're departmentalized at the middle school, but our four-member team has a teacher from each of the four major subject areas. We have two periods a day for planning so that we can do just what you're talking about. We make sure that at least a third of our units are integrated with the other three subject areas. We use either science or social studies as the focal point for each of our units. When I'm about to begin a social studies topic, the science, English and math teachers work with me to find connections to their disciplines. The English teacher finds a book about our social studies topic for the kids to read and discuss. The science teacher finds some biology or earth science topic for the students to study related to the region we're studying in social studies. The math teacher always has the hardest time making the connections. Usually, we find a way to work math in by creating word problems related to our social studies or science content. That way the kids have a sustained and long-term exposure to the topic."

The examples cited above could be used to describe the state of integrated curriculum development in most school districts throughout the country. The concept of integration is appealing to many of us, largely because of the opportunities it seems to afford for collaboration, teaming, and time management. However, structured, collaborative time to research content prior to writing curriculum and time for brainstorming, planning, decision making, and revision is scant. As a result, many integrated curriculum units fall short of hitting their mark with regard to the rigor, power, and meaning that is central and authentic to the disciplines. Until more teachers have greater opportunities to plan collaboratively, to receive and provide constructive criticism on their work, to sample students' work products for the quality of ideas and skills they demonstrate, and to rework lessons and unit plans, the promise of meaningfully integrated curriculum units remains out of reach.

If we were to fine-tune and remodel the "integrated" units cited above, students might still be using picture books as resources, but there would be two or more books that students would use to compare and contrast content, concepts, processes, dispositions, or principles. Pilgrims could be compared to newcomers to a school, neighborhood, or town. Thanksgiving could be contrasted with harvest festivals in Alaska, China, or Egypt. Mexico could be compared with other Central American countries or with California and Texas. The Aztecs could be contrasted with the Mayans or the Incas. The "integrated" middle school science, social studies, and language arts units would all be remodeled to focus on a macroconcept, such as diversity, a theme such as man's continual search for knowledge, or the interdisciplinary skill of observation and perspective. This approach is vastly different from concurrent study of *Grapes of Wrath* in English, the water cycle in science, and the Great Depression in social studies.

Despite the popularity of the three scenarios, there is no unifying macroconcept or generalization that connects all three units. The language arts curriculum focuses on a resource and not a skill, the social studies curriculum focuses on an event and not a concept or principle, and the science curriculum focuses on a system without connecting it to other systems or cause and effect relationships.

Less common, and far more powerful, is the use of the strategies described in this section coupled with a conscious decision to focus the integration of common concepts, principles, dispositions, and skills across topics, time, cultures, and disciplines. To develop a truly powerful and overarching Curriculum of Connections, teachers must first ask the three questions posed at the outset of the chapter: What are the major concepts and principles in the discipline that are related to this topic or unit? What other topics or problems in this discipline address these same concepts and principles? How might I develop a connection between these topics and problems to encourage a deeper understanding of these concepts and principles? Planning the Curriculum of Connections, then, becomes the teacher's journey in answering those questions and then gathering resources and designing tasks and products that will enable learners to make those connections as well.

Summary

Although both the Core Curriculum and the Curriculum of Connections address content knowledge, concepts, skills, and principles, one of the greatest differences between the two curriculum models is the degree of importance the Curriculum of Connections places on the ability to see relationships. The Curriculum of Connections emphasizes (a) common concepts, principles, generalizations, and/or skills across topics, individuals, events, cultures, and/or time periods, (b) common concepts, principles, generalizations, and/or skills across disciplines, (c) the identification of macroconcepts across multiple concepts, and (d) and the discovery of generalizations across principles.

Reconfiguring Other Curriculum Components for the Curriculum of Connections

Assessment Strategies in a Curriculum of Connections

In Chapter 4 we discussed the characteristics of exemplary assessment. To be effective, assessments must be aligned to the learning goal. Second, they should be honest and accurate measures of students' learning over time. Third, they must provide some kind of performance or product with which to evaluate student learning. These characteristics are as valid for an assessment used within a Curriculum of Connections unit as they are for any of the assessments designed for use with the other three curriculum models described in this book. However, the nature of the learning goals within the Curriculum of Connections Parallel requires special attention to the design of appropriate rubrics and assessment formats.

A comparison of the assessment components in both models reveals subtle differences in both the rubric design and the assessment strategies. Although best practices for both models support the use of a four- or five-level rubrics, rubrics in a Curriculum of Connections until frequently contain descriptors of greater student expertise as well as criteria related to students' ability to demonstrate knowledge of patterns, principles, and themes across topics, time periods, and disciplines. In turn, the performance assessment must be aligned with this purpose and allow students to communicate growth, over time, in their ability to see larger and broader classifications for facts, concepts, and principles. The use of concept maps, graphic organizers, reflection journals, and dual-entry logs are common formats for assessments that support the analysis of students' understanding of principles and generalizations.

Take, for example, a learning goal that addresses core concepts in a discipline or field of study. To design an appropriate rubric to measure growth in concept attainment, the levels within the rubric must attend to ever-increasing levels of knowledge acquisition. However, within an integrated curriculum unit, the concept being assessed is generally a macroconcept that crosses disciplines, fields, or topics. To ensure a valid assessment, the accompanying rubric must address interdisciplinary connections at the upper levels of the rubric. Figure 5.7 provides an example for the concept of "migration."

As with other rubrics, a student's understanding of a macroconcept could be measured during both preassessment and postassessment. If, on the other hand, the

Figure 5.7. A Rubric for Measuring the Attainment of a Macroconcept

	Beginning	*Developing*	*Competent*	*Proficient*	*Expert*
Level of Understanding	The learner can define and provide key attributes that distinguish a concept in a given field or discipline.	The learner can use the concept to categorize and understand new information in the same field or discipline.	The learner can identify commonalities between concepts in one field or topic and concepts in another field or discipline.	The learner can classify and name comparable concepts in two or more fields as macroconcepts.	When confronted with new information in another discipline students attempt to classify the new information using an interdisciplinary macroconcept.
Example	"Migration is the purposeful movement of living things across regions."	"Migration is evident during the 1880s, the early 1900s, the 1930s, and the 1940s in various part of the United States."	"The migration of whales has several things in common with the migration of human beings."	"The concept of beneficial movement is evident in both biology and anthropology."	"The population in our small, rural town experienced a decline in the 2000 census. I wonder if migration is a factor?"

Figure 5.8. A Rubric for Measuring the Acquisition of an Interdisciplinary Rule, Principle, or Generalization

	Beginning	Developing	Competent	Proficient	Expert
Level of Understanding	The learner can identify and explain a principle or relationship within a topic or field of study.	The learner can provide novel examples of the principle, theme, or generalization across events, topics, field of study, or disciplines.	The learner can use knowledge about principles in various disciplines or topics to develop an interdisciplinary theme or generalization.	The learner searches for interdisciplinary themes or generalizations in unfamiliar information in order to identify analogous or equivalent situations.	The learner searches for interdisciplinary themes or generalizations in unfamiliar information in order to identify analogous or equivalent situations and develop creative solutions to real-world problems.

knowledge goal in the unit addresses the acquisition of an interdisciplinary rule or a generalization, the rubric shown in Figure 5.8 might prove useful.

An appropriate assessment for the rubric in Figure 5.8 might ask students to explain the theme or generalization orally or in writing or to provide appropriate examples. As an alternative, students might be asked to analyze teacher-provided examples and develop related hypotheses or generalizations.

The need for valid and reliable pre- and postassessments is as vital within the Curriculum of Connections as it is within any kind of curriculum unit. The format for the assessment, however, varies in order to conform more readily to measuring changes in students' acquisition of macroconcepts and generalizations across topics and disciplines.

Introductory Activities in a Curriculum of Connections

Students about to participate in a Curriculum of Connections benefit from introductory activities that carefully explain the nature of the unit and teacher's expectations for students' learning. Unless the students clearly understand that their role involves a search for overarching connections, they are likely to get mired in the details and specifics of the cases, events, topics, and people they study and examine during the course of the unit. The use of focusing questions, reframed as questions that address the essential nature of knowledge, are extremely useful in helping students understand the focus of the unit.

In a Curriculum of Connections unit, one is unlikely to hear Lydia tell students "During this unit we will be studying the Civil War." Instead, her introductory comments might ask students what they think the word *civil* means, what a war is, and whether or not they think other countries, or other time periods, experienced civil wars. She might ask students about conflicts in their families and ask them to share stories of compromises made because of conflicts between needs and wants, rights and responsibilities. Beginning the curriculum unit with connections to personal conflicts helps students begin the process of developing analogies between what they are about to study and prior experiences in their own lives. Periodic reminders to make connections, modeling the making of connections, use of active teaching and learning strategies, debriefing opportunities and reflective journals must follow such an introduction to ensure its effectiveness in helping students assume the appropriate role during the remainder of the unit's learning activities.

In addition, introductory activities in this parallel might include preassessments to identify students' skill in making analogies, in comparing and contrasting, and in classifying—essential skills in this parallel. Advance organizers might list the related topics, events, time periods, cultures, people, and/or disciplines students will compare. Further, teachers must be sure to emphasize the relevance of this approach to learning for improving students' abilities to find commonalities across topics, thereby accelerating and deepening the learning process.

Teaching Strategies in a Curriculum of Connections

A third difference between the models has to do with the teaching strategies selected for each lesson. Although both the Core Curriculum and the Curriculum of Connections incorporate varied pedagogy, coaching, and scaffolding, the pedagogies used most often in the Curriculum of Connections promote students' ability to perceive, understand, and appreciate the connections across topics, disciplines, and concepts. Among teaching strategies most likely to be used within the Curriculum of Connections are Socratic questioning, synectics, metaphorical thinking, cooperative learning, debriefing, problem-based learning, and inquiry-based teaching.

The essential role for the teacher is that of mediator between the student and the new learning. As such, the teacher builds bridges that enable students to perceive or demonstrate a connection between two different sets of information, two or more concepts, or two or more principles. Using two or more topics, events, pieces of literature, time periods, or disciplines, the teacher scaffolds for students as they treat knowledge like a set of Russian Petrushka dolls. Under the teacher's guidance, students attempt to "nest" and classify knowledge as they search for overarching connections by noting common features and attributes. It is a search for commonalties not unlike the thinking that goes into playing that old television game show "The $100,000 Pyramid."

Figure 5.9. Some Key Process Skills in the Curriculum of Connections

- Making metaphors and analogies
- Comparing and contrasting
- Finding key attributes
- Classifying
- Sequencing
- Noting patterns
- Detecting relationships
- Interpreting
- Inferring
- Drawing conclusions
- Relating
- Identifying part and whole
- Inventing
- Constructing meaning
- Pursuing insight

Learning Activities in a Curriculum of Connections

Although both the Core Curriculum and the Curriculum of Connections promote students' active learning and cognitive involvement with new knowledge, the Curriculum of Connections tends to rely on students' use of a specific subset of analytic thinking skills to support their ability to make and understand these connections. These analytic thinking skills are listed in Figure 5.9.

If teaching and learning activities begin by providing students with an explanation of a macroconcept or generalization, then students are most likely to use deductive thinking to analyze raw data so as to determine the extent to which their characteristics fit the concept or theme. If, on the other hand, the teacher shares multiple examples across time periods, topics, events, or disciplines and asks students to form hypotheses or generalizations, then students are most likely to use inductive thinking to reach conclusions regarding the patterns they observe. Regardless of the approach, inductive or deductive, it is the teacher's skilled used of questioning, feedback, and debriefing that cements students' ability to make interdisciplinary connections and perceive overarching relationships.

Resources in a Curriculum of Connections

An analysis of the resources used in a Core Curriculum and a Curriculum of Connections unit also reveals subtle differences. Both models encourage use of primary source documents, varied media, and appropriate reading levels, but the materials in Connections lessons usually include content from more than one author, event, culture, topic, or discipline. A unit that seeks to teach students the common literary elements and devices in a given genre, folktales, for example, would likely include numerous myths, fables, and folktales from various cultures or time periods for students to read and analyze. If, on the other hand, students are searching for connections across disciplines, time periods, or cultures, teachers must have access to print materials that students can read or examine to identify patterns and common attributes. The collaboration of the school media specialist or librarian can be very helpful in supporting teachers' ability to plan for and implement a Curriculum of Connections.

In addition, students are likely to use graphic organizers that support their use of the analytic thinking skills and their search for universal concepts and generalizations. The availability of concept maps, double-entry journals, Venn diagrams, and reader response questions also supports the student's role in the Curriculum of Connections.

Products, Grouping Strategies, and Extension Activities in the Curriculum of Connections

There are few tangible differences in the products, grouping strategies, or extension activities used in a Core Curriculum unit and in a Curriculum of Connections unit. Students who participate in both kinds of units benefit from opportunities to produce open-ended products and assignments that enable them to explain their conclusions, demonstrate their thinking process, share supporting evidence, and reflect on the personal and conceptual connections they forged as they studied the data and information within the unit. Essays, collages, PowerPoint presentations, concept maps, theories, hypotheses, and scholarly treatises are excellent examples of appropriate product formats. As noted at several earlier points in the chapter, the difference between product assignments in a Core Curriculum and Curriculum of Connections is that the former would call on students to identify, apply, and illustrate frameworks of meaning and skill within a particular discipline, whereas the latter calls on students to deal with those frameworks across disciplines, topics, time periods, cultures, and so on.

Small groups and dyads allow students to work collaboratively, provide constructive feedback to each other, and participate in the critical thinking, deductive, and inductive thinking so closely associated with the Curriculum of Connections. Students need opportunities to make hypotheses, argue the merits of their conclusions, listen to others' perspectives, and refine their own thinking. In a well-constructed Curriculum of Connections, the room is a busy place, filled with students engaged in speculation, debate, and a search for corroboration evidence.

Extension activities are a natural in the Curriculum of Connections. Because of the interrelatedness of knowledge, it is simple for a teacher to help students explore key macroconcepts and generalizations in areas of particular interest to students. These sorts of extensions can occur as a result of teacher illustrations in class, through individual or small group investigation, via strategies such as Group Investigation that invite student selection of topic, and by encouraging students to make connections in culminating products between required topics and concepts and related ones in fields or topics of interest to them.

Differentiation and Ascending Intellectual Demand in the Curriculum of Connections

Teachers can support differences among students' cognitive abilities and prior knowledge or experience through use of tiered assignments, scaffolded questioning, student conferences, two-way journaling, and ongoing assessment. Carefully crafted sequences of questions and graphic organizers support students who might be easily frustrated with open-ended assignments to identify macroconcepts and overarching themes and generalizations. It may also be useful for students who need extra support in the Curriculum of Connections, at least in the beginning, to interpret and apply teacher-generated analogies, metaphors, and generalizations prior to generating their own.

As students show evidence of advancing understanding and skill in the Curriculum of Connections, teachers can generate tasks with ascending intellectual challenge or demand by using the "generic" strategies listed in Chapter 4, Figure 4.8. In addition, Figure 5.10 suggests additional strategies to provide appropriate demand for students moving notably toward expertise in the discipline or topic being studied.

As was the case with the Core Curriculum Parallel, it is our belief that all students should work with connections-making curriculum. It is also our belief that as students continue to develop along a continuum toward expertise, an effective teacher provides ascending challenge and support for reaching that challenge. This is the case with highly advanced students as much as with students who need support to reach more basic or moderate levels of challenge. Only when there are continually escalating expectations for each student, and a support system for the ascent, do students grow cognitively, in independence, and in self-efficacy as learners.

Lydia's Civil War Unit Using the Goals of the Curriculum of Connections Parallel

In the past, Lydia Janis developed two related Civil War curriculum units, one that aligned with the components of the Comprehensive Curriculum Framework and one that was adjusted to address the goals of the Core Curriculum Parallel. We now describe her third revision, one that is based on the goals of the Curriculum of Connections Parallel.

Content Connections

Lydia began by asking herself some key questions related to the Curriculum of Connections Parallel—questions that would help her focus her curriculum writing.

To organize her search for the answers to these questions, Lydia developed a chart (see Figure 5.11 on page 152). In the first column, she listed the major con-

Figure 5.10. Some Paths to Achieve Ascending Intellectual Demand in the Curriculum of Connections

- Increase the unfamiliarity of the context or problem in which understandings or skills are applied.
- Ask students to generate defensible criteria against which they then weigh diverse perspectives on a problem or solution (or use professional criteria for the same purpose).
- Call on students to develop solutions, proposals, or approaches that effectively bridge differences in perspective but still effectively address the problem.
- Ask students to make proposals or predictions for future directions based on student-generated, discipline-related patterns from the past in a particular domain.
- Have students search for legitimate and useful connections among seemingly disparate elements (for example, music and medicine or law and geography).
- Develop tasks or products that seek patterns of interaction among multiple areas (for example, ways in which geography, economics, politics, and technology affect one another).
- Call on students to look at broad swaths of the world through a perspective quite unlike their own (for example, how an age mate from a culture and economy very different from the student's would react to the student's house, slang, religion, clothing, music, relationships with adults, toys or gadgets, plans for the future, and so on).
- Develop tasks and products that seek out unstated assumptions beneath the surface of beliefs, decisions, approaches, or perspectives.
- Ask students to develop systems for making connections, drawing generalizations, achieving balanced perspectives, or addressing problems.
- Design criteria for students' work that call for a higher standard of quality (such as insightful, highly illustrative, highly synthetic, unusually articulate or expressive, and so on) as opposed to a less demanding but still positive standard of quality (such as appropriate, accurate, feasible, informed, defensible, and so on).

cepts she had used in her work with the Core Curriculum Parallel to revise and reorganize her original textbook unit. In the second column, she listed all the events, people, products, and topics that her students studied in the Core Curriculum unit

Lydia's Focusing Questions for the Curriculum of Connections

What are the major concepts and essential knowledge related to this topic or unit?
What are the comparable macroconcepts in this or other disciplines?
How might I develop a deeper understanding of these concepts within or between disciplines through the study of related topics, events, people, and/or problems?

Figure 5.11. Lydia's Ideas About Possible Connections With the Unit's Key Concepts

Key Concepts Related to the Civil War	Topics, Events, Products, and People Related to the Study of the Civil War	Related Concepts From Other Topics, Subjects, or Disciplines	Related Topics, Events, Products, and People From Other Time Periods, Cultures, or Disciplines
Culture Perspective Time Period	Northern States Southern States Slave Culture	Culture Perspective Time Period	Taliban Regime Indian Reservation System Apartheid in South Africa The U.S. in the 1960s U.S. Women's Culture from 1820 to 1920
Labor Resources Goods and Services	Dred Scott Decision Frederick Douglass Factories Plantations Slave Trade Industrialization Slavery	Property Human Rights Civil Rights Immigration Prejudice	Child Labor Unionism Great Migration
Abolitionist Movement Emancipation	Harper's Ferry John Brown Sojourner Truth Harriet Tubman *Uncle Tom's Cabin* Harriet Beecher Stowe Levi Coffin Lucretia Mott Underground Railroad	Freedom Movements Trends Change Loss	The Suffrage Movement The Civil Rights Movement of the 1960s Women's Rights Movement Peace Movement Native American Movement Americans with Disabilities Movement War on Poverty Green Revolution Nationalism in South Africa
States' Rights Federalism Balance of Power	Secession Confederacy United States Westward Movement Territories	Colonialism Nationalism Balance of Power Independence	Bill of Rights British Colonies Ireland Branches of Government

Conflict	Missouri Compromise	Conflict	Egypt-Israel Peace
Compromise	Compromise of 1850	Compromise	Accord
Consensus	Fort Sumter	Consensus	Vietnam War
Civil War/Unrest	Battle of Gettysburg	Treaties	Great Plains Wars
Resolution	Antietam	Civil War/unrest	Bosnia War
	Battle of Vicksburg	Revolution	Irish Conflict
	Sherman's March	Revolt	Indian Revolution
	Appomattox	Demonstrations	
Leadership	Abraham Lincoln	Change Agents	Nelson Mandela
	Jefferson Davis	Leadership	Martin Luther King, Jr.
	General Grant		Elizabeth Cady Stanton
	General Lee		Betty Friedan
	General Sherman		Gloria Steinham
	Stonewall Jackson		Thurgood Marshall
	Henry Clay		Mahatma Ghandi
	Nat Turner		Susan B. Anthony

to address and understand the concepts in the first column. In the third column, she attempted to identify intradisciplinary or interdisciplinary concepts or macro-concepts aligned with the concepts in the first column. In the fourth column, she attempted to identify and list topics, events, people, and products from a variety of time periods, cultures, and disciplines that could be used to illustrate the multitude of connections between these topics and their related concepts and macroconcepts.

When Lydia stopped to analyze the content of the fourth column in her lists, she noticed that most of the connections were to other time periods, people, problems, issues, and cultures. As she intended, the connections came from the four disciplines within the social sciences: history, geography, economics, and government.

Lydia considered related connections in math, science, and the language arts. She could, for example, ask her students to read historical fiction about the Civil War, research leadership in the field of science, or examine conflict and resolution as a component of writer's craft, but those connections felt awkward for her current purposes. Instead, she decided that her decisions regarding the three focusing questions would revolve around connections made within the social sciences. She chose to make intradisciplinary connections among concepts rather than interdisciplinary connections.

Next, she chose five topic-based concepts as key concepts for the unit: slavery, emancipation, industrialization, plantation, and abolition. She then selected 11 intradisciplinary concepts that she believed were crucial to deep understanding: culture, time period, labor, resources, goods and services, prejudice, rights, compromise, consensus, leadership, and civil war. Last, she choose five interdisciplinary macroconcepts as the overarching ideas she wanted to foster in her Curriculum of

Connections: perspective, balance, change, loss, and conflict. She recognized that up to this point, she had made similar decisions when she organized her unit around the goals of the Core Curriculum Parallel. Just as she had done in the Core Curriculum unit, Lydia decided to teach the topic and discipline-based concepts through an examination of the information and evidence about the people, events, products, and topics surrounding the Civil War.

However, with this revision she went a step further. She decided to use a compare-and-contrast focal point to help students build a bridge between the information and concepts they would learn about the Civil War and related examples of these concepts and principles in other events, people, time periods, and cultures. If she succeeded, she was convinced her students would understand that history truly does repeat itself. They would come to appreciate the fact that the same overarching concepts and principles resurface and help explain the actions of different people in other time periods who also struggled with issues that were explained by perspective, change, balance, loss, and conflict. In addition, she hoped the students would come to value the search for relationships, analogies, and metaphors because the ability to make such connections makes it easier to understand novel problems and unfamiliar situations.

Resources

To implement her dual goal of using macroconcepts and a compare and contrast focal point to foster student learning, Lydia needed to select compatible content for students to examine in other cultures and time periods. Her list of potential compare and contrast topics, events, issues, and people was fairly lengthy (see column 4 of Figure 5.11). She could have her students compare Lincoln to Martin Luther King, Jr. in order to study the concept of leadership. They could compare the Civil War to the present-day conflict in Ireland in order to study perspective, compromise, and conflict. They could compare the abolitionist movement to the suffrage movement to analyze the effects of change, loss, and balance of power. However, she reminded herself that planning time was short and that it might be harder to find materials about some topics than others, especially when she had to take into account the fact that the instructional reading levels of the students in her classroom usually spanned at least four grade levels.

Although it seemed more logical to make assessment decisions after she selected the content for the unit, she realized that in this case she might have to put the cart before the horse and select content that was both relevant and accessible. She also had to be practical. She had to consider the type and number of resources she could locate and the speed with which she could access these materials. Ideally, she would need newspaper articles, diaries, photographs, books, videotapes, and even access to community members who had experienced events connected with the concepts and macroconcepts.

It occurred to her that the search for these materials would progress faster if she had help. A call to the others teachers on her grade-level team, to the media specialist, and to the special education and gifted education teachers garnered more support than she had anticipated. Using the "divide and conquer" approach, the four other teachers who demonstrated enthusiasm for the curriculum revision project conducted a quick search of library databases, publishers' catalogs, the school's book depot, and related Web sites. In a brief time, they had conducted their search and narrowed their choice of topics to those most easily accessible for their Grade 5 students.

The Jackdaws Company sold artifacts related to the women's suffrage movement and the civil rights movement. Discovery Enterprises published appropriate Grade 5 materials about child labor and the great migration north. Scholastic Book Company published several materials about the civil rights movement in South Africa, its leaders, and cornerstone events. In addition, they discovered six videos in the school and town library about child labor, the great migration, the Vietnam War, South Africa, and the civil rights movement.

While the teachers were searching through catalogs, the librarian looked for Web sites. She discovered 120 sites about the women's movement, 311 sites about the Vietnam War, 82 sites about child labor, 96 about the suffrage movement, 92 sites about the civil rights movement, and 112,613 sites about the Irish conflict! Martin Luther King, Jr., garnered 153 sites, Nelson Mandela had 2,331, Bosnia had 23, and Elizabeth Cady Stanton had 18 sites in her name. Even if only 10% of the sites proved useful and appropriate for Grade 5 students, there seemed to be more than enough materials to make connections across three or four events and or individuals.

Blending Content Decisions and Grouping Strategies

The good news about the wealth of materials and sites gave rise to yet another decision. With all that information available to Lydia and her students, she decided on three topics and the key individual associated with each as the focal points for comparisons with the Civil War and its leaders: suffrage and Elizabeth Cady Stanton, apartheid in South Africa and Nelson Mandela, and the civil rights movement of the 1960s and Martin Luther King, Jr. Lydia noticed that she seemed to be jumping around from content to resources to grouping decisions. So much for following a precise sequence for making her curriculum decisions and plans related to the ten curriculum components! Lydia decided that maybe the sequence wasn't quite as important as the quality of the decisions and the alignment of the components.

During the Core Curriculum unit, Lydia had divided her 20 lessons into 6 segments, each segment addressing one core concept. Her original list included (1) culture, perspective, and time; (2) labor, resources, goods, and services; (3) the abolition movement; (4) states' rights, federalism, and the balance of power; (5) conflict, compromise, consensus, civil war, and resolution; and (6) leadership. Students used information and evidence about people, events, and situations surrounding the Civil War to develop their own explanations for these concepts and related principles.

During her Curriculum of Connections, Lydia decided to maintain the same number of segments with slight changes in conceptual emphasis. Her first, fifth, and sixth focal point would remain the same because these concepts transcended the topic of the Civil War and reflected big ideas in several social science disciplines. Her second conceptual focus would broaden from a concentration on goods, services, labor, and resources to a broader look at property, human rights, civil rights, and prejudice. Her third focal point, abolition and emancipation, would be revised to address freedom, movement, trends, and change. Her fourth conceptual lens, states' rights and federalism, would now broaden to incorporate the macroconcepts of independence, dependence, and balance.

Lydia knew that these time/content decisions had to be directly related to her choices for student groups. Choosing the concepts, macroconcepts, topics, events, time periods, and individuals to foster her Curriculum of Connections was one thing. Finding the time to conduct the study and a way to manage and organize the content and the groups of students was yet another.

After considering and abandoning several ideas, Lydia decided to use a large group setting for her unit introduction, her sharing, and her debriefing sessions. She would use both homogeneous and heterogeneous cooperative small groups to conduct evidence and information analysis about the concepts, macroconcepts, the Civil War, key leaders, and the related topics and leaders from other time periods and culture. Sometimes, the groups would be based on common interests among students and sometimes based on similar or mixed readiness, depending on student needs and availability of resource materials.

Teaching Methods and Learning Activities

Lydia's next two decisions were fairly easy. When considering her role and chosen teaching methods for this unit, she decided to use the same pedagogies she had used in the majority of the Core Curriculum unit: Socratic questioning, concept attainment, inductive teaching, scaffolding, and coaching. The use of simulations and problem-based learning didn't seem appropriate, given the time constraints and the fact that she would have to juggle multiple sets of content.

While her students were examining the evidence she put before them, she would ask them to search for patterns, identify relationships, classify information, and define concepts. They would search evidence inductively in order to build the concepts and define the principles that explained the big ideas surrounding the Civil War. When they examined information about individuals and issues across time periods or cultures, such as Nelson Mandela and Jefferson Davis or suffrage and the Civil War, she would support their use of compare and contrast strategies, analogy making, and deductive thinking. She knew these skills were particularly appropriate in helping them determine the extent to which the content and principles they created to explain the big ideas in the Civil War also worked to explain the events, issues, and conflicts in South Africa and the United States during both countries' civil rights movements and during the women's suffrage movement in America.

Student Products and Assessments

Lydia's decision to structure the Civil War unit around the goals of the Curriculum of Connections would require a substantial amount of teaching and learning time. To save as much time as possible for these valuable activities, Lydia decided to dovetail her selection of students' short-term products with her assessment formats. She would assess students' short-term or daily products (their document analysis worksheets, their graphic organizers, Venn diagrams, and persuasive essays comparing two or more events, people, concepts, or issues) to measure growth and development. The rubrics for assessing macroconcepts, generalizations, and themes, detailed in Figures 5.7 and 5.8, would be especially useful. They simply needed to be revised to suit the specific concepts and macroconcepts related to this unit.

In addition, the skill proficiency rubrics Lydia created for the Core Curriculum unit (see Chapter 4) would come in handy as she assessed students' ability to apply learned analytic reasoning skills to novel content and information. Specifically, she would assess students' skill at comparing and contrasting, deductive reasoning, inductive thinking, and making analogies. She would also assess their ability to make warranted claims about observable patterns, claims that were backed up with evidence from the numerous sources they consulted as they became more knowledgeable about people and events of the Civil War, the civil rights movement, South Africa, and suffrage.

Concept maps and compare and contrast charts would be especially useful to measure students' acquisition of declarative knowledge, both specific information about various events, people, and issues and knowledge of key concepts, principles, macroconcepts, and themes. Essays and reflective journals might also prove helpful.

For a culminating product, Lydia decided to ask her students to make connections drawing on some of their particular interests. Each student was to examine a leader to help the class understand the struggle for civil rights and that leader's time period. In each instance, students would use a variety of resources to gather information about the person and time they selected. Ultimately, students would show how the person and time period they selected were like and different from the Civil War time period and its leaders. They would also need to show how culture, perspective, change, loss, conflict, and conflict resolution were at work in the person's life and time period. Their findings would be compiled in a *Who's Who of Civil Rights* anthology. To support student work, the teacher assumed the role of Editor-in-Chief of the anthology and created an editor's guide for her "staff" to use in preparing their entries to the anthology. In addition to prompting her students to examine the central macroconcepts across contexts, the product would call on them to use key skills of drawing conclusions, comparing and contrasting, detecting relationships, inference, constructing meaning, and pursuing insight.

Introductory Activities

Next, Lydia turned her attention to the introductory activities she would design for this Curriculum of Connections unit. She knew that one of the most important things she could do during the introduction was to reinforce her vision for this unit. Students needed to understand that they were not merely taking on the role of knowledge consumers. They were expected to be analyzers, inductive thinkers, detectives, and metaphoric bridge builders. How to explain that to 10- and 11-year-olds was another matter!

Lydia's librarian introduced her to a book by Paul Fleischman (1996) titled *Dateline: Troy*. In the book the author compares the ancient Greek story of Ulysses and his adventures with current-day events and individuals. It was a perfect metaphor for the kind of thinking she wanted students to do in this unit. Previewing the book and the author's purpose during her introductory activities seemed like an ideal way to acquaint students with their role as analogy makers. In addition to this read-aloud, Lydia would also conduct a discussion to probe students' interests in civil rights, South Africa, the Civil War, or women's rights. She could use this information to decide on membership in some of the small group activities.

Lydia knew that in a Curriculum of Connections unit it was unlikely she would tell students "During this unit we will be studying the Civil War." Instead, her introductory comments might ask students what they think the word civil means, what a war is, and whether or not they think other countries, or other time periods, experienced civil wars. She decided to ask students about conflicts in their families and ask them to share stories of compromises made because of conflicts between needs and wants, rights and responsibilities. She knew that beginning the curriculum unit with connections to personal conflicts would help her students begin the process of developing analogies between what they are about to study and prior experiences in their own lives.

Extension Activities

In thinking about her students, Lydia recognized real differences in the interests of her 24 fifth graders. Although she couldn't be positive until she began the unit and had the students in front of her, Lydia made some educated guesses about why and how she might want to extend this Curriculum of Connections unit.

For one thing, she knew she would want to have varied resources, materials, and documents available for the students. She would create a library corner with artifacts and materials. Students would have access to the materials throughout the unit. She would spotlight materials at appropriate times in the unit—sharing with students her own feelings about particular materials. She would also encourage students to work in the library corner when they finished assignments in class and to sign out materials for overnight use at some points. In fact, she might develop a couple of "free choice" homework assignments through which students would have a chance to explore and briefly report on some of the extension materials. Of course, as students raised questions during the Civil War unit, she hoped the materials would be a good source for finding answers.

Lydia would align some learning activities with certain materials she would specially select with students' interests in mind. Not everybody in the room would want to read everything she was beginning to collect. On the other hand, some of her students would probably be fascinated with opportunities to read firsthand Civil War diaries and accounts from big city newspapers like *The Washington Post* and *The New York Times*. Some students would be drawn to biographies or even novels about the Civil War and civil rights struggles in other times and places. Videos and audiocassettes provided other good extension options besides the print sources she was gathering. The Internet, too, would be a source of good information, as well as an attractive vehicle for learning for many of her students.

In addition to linking extension materials to short-term learning activities and products, Lydia would also coordinate the extension opportunities with the culminating anthology product students would develop during the latter stages of the unit. By giving students a chance to learn about a range of civil rights leaders though exploration of extension materials, she would assist students in making informed choices about who to study for the culminating product. The extension materials would also help students begin to gather data for their anthology pieces and reinforce their awareness of the sorts of research materials available.

Lydia also planned to work with her students to find some parents or community members who had personal experiences with civil conflicts in other times or places. In past years, parents who had been a part of our nation's struggle during Vietnam, who had lived through conflicts in the Middle East or Ireland, or who had participated in the struggle for civil rights or women's rights in the United States or elsewhere had talked with her class. Discussions based on presentations such as those would be great for helping her students learn how to connect time, cultures, places, and perspectives using the unit's macroconcepts and skills.

Modifications in Response to Learner Need, Including Ascending Intellectual Demand

In addition to addressing differences in her students' interests, Lydia would also have to address differences in student readiness or learning sophistication. She knew that most of her students could compare and contrast, categorize, sequence, and classify. But several of them had difficulty explaining key features in a relationship, and few of them had experience in making their own analogies. She wanted to make this unit challenging for everyone, without overwhelming any of her students. To accomplish that goal, she knew she might need to pull some students into small groups to share cognitive strategies, offer coaching, and increase scaffolding to improve their likelihood of success with concept development and metaphoric thinking.

Her more advanced thinkers would probably be challenged by the expectation to cross topics, cultures, and time periods, compare, contrast, and make analogies. She could ensure that these students had the opportunity to work with disparate context, at least in part, by including in the extension library corner materials about countries and time periods less familiar to the students and about conflicts related to individual rights in fields such as science, technology, and so on.

If the advanced students needed additional challenge, Lydia decided that she could escalate the quality of their thinking through the use of persuasive essays and some mini-lessons on logic and reasoning. Other students might want to use their strong verbal and logical thinking skills to get involved with debates about issues relating to civil rights, prejudice, slavery, and so on. In either case, Lydia would ensure that her directions and criteria for these students' work emphasized complex skills such as artful expression of ideas, well-constructed arguments, and identifying the assumptions of people with varying perspectives on a topic or issue.

Lydia would also meet with students who needed to think at a more expert-like level as they selected and developed their anthology entries. She would reinforce their need to use elegant language and high-quality logic in their work, as they had in their essays and debates. She would also have them include in their anthology entries criteria to weigh diverse perspectives on the issues central to the leader they selected and then to weigh the actions and solutions of the person based on those criteria. She would be able to conduct mini-lessons to support this sort of language, logic, and abstraction in the same way she would conduct mini-lessons to help other learners learn to draw conclusions, infer, or make analogies.

Lydia's Reflections

Lydia was satisfied that she had considered all 10 of the curriculum components in making decisions and developing her plan for a Civil War unit that revolved around the Curriculum of Connections. She was struck by the fact that, in the end, she didn't need to follow a specific sequence for her planning. In reality, she often found herself moving from planning one component to another and back to a previously considered component to make revisions and slight alterations. In the end, however, she was sure the components were aligned, powerful, and would lead to a much deeper understanding of the content. She knew she was already wiser for the process!

The shift from planning to implementation would be an interesting one. How well could her students think their way through the content? What kind of conceptual explanations would they build? How much help would they need? How motivated would they be to make connections to other "grown-up" topics? Would they gain an appreciation for connection making and analogies? How well would this whole curriculum development process work with younger students, or in other subject areas? What would happen if Lydia had revised only part of her unit to attend to the purposes of the Curriculum of Connections? What if she had used this model with some but not all of her students? These would be interesting questions to contemplate as Lydia reflected on the impact of her new unit on her students and on her own professional growth.

Looking Back and Ahead

The Curriculum of Connections provides teachers and students with opportunity to learn an extremely valuable life skill—the ability to make connections, analogies, and metaphors. No other cognitive skill is as important as metaphoric thinking in supporting a student's ability to analyze new information and data independently. Once acquired, the ability to make connections, see relationships, and "make the strange familiar" empowers students to continue a life's search for connections among all pieces of information, all facets of knowledge, all topics and disciplines, and their own prior knowledge. Prolonged opportunities to make connections, see relationships, and develop inductive and deductive conclusions empower a student to pursue learning and the search for universality as a lifelong vocation.

It is also crucial, however, for students to see themselves at work in the various disciplines—to understand that people make contributions to our world every day through their active involvement with the ideas, issues, and skills rooted in the disciplines. The Curriculum of Practice Parallel, discussed next in Chapter 6, retains the Core Curriculum focus on the key concepts, principles, and skills of the disciplines and invites students to become practitioners who not only think about important ideas but also apply what they learn to address meaningful problems.

6

The Curriculum of
Practice Parallel

A group of sixth grade students in the state of Oregon has just completed a unit on World War II in Mrs. DeFranco's classroom. To bring closure to the unit, she asks them if there are any other questions that they have about this topic. Charles, who is fascinated by this time period innocently states, "I know the causes of the war, who the great leaders were, but I still would like to know what was happening in our town during the war." This question causes Sarah to raise her hand and ask, "How was our town affected by the war?" Then Alyssa asks, "How were children my age affected by the war?" Mrs. DeFranco seems a bit surprised by these questions, but the students seem eager to have their questions answered. Mrs. DeFranco takes the opportunity to ask students to consider the time period and to generate any other questions that seem personally relevant to them. After spending a few days generating these inquiries, it appears as if the questions require the students to learn a series of new skills that she hadn't thought of using—teaching students to conduct oral histories and analyze historical documents. What she does recognize is that the questions are personally motivating to the students and require the students to learn skills that "real" researchers use. Additionally, she has arrived at the conclusion that there are no predetermined answers to these questions and more important, SHE DOESN'T KNOW THE ANSWERS! Thus her journey begins in facilitating research with her students.

Like this example, most students ask questions that seem quite innocent, but if examined closely parallel the questions asked by researchers in various disciplines. These questions might emerge when (a) students personally interact with the content and emotionally become invested in a specific topic, (b) what they have read or experienced does not match their understanding, or (c) intriguing ideas are generated as they try to make connections between and among contexts to extend their understandings. Therefore, throughout all grades, teachers should systematically assist students in developing curiosity, pursuing topics that interest them, identifying intriguing questions, learning the skills used by professionals to answer their questions, developing plans to find out more about those questions, managing time, setting goals and criteria, and presenting new understandings to audiences who can appreciate them.

The Curriculum of Practice has been designed to emphasize opportunities for students to learn the skills that professionals use in various disciplines to construct new knowledge in their fields and to extend their understandings about a particular topic or idea. Additionally, the Curriculum of Practice encourages educators to design learning experiences where students apply the methods of the practitioner in a discipline to problems or inquiries that are of importance and interest to them. The Curriculum of Practice builds on the Core Curriculum, still focusing on key information, concepts, and principles, by guiding students in the journey of researching questions or solving problems as scholars or expert practitioners in the discipline would. To accomplish this, the Curriculum of Practice guides students in learning the skills and methodologies used by professionals in various disciplines. In learning how professionals study their field, what questions they explore, and how they move knowledge forward, it is possible that many students will learn and retain far more than through more direct, but limited, approaches to teaching and learning.

In this chapter, a format similar to that of other chapters in the book provides an overview of the Curriculum of Practice Parallel. Readers will find (1) a definition of the Curriculum of Practice, (2) a rationale for using this approach to curriculum development, (3) an explanation of key features and exemplary characteristics inherent in this design, (4) an example of this process in action, (5) specific procedures and techniques for adapting the components of the Curriculum of Practice for ascending intellectual demand, and (6) an explanation of the curriculum parallel's relationship to the three other curriculum parallels described in this book.

What Does It Mean to "Practice" in a Curriculum?

Every field of knowledge has a set of key facts, concepts, principles, and skills that helps define the discipline. Concepts help us label and make sense of large amounts of information and serve as the speaking vocabulary of a discipline (e.g., interdependence, systems, change, adaptation, and patterns). Unlike facts, which are limited to specific situations, concepts are broad enough to apply to many situations. Some concepts are domain specific, whereas others are more connective or interdisciplinary in nature. Principles are generally agreed-on truths that have been arrived at through research and experience. Some of these principles can be factual (e.g., "In order to survive, a civilization must be able to answer the basic biological needs of its members: food, drink, shelter, and medical care"), whereas others can be more abstract (e.g., "Each culture views the physical environment in a unique way, prizing aspects of it that may be different from those prized by others"). Principles help learners probe the governing ideas of a discipline and help teachers get to the heart of the content. Using principles and concepts at the center of curricular planning is particularly useful because of the potential they hold for organizing large quantities of information in a meaningful manner.

In addition to core concepts and principles, every field of knowledge has a set of skills and methodologies that professionals use to (a) answer questions about a particular idea or to solve problems within a discipline, (b) acquire and use information, (c) analyze and organize data, and (d) reach conclusions. These skills, when taught directly to students, can equip them with the "tools" used by professionals to uncover important ideas in the field, pursue answers to their probing questions, and experience firsthand what it is like to be a practicing professional within any field of knowledge. These skills and methodologies define the work or "practice" of the professional and define the mode of inquiry that is used by scholars to figure out correct or reasonable answers to a certain set of questions. This is the type of practice used in lessons or units based on the Curriculum of Practice Parallel.

Skills and methodologies used in various disciplines assist professionals in constructing knowledge that is ever changing. These skills also encourage professionals to be open-minded, skeptical, willing to suspend initial judgments, curious, creative, able to collaborate with others, and persistent in the face of failure. In most cases, the activity and pleasure derived from the experience of finding out is as important as knowing the answer. In science, the inquiry process relies on the skills of asking questions, making observations, setting up experiments, refining and validating hypotheses, and drawing conclusions. Historians use the skills of seeking evidence and determining the authenticity of documents, documenting bias, and a host of other skills to find out about the past. In all disciplines, a certain mode of inquiry directs the learning process and requires scholars to use certain thinking skills, tools, and procedures to systematically answer their questions.

The intent of the Curriculum of Practice is to arrange opportunities for students to use the skills and methodologies of a discipline by asking students to function as a practicing professional in a discipline. In some situations, the student will be asked to function as a "scholar"— use the knowledge, skills, and tools to develop a fuller understanding of the domain. At other times the student will be the "expert practitioner—using the knowledge, skills, and tools of the discipline to produce new knowledge. Figure 6.1 lists focusing questions in the Curriculum of Practice.

In essence, the Core Curriculum begins with students acquiring knowledge of the key facts, concepts, and principles within a discipline. The Curriculum of Practice extends these understandings by enabling students to "practice" or to learn firsthand how to use the skills and methodologies used by practicing professionals in various disciplines to answer their questions, to probe the meaning of the key ideas of the discipline, and to test their adaptability with those ideas. Therefore, it is important to note that one educator might be able to use the Curriculum of Practice as a curricular approach to arrive at the same destination as the teacher who uses the Core Curriculum, or the Curriculum of Practice can be used to extend and deepen an understanding of the principles and concepts as students move from novice to expert production in a field of study. While the two approaches to curriculum development are certainly related, a way of thinking about a key difference in them is that the Curriculum of Practice places in the foreground of consideration the methods and skills used by practicing experts or scholars in a discipline.

Figure 6.1. Some Focusing Questions in the Curriculum of Practice

- What are the theories that govern the field of knowledge?
- How do practitioners organize their knowledge and skill in this field?
- How do the concepts and principles that form the framework of the discipline get translated into practice by those in this field?
- What are the features of routine problems in the field?
- How does a practitioner know which skills to use in given circumstances?
- What strategies does a practitioner use to solve nonroutine problems in the discipline?
- What tools does a practitioner use in his or her work?
- How does one gain access to and skill in using those tools?
- How does a practitioner sense whether approaches and methods are effective in a given instance?
- What constitutes meaningful evidence versus less significant information in this field or in instances in the field?
- On what basis does a practitioner in the field make educated guesses?
- On what basis does a practitioner in the field draw conclusions?
- What are the methods used by practitioners and contributors in the field to generate new questions, to generate new knowledge, and to solve problems?
- What personality traits support productivity in the field?
- What drives the work of practitioners in the field?
- What are indicators of quality in the field?
- According to what standards does the field measure success?
- What are the ethical issues and standards of the field?

Why Does It Matter to Have Students Engage in a Curriculum of Practice?

The importance of teaching students the methodologies used in various fields has been long advocated by researchers. In the later 1800s and early 1900s, John Dewey proposed creating schools around the practice of problem solving through the scientific method. Life and society outside the school were viewed as relevant, and it was suggested that curricular experiences should prepare students for their future role as citizens and workers. He suggested that student learning should be shaped by problems they encounter and that their involvement in research and activity would teach them a model or process of problem solving that would be applicable in school and in life (Dewey, 1938).

Upon a closer look at the knowledge level of the "cognitive taxonomy" developed by Benjamin Bloom and his colleagues (1956), there is further evidence of the importance of teaching students the methodologies of a discipline. "Cognitive taxonomy" describes three types of knowledge: (1) knowledge of specifics; (2) knowledge of ways and means of dealing with specifics; and (3) knowledge of the universals and abstractions in a field. The first category deals with the basic elements a learner must know to become acquainted with a field, which centers on knowledge of terminology and knowledge of specific facts—somewhat as a high-quality Comprehensive Curriculum might call on learners to do. The third category focuses on the key concepts and principles of the disciplines—as an effective Core Curriculum or Curriculum of Connections would do. It is the second category in Bloom's thinking that is reflected in the Curriculum of Practice. The second category includes ways of organizing, studying, judging, and critiquing ideas, events, and phenomena in a field and closely approximates the idea behind the Curriculum of Practice. Bloom and his colleagues felt a student should come to understand the modes of inquiry, techniques, and procedures that characterize a particular field and assist the professional in investigating problems.

Research and theories put forth by Jerome Bruner, Phil Phenix, Hilda Taba, Joseph Renzulli, and others are testimony to the importance of students learning how to use the methodologies in various disciplines to construct and apply knowledge. Bruner (1960) explained the importance of being the professional when he stated "that intellectual activity anywhere is the same, whether at the frontier of knowledge or in a third-grade classroom. What a scientist does at his desk or laboratory, what a literary critic does in reading a poem, are of the same order as what anybody else does when he is engaged in like activities—if he is to achieve understanding" (p. 14). Renzulli (1977) has long advocated placing students in the role of the "practicing professional" to pursue problems or questions based on individual or group interests. The goals are to acquire advanced-level understanding of the knowledge and methodology used within particular disciplines, artistic areas of expression, and interdisciplinary studies.

Helpful to educators today is to realize that inherent in every high-quality standards document is careful attention to the modes of inquiry in each discipline. For example, within *National Science Education Standards* (National Academy Press, 1996) is a chapter devoted to "Science as Inquiry" and guidelines for how it should be taught at each grade level. Accordingly, a set of historical thinking skills is outlined in *National Standards for History* (National Center for History in the Schools, 1996). These skills are summarized in Figures 6.2 and 6.3.

Clearly, it benefits society for its members to understand and appreciate how to learn and how to use inquiry skills to solve problems that affect present and future generations. It also benefits teachers and students to focus on such knowledge, understanding, and skill because it:

1. Provides them with a means for continued learning
2. Assists them in knowing how to respond when answers to problems are not immediately apparent
3. Teaches them to use data in valid and reliable ways
4. Promotes and values the questioning of assumptions
5. Expands their fluency and flexibility as problem solvers in the field

(Text continues on page 173

Figure 6.2. Science as Inquiry

Understandings About Scientific Inquiry and the Abilities Necessary to Do Scientific Inquiry in Grades K-4	Understandings About Scientific Inquiry and the Abilities Necessary to Do Scientific Inquiry in Grades 6-8	Understandings About Scientific Inquiry and the Abilities Necessary to Do Scientific Inquiry in Grades 9-12
Scientific investigations involve asking and answering a question and comparing the answer with what scientists already know about the world. Ask a question about objects, organisms, and events in the environment.	Different kinds of questions suggest different kinds of scientific investigations. Some investigations involve observing and describing objects, organisms, or events; some involve experiments; some involve seeking more information; some involve discovery of new objects and phenomena; and some involve making models. Identify questions that can be answered through scientific investigations.	Scientists usually inquire about how physical, living, or designed systems function. Conceptual principles and knowledge guide scientific inquiries. Historical and current scientific knowledge influence the design and interpretation of investigations and the evaluation of proposed explanations made by other scientists. Identify questions and concepts that guide scientific investigations.
Scientists use different kinds of investigations depending on the questions they are trying to answer. Types of investigations include describing objects, events, and organisms; classifying them; and doing a fair test (experimenting). Plan and conduct a simple investigation.	Current scientific knowledge and understanding guide scientific investigations. Different scientific domains employ different methods, core theories, and standards to advance scientific knowledge and understandings. Design and conduct a scientific investigation.	Scientists conduct investigations for a wide variety of reasons. For example, they may wish to discover new aspects of the natural world, explain recently observed phenomena, or test the conclusions of prior investigations or the predictions of current theories. Design and conduct scientific investigations.
Simple instruments, such as magnifiers, thermometers, and rulers, provide more information than scientists obtain using only their senses. Employ simple equipment and tools to gather data and extend the senses.	Mathematics is important in all aspects of scientific inquiry. Technology used to gather data enhances accuracy and allows scientists to analyze and quantify results of investigations. Use appropriate tools and techniques to gather, analyze, and interpret data; Use mathematics in all aspects of scientific inquiry.	Scientists rely on technology to enhance the gathering and manipulation of data. New techniques and tools provide new evidence to guide inquiry and new methods to gather data, thereby contributing to the advance of science. The accuracy and precision of the data, and therefore the quality of the exploration, depends on the technology used.
		Mathematics is essential in scientific inquiry. Mathematical tools and models guide and improve the posing of questions, gathering data, constructing explanations and communicating results. Use technology and mathematics to improve investigations and communications.

Scientists develop explanations using observations (evidence) and what they already know about the world (scientific knowledge). Good explanations are based on evidence from investigations. Use data to construct a reasonable explanation.

Scientific explanations emphasize evidence, have logically consistent arguments, and use scientific principles, models, and theories. The scientific community accepts and uses such explanations until displaced by better scientific ones. When such displacement occurs, science advances. Develop descriptions, explanations, predictions, and models using evidence; Use mathematics in all aspects of scientific inquiry; Recognize and analyze alternative explanations and predictions.

Scientific explanations must adhere to criteria such as: a proposed explanation must be logically consistent; it must abide by the rules of evidence; it must be open to questions and possible modification; and it must be based on historical and current scientific knowledge.

Formulate and revise scientific explanations and models using logic and evidence; Recognize and analyze alternative explanations and models.

Students make the results of their investigations public; they describe the investigations in ways that enable others to repeat the investigations. Communicate investigations and explanations.

Science advances through legitimate skepticism. Asking questions and querying other scientists' explanations is part of scientific inquiry. Scientists evaluate the explanations proposed by other scientists by examining evidence, comparing evidence, identifying faulty reasoning, pointing out statements that go beyond the evidence and suggesting alternative explanations for the same observations. Communicate scientific procedures and explanations.

Results of scientific inquiry—new knowledge and methods—emerge from different types of investigations and public communication among scientists. In communicating and defending the results of scientific inquiry, arguments must be logical and demonstrate connections between natural phenomena, investigations, and the historical body of scientific knowledge. In addition, the methods and procedures that scientists used to obtain evidence must be clearly reported to enhance opportunities for further investigation. Communicate and defend a scientific argument.

Students review and ask questions about the results of other scientists' work. Communicate investigations and explanations.

Scientific investigations sometimes result in new ideas and phenomena for study, generate new methods or procedures or an investigation, or develop new technologies to improve the collection of data. All of these results can lead to new investigations. Communicate scientific procedures and explanations.

SOURCE: National Academy Press (1996).

Figure 6.3. History as Inquiry

Type of Thinking Skill	Explanation of the Skills	Student Example
Chronological Thinking Students develop a clear sense of historical time—of when events occurred and in what temporal order—so they can examine relationships among them or to explain historical causality.	Distinguish between past, present and future; identify the temporal structure of a historical narrative or story; establish temporal order in constructing their own narrative stories; measure and calculate calendar time; interpret data presented in timelines; create timelines; and explain change and continuity over time.	Investigate a family history for at least two generations, identifying various members and their connections in order to construct a timeline.
Historical Comprehension Students understand the chronology of events, that events in history reflect stories or narratives that allow us to interpret, reveal conditions, changes, and consequences, and explain why things happened like they did.	Identify the author or source of the historical document or narrative; reconstruct the literal meaning of a historical passage; identify the central question(s) the historical narrative addresses and the purpose, perspective, or point of view from which it has been constructed; read historical narrative imaginatively, taking into account the historical context in which the event unfolded (the values, outlook, crises, options; and contingencies of that time and place); and what the narrative reveals of the humanity of the individuals involved (their probable motives, hopes, fears, strengths, and weaknesses); appreciate historical perspectives; draw upon data in historical maps; draw upon the visual and mathematical data presented in graphs; and draw upon the visual data presented in photographs, paintings, cartoons, and architectural drawings in order to clarify, illustrate, or elaborate upon information presented in the historical narrative.	From data gathered through family artifacts, photos, and interviews with older relatives and/or other people who play a significant part in a student's life, draw possible conclusions about roles, jobs, schooling experiences, and other aspects of family life in the recent past. Draw upon a variety of stories, legends, songs, ballads, games, and tall tales in order to describe the environment, lifestyles, beliefs, and struggles of people in various regions of the country.

Historical Analysis and Interpretation

Students examine historical situations and raise questions or define problems for themselves; compare differing ideas, interests, perspectives, actions, and institutions represented in these sources; and elaborate upon what they read and see to develop interpretations, explanations, or solutions to the questions they have raised.

Formulate questions to focus their inquiry and analysis; compare and contrast differing sets of ideas, values, personalities, behaviors, and institutions by identifying likenesses and differences; analyze historical fiction on such criteria as the accuracy of the story's historical details and sequence of events, and point of view or interpretations presented by the author; distinguish fact and fiction by comparing documentary sources; compare different stories about a historical figures, event, or era; analyze illustrations in historical stories for information they reveal and compare to other documents to judge their accuracy; consider multiple perspectives; explain causes in analyzing historical actions, including the importance of the individual in history, the influence of ideas, human interests, and beliefs; and the role of chance, the accidental and the irrational; challenge arguments of historical inevitability by giving examples of how different choices could have led to different consequences; and hypothesize the influence of the past, including both the limitations and opportunities made possible by past decisions.

For various cultures represented in the classroom, compare and contrast family life now with family life over time and between various cultures and consider such things as communications, technology, homes, transportation, recreation, school, and cultural traditions.

Draw upon data from charts, historical maps, nonfiction and fiction accounts, and interviews in order to describe "through their eyes" the experience of immigrant groups. Include information such as where they came from and why they left, travel experiences, ports of entry and immigration screening, and the opportunities and obstacles they encountered when they arrived in America.

(Continued)

Figure 6.3. Continued)

Type of Thinking Skill	Explanation of the Skills	Student Example
Historical Research Capabilities Students engage in "doing history" by formulating problems or a set of questions worth pursuing. Students are encouraged to analyze historical documents, records, or a site itself. The historical inquiry is a search in which answers are not known in advance, and finding and interpreting the results is a genuine process of knowledge building.	Formulate historical questions from encounters with historical documents, eye-witness accounts, letters, diaries, artifacts, photos, historical sites, art, architecture, and other records from the past; obtain historical data from a variety of sources; interrogate historical data by determining by whom and when it was created; testing the data source for its credibility, authority, and authenticity and detecting and evaluating bias, distortion, and propaganda; and marshal information of the time and place to construct a story, explanation, or historical narrative.	Examine and formulate questions about early records, diaries, family photographs, artifacts, and architectural drawings obtained through a local newspaper or historical society in order to describe family life in their local community or state long ago.
Historical Issue Analysis and Decision Making Students are asked to consider the historical dilemmas with which people have coped at critical moments in the past and near present. Problems confronting people in historical fiction, fables, legends, and myths, as well as in historical records of the past are usually value-laden. Examining these dilemmas, the choices before the people who confronted them, and the consequences of the decisions they made provides opportunities for children to consider the values and beliefs that have influenced human decisions both for good and for ill.	Identify problems and dilemmas confronting people in historical narratives; analyze the interests, values, and points of view of those involved; identify causes of the problem or dilemma; propose alternative ways of resolving the problem or dilemma and evaluate each in terms of ethical consideration (is it fair? just?), the interest of the people involved, and the likely consequences of each proposal; formulate a position or course of action on an issue by identifying the nature of the problem, analyzing the underlying factors contributing to the problem, and choosing a plausible solution from a choice of carefully evaluated options; identify the solution chosen by characters in the story or in the historical situation; and evaluate the consequences of the actions taken.	Identify a problem in the community's past, analyze the different perspectives of those involved, and evaluate choices people had and the solution they chose.

SOURCE: National Center for History in the Schools (1996).

6. Organizes their understandings in ways useful for accessing information in the various fields
7. Encourages the development of a community of learners
8. Expands their learning environments by using professionals in the field and the community at large
9. Requires that they learn how to effectively communicate their understandings to others
10. Makes learning enjoyable and personally relevant

This section on the Curriculum of Practice has focused on the importance and the benefits of using the Curriculum of Practice to develop comprehensive curriculum. In the next section, we explore how the Curriculum of Practice is designed. Figure 6.4 may serve as an advance organizer for the ideas that follow.

Key Features of the Key Components of Curriculum in the Curriculum of Practice

When teachers identify the principles and concepts to be explored in a curricular unit, student understanding and involvement can be enhanced by generating a series of **essential questions** that can be used by the students to probe the meaning behind these ideas. Essential questions are the questions that touch our hearts and souls and help us to become engaged with knowledge. They are central to our lives and help to define what it means to be human. In the social studies curriculum, essential questions probe the deepest issues confronting us: perspective, identity, revolution and change, leadership, invention, inspiration, culture, honor, integrity, courage, and power. In science, we explore our natural surrounding and its related concepts so that we can protect it for future generations. In literature, we explore ideas such as truth, love, wisdom, myths, and perspective so that we become more human. While some student-generated questions seem simplistic in nature, educators can assist students in probing the meaning behind these ideas in order to bring to light more abstract questions (e.g., Why are wars fought? How much diversity can any nation tolerate? What does it mean to be a citizen? How are relationships sustained? What is meant by friendship?). The Curriculum of Practice helps us probe these meanings in a way that helps us retain childlike wonder and awe in our discoveries.

Content/Standards in the Curriculum of Practice

Educators who are planning a Curriculum of Practice unit must first identify the goals students must achieve within the unit. Depending on the method a teacher selects to direct the inquiry, students must come to understand the role they play in learning and applying certain principles, concepts, and skills within a discipline, since we are asking that they assume the role of producer or scholar in the discipline. These roles may be new or different to the students. Additionally, students need to understand the role that the teacher plays in facilitating the inquiry in order

(Text continued on page 176)

Figure 6.4. The Comprehensive Curriculum Components Illustrated in the Curriculum of Practice Parallel

Curriculum Component	Modification Techniques
Content/ Standards	• Consider which methodologies (tools, procedures, and skills) of a specific discipline might assist students in: answering their own research questions, probing the meaning of the key ideas of the discipline, and testing the adaptability of those ideas in other contexts. • Determine the types of questions, problems, or discrepant events that will be uncovered by the students as they apply the research methodologies. • Consider how the students will use the information they discover in their investigations to deepen their understanding of key principles and concepts and their relationships. • Determine the type of problem-solving process or modes of inquiry that will be used to solve problems or to investigate questions. • Work with students to generate questions, determine the methodologies and procedures for carrying out the investigation, gather and analyze data, reach conclusions, and determine the implications of the research findings. • Identify which habits of mind are to be developed through the use of this learning experience (e.g., independence, persistence, and dealing with ambiguity). • Consider which ethical issues or problems can be used as subjects for the investigation. • Identify the modes of inquiry that are listed in national standards documents (e.g., NSTA, NCTM, NCSS, and NTE).
Assessments	• Determine the varying levels of sophistication, expertise, or technical proficiency in the use of methodological skills to assist learners toward continued growth. • Consider how students will demonstrate their understanding in using the methodological skills, how their knowledge has changed over time, and the degree to which they interpret, apply, and transfer the knowledge and skills that they have gained to new contexts. • Determine which products will be used to communicate new understandings and document growth. • Consider a variety of products that can be used to show evidence of understanding of new ideas, new connections, transformations of existing ideas in new contexts, and flexibility in acquiring data. • Provide ample opportunities for students to communicate their findings in a variety of formats. • Observe and note changes in behavior (e.g., persistence, independence, and skepticism) over time.
Introductory Activities	• Use focusing questions, problems, dilemmas, and discrepant events to justify the need for methodological skills. • Identify experts who can assist students in identifying problems, developing technical expertise in the use of inquiry skills, and knowing which tools and procedures to use to best address these problems.

Teaching Methods	• Use a variety of teaching methods to support and scaffold learning. • Develop a repertoire of teaching strategies that are more inductive and more inquiry based in accordance with the goal of developing behaviors used by scholars (e.g., investigative studies, problem-based learning, independent studies, Socratic questioning, small and large group investigations, simulations). • Adjust and match teaching methods to the learners as they demonstrate continued growth in using the tools and procedures of the professional.
Learning Activities	• Make sure that the learning activities are those that provide opportunities for students to use the tools of the professional to acquire new information, enhance learning, and engage in research. • Select activities that target the development of essential principles and concepts, or encourage the inquiry process. • Introduce students to the inquiry process or steps to research. • Acquire tools and technologies to advance the level of research that students conduct (e.g., probes and sensors, statistical software, word processor, data collection devices). • Use graphing techniques to analyze data.
Grouping Strategies	• Employ a variety of grouping arrangements (flexible, small group, individual, interest-based, across grade levels, multi-aged) based on students' readiness levels, learning styles, skill accomplishment.
Resources	• Locate methodological tools that can be used to collect data. • Identify community experts who can help students learn the skills and methodologies used in various disciplines. • Locate videos, books, artifacts, photographs, artwork, electronic information, community members, experts in the field, primary and secondary source documents, and methodological guides (how-to books) to support student research.
Products	• Determine the variety of products that can be used to provide evidence of increased understanding of the principles and concepts in a particular field, research procedures, and new discoveries made about an area of study. • Select the types of products that are close approximations of the types of products that practicing professionals create in their fields (e.g., gallery displays, documentaries, books, articles, social action plans, compositions, and scientific studies). • Consider the audience that can best provide students with authentic evaluation of their work.

(Continued)

Figure 6.4. Continued

Curriculum Component	*Modification Techniques*
Extension Activities	• Listen carefully for other questions that students raise prior to, during, and after instruction. • Consider community experts who can provide advanced technical assistance to those students who are ready. • Determine other areas in which students want to explore, practice, or apply newly acquired skills of practice.
Modification Based on Learner Need, Including Ascending Intellectual Demand	• Provide opportunities for students to guide their own inquiries. • Devise tasks and products that cause students to develop, through application, personal frameworks of knowledge, understanding, and skill related to the discipline. • Escalate the level of resource materials that are used by the students during their research. • Identify new contexts for transferring and applying knowledge. • Guide students in establishing their own goals for work at what they believe to be the next steps of research. • Escalate the level of analysis for the investigation. • Network students with mentors in the field to advance their knowledge and research skills. • Use the Parallel's guidelines for Ascending Intellectual Demand in selecting resources and designing learning activities and products.

to seek assistance and to understand the types of questions that teachers will be asking them throughout the Curriculum of Practice unit. Sharing these goals with the students establishes the student's role and assists educators in selecting the types of instructional strategies and activities that will facilitate student understanding and accomplish the intended goals.

It is also helpful to teachers to focus on skills students will need during the learning process. These skills will guide teachers in developing an extended set of goals. As a result of engaging in learning activities that help them to probe a discipline at a deeper level of understanding, students will learn how to use and apply the skills (strategies and tools) practitioners use to solve nonroutine problems or answer their questions; acquire advanced understanding of how the field translates concepts and principles into practice; and learn new applications of the theories that govern the knowledge of a particular field of study. It is also probable that the students will confront the ethical issues and standards of the field.

Finally, when students tackle meaningful problems or employ the methodologies of researchers, they are likely to develop productive dispositions or habits. These "habits of mind" described by Costa and Kallick (2000) reflect attributes of humans who behave intelligently. Although the list of attributes that follows is not meant to be complete, teachers may notice several of these attributes resulting from prolonged engagement with the types of learning experiences offered in the Curriculum of Practice. These attributes of intelligent behavior include the following:

- Persisting
- Managing Impulsivity
- Listening to Others With Understanding and Empathy
- Thinking Flexibly
- Thinking About Our Thinking (Metacognition)
- Striving for Accuracy and Precision
- Questioning and Posing Problems
- Applying Past Knowledge to New Situations
- Thinking and Communicating With Clarity and Precision
- Gathering Data Through All Senses
- Creating, Imagining, and Innovating
- Responding With Wonderment and Awe
- Taking Responsible Risks
- Finding Humor
- Thinking Interdependently
- Learning Continuously

Based on these goals and the focusing questions for the Curriculum of Practice (See Figure 6.1), teachers can develop standards to guide their selection of instructional activities for the Curriculum of Practice.

Students will be able to:

1. Define, refine, and refocus broad questions or problems within a particular unit of study
2. Design, conduct, and execute an investigation by formulating questions and designing a plan for the investigation
3. Use appropriate skills, tools, and techniques to gather, analyze, and interpret data
4. Develop descriptions, explanations, predictions, and models using evidence gathered
5. Communicate findings of the inquiry with an audience

6. Explain how the findings relate to, illustrate, or extend the understanding of a principle or concept in a particular unit of study
7. Demonstrate dispositions that approximate those of the professional

These standards are quite broad, and a teacher can develop more specific objectives that correlate with the content of a particular unit. For example, a teacher who is working with students to identify the causes of conflicts prior to the start of a unit on the American Revolutionary War might ask his or her students to survey all sixth graders to gather information about the perspective of conflict in the lives of sixth graders. Upon gathering the data, students will analyze it to see what categories emerge. In most cases, the data can be grouped in the following categories: economic, religious, social, and political. These categories can then be used to assist students in organizing the information they will learn about during this unit of study and enable them to make connections between and among other wars that are fought. For this activity, then, the teacher can generate a more specific set of objectives that address the broader ones noted above. For example, some of the objectives for this lesson might include the following:

Students will be able to:

1. Generate a series of questions that can be used to guide the investigation
2. Design and conduct a survey that can be used to gather data about the perspectives of sixth graders in regard to conflict
3. Analyze the survey data to determine the categories it represents
4. Use the categories to compare factors that influenced conflict in the American Revolutionary War with factors that influence conflict in the sixth graders' lives
5. Provide evidence of these factors through written and visual examples

In the end, these objectives combine knowledge, understanding, and skills stated (or implied) in text and standards documents with the goal of the Curriculum of Practice to have students develop and use critical knowledge, understanding, and skill while acting as a scholar or expert practitioner would.

Assessment in the Curriculum of Practice

In the Curriculum of Practice, students are invited to learn how to construct knowledge by applying the skills, methods and procedures, and strategies of the professional. By engaging in this type of work, students demonstrate important qualities of understanding that can be assessed in a variety of formats (e.g., student reflections, products, observations, performances, or conferences) and by using a rubric that articulates a continuum of expertise, from novice through apprentice to expert. This rubric also allows for the diagnosis and coaching of student's progress along this continuum. In writing these rubrics, an educator may find it helpful to use the four qualities of understanding defined by Mansilla and Gardner (1998): (1) ability to refine, transform, or replace naïve content understandings with more sophisticated levels of understanding; (2) application of research methodologies to build reliable data; (3) ability to recognize the purposes and interests that drive knowledge construction; and (4) level of expertise used in creating performances or products that communicate new understandings. In formulating the assessment portion of a unit that focuses on the Curriculum of Practice, educators can identify a range of instructional techniques that will facilitate student understanding in these four areas, and generate learning activities through which understanding can be achieved. This reinforces that tightly forged link in excellent curriculum between content goals, assessment strategies, and instructional techniques.

Introductory Activities and the Curriculum of Practice

Every discipline has a set of skills and research procedures that a scholar uses to answer questions or study problems, and to make contributions to a discipline. The essence of a discipline is not so much the accumulated knowledge and ideas but, rather, the ongoing struggle and persistence required to find out how these ideas change, adapt, or affect other things. From a disciplinarian's perspective, answers to questions are often elusive and require systematic study. And in this journey, a researcher seldom stops in any particular place for long because questions sometimes lead to answers and invariably lead to other questions.

In the beginning, educators must plan opportunities for introducing students to the dispositions used by scholars in a particular discipline so that, they too, can understand what it takes to pursue this type of work. Educators can read stories about historians who have uncovered new information relating to a particular topic that has been studied in class, invite guest speakers into the classroom who can be asked to demonstrate particular skills that they use in answering their questions, or view multimedia resources that illustrate strategies practitioners use to solve nonroutine problems in the discipline. The purpose of these introductory activities is to establish a classroom environment that promotes active inquiry in students. Students must feel that their ideas and inquiries are respected, that they are capable of uncovering the answers to their questions, and more important, feel safe in questioning assumptions and being somewhat skeptical of knowledge as it is presented in text resources.

Some educators begin this type of unit with a brainstorming session or through a series of questions designed to activate students' background knowledge and introduce the Curriculum of Practice unit in an accessible manner. Other educators tell effective stories that provide a "hook" to demonstrate the relevance of the topic to the real world, or to clarify a misunderstanding through sustained research. Whichever strategy is used, it should serve to plant the seed for further inquiry into a unit of study and clarify the role that students will assume in this unit.

Teaching Methods and the Curriculum of Practice

Within this curricular unit, teaching methods will be varied. Because the primary purpose of the Curriculum of Practice is to help students extend and apply their understandings and skills in a discipline in much the same way as scholars study their field, educators will find themselves moving in and out of instructional techniques that best facilitate their students' understanding and application of the methods. At times, educators will use more direct methods of teaching (e.g., teaching students background information for the unit or teaching students how to conduct interviews with community members). At other points, teachers will need to use more indirect methods of teaching (e.g., facilitating a group discussion about the ways to organize data that students have collected). However, the Curriculum of Practice does place a premium on those teaching methods that are more inductive and more inquiry based in accordance with the goal of developing behaviors used by scholars. Depending on the nature of the skill and the readiness levels of the students, some teaching strategies may better facilitate student understanding. More important, the methods of teaching should put the learner in the role of a scholar or an inquirer in each subject or discipline area being taught.

Educators not only need to be familiar with using a variety of teaching methods, they must also be knowledgeable about the concepts and principles of a discipline and the characteristic methods of inquiry used in that discipline. Throughout a Curriculum of Practice unit, students will require feedback on the accuracy of their information and suggestions for designing better questions, analyzing data, conducting interviews and using other data collection methods, as well as methods of acting on problems in a discipline.

Learning Activities and the Curriculum of Practice

When students behave as scholars, they will use rather than simply acquire information. The learning activities component of a Curriculum of Practice unit are arranged to provide opportunities for using methodological skills to acquire new information and to use this new information to form products new to the students. First and foremost, the learning activities should engage students in using the research process (the strategies, methods, and procedures) to acquire information. Although these methods may vary across disciplines, they generally involve a series of investigative procedures that include the following:

1. Identifying a problem within a content field
2. Finding and focusing a problem within an area of study
3. Posing research questions or generating hypotheses
4. Gathering information from a variety of sources
5. Locating and constructing appropriate data-gathering instruments
6. Classifying and categorizing data
7. Summarizing and analyzing data
8. Reporting findings through a variety of products

A second type of learning experience that will be provided to the students will focus on the domain-specific skills researchers use in completing the more comprehensive tasks outlined above. For example, students might need to learn a series of how-to skills to carry out their research (e.g., how to set up a scientific experiment by controlling variables; how to develop a survey to gather data; how to analyze historical photographs and documents; how to critique a piece of writing). Collectively, these two types of learning experiences equip students with the know-how of investigative methodology, which moves them closer to the goal of behaving like scholars.

In addition to the skills of problem finding and problem solving, and the more specific skills a researcher uses in the research/problem solving process, certain creative and analytical thinking skills are also well suited to the goals of the Curriculum of Practice and to helping learners work like scholars or expert practitioners. Figure 6.5 illustrates, with examples, some of the skill categories important for student learning activities in the Curriculum of Practice.

Recall, too, that some learning activities in the Curriculum of Practice might ask students to function as scholars, developing an appreciation for the contribution of individuals to the body of knowledge, skills, tools, and methodologies of a domain. Other activities in the Curriculum of Practice might ask students to function as expert practitioners, actually using the body of knowledge, skills, tools, and methodology of the domain. In this regard, it is important for educators to be mindful of the developmental and readiness levels of their students. In some cases, a student will be ready to *assume* the role of an expert practitioner, whereas another student will be ready only to *simulate* the role of an expert practitioner. A student's cognitive and affective development should signal which of the two approaches or combination of approaches is best suited to that particular learner at a particular time. Examples of these two types of experiences follow.

An Example of Simulating the Role of an Expert Practitioner

The students in Mr. Harper's third grade class are studying the characteristics of organisms and have recently become intrigued by the earthworms they found on the playground after a recent rain shower. After visiting with the science coordinator at the school, Mr. Harper found out that the coordinator could order earthworms, egg cases, and baby earthworms from a biological supply company. This would allow his students to observe adult earthworms, the egg cases, the young earthworms, and some of the animal's characteristics.

While waiting for the earthworms to arrive, Mr. Harper took his students outside and asked the students to make observations of the earthworms in their natural habitat. Then he posed the question, "If we wanted to study how earthworms behave, how would we set up an environment in our classroom that closely resembles the natural setting?" This stimulated the students to gather books from the library to draw plans for a simulated environment that would be arranged in the classroom.

After discussing their plans, the students decided to create a habitat for an earthworm by using a terrarium strategically placed away from direct sunlight. The students covered the sides of the terrarium with black paper, then added soil, leaves, and grass to the habitat. After the other earthworms arrived from the supply company, they were placed into the terrarium.

In the first weeks of instruction, students were asked for many observations that would record how earthworms move, a description and an illustration of what they looked like, and what the students thought the earthworms were doing. They described the earthworm's color and shape; they weighed and measured the earth-

Figure 6.5. Critical and Creative Thinking Skills

Type of Thinking Skills	Student Examples
Information-Processing Skills Students locate and collect relevant information to sort, classify, sequence, compare and contrast, and analyze part to whole relationships.	• Ask students to write out their addresses. Ask the children to draw a map of their route from home to their classroom and describe their route to a partner. Discuss with the children who lives the farthest away and who lives the nearest. • With the children's help, design and carry out a survey of how children come to school. Help students use the information to draw a graph, which can be computer generated, and analyze the findings. • Have students observe and take photographs in the local community. Using these photographs, students research the history behind the locations. Conduct interviews with local residents to gain historical information about the community.
Reasoning Skills Students provide reasons for opinions and actions, draw inferences and make deductions, use precise language to explain what they think, and make judgments and decisions informed by reasons and/or evidence.	• Using the data collected in the activities listed above, have students design a historical walking tour map of the area. Students will make recommendations of places to see, describe their historical relevance, and add pictures of historical statues or sculptures that merit recognition. • Present these recommendations and the tour guide to an audience, such as a local historical museum.
Inquiry Skills Students ask relevant questions, pose and define problems, plan what to do and ways to research, predict outcomes and anticipate consequences, and test conclusions and improve ideas.	• Arrange for the children to complete a simple traffic survey on the road outside the school. With the children's help, label a wall display of photographs of the road outside the school to show aspects related to traffic (e.g., road signs, road markings). • Ask the children to think about their own road at home and decide whether it is quieter or noisier than the school road. Encourage the children to think up their own questions about traffic around the school. Discuss with the children what makes a "fair" test in a survey (e.g., times, frequency, place). With the children's help, design and carry out a survey of the numbers of cars parked in the street. Ask the children to present the results as a graph, using simple graphing software, and analyze the results. Ask the children to consider questions like: Are the parked cars there all day? Where do people go when they park their cars?

Creative Thinking Skills Students generate and extend ideas, suggest hypotheses, apply imagination, and look for alternative innovative outcomes or solutions.	• Ask the children to identify methods of making an area safe (e.g., bicycle paths, pavements, fencing, "no parking" zones, road signs, pedestrian crossings), and to think about how the school grounds and other streets they know are made safe. • Ask the children to make use of all the evidence they have collected (photographs and survey results) to write a letter to the transport department at the local council to ask about the possibility of a safety feature (e.g., a pedestrian crossing) being constructed.
Evaluation Skills Students evaluate information; judge the value of what they read, hear, and observe; develop criteria for judging the value of their own and others' work or ideas; and provide reasons for their decision.	• Students will discuss the pros and cons of building a hotel near a small coastal region. • Divide the children into five groups, each assuming one of the following roles: fisherman, local government official, travel company representative, store owner, and local resident. • Students will first work in small groups with peers portraying the same role to develop information and prepare statements that support their viewpoints about building the hotel. • Next, new groupings will be formed, this time composed of one representative from each role group. In these new groups, all participants will listen to, take notes on, and discuss the varying viewpoints on the hotel project. • After students have had a chance to revise their statements, the class will stage a mock public hearing on the hotel project. A vote will be taken to determine the outcome.

worm and designed large data charts to record their observations. The focus of their observations was mainly descriptive at this point.

As the unit progressed, students began to generate questions that were recorded on the chart by Mr. Harper. These questions were used to develop several explorations for the students to conduct. One group chose to investigate the life cycle of earthworms. They found several egg cases in the soil and this led them to books in the library that described the life-cycle process. They were also interested in trying to figure out a way to keep track of the growth of a baby earthworm as it developed over time.

Three other groups of students were trying to investigate the types of environments that earthworms prefer. Mr. Harper suggested that they try different things—

light, moisture, and temperature—and then coached them through the process of controlling variables.

A fourth group was trying to decide what the earthworms liked to eat. The students had read about the kinds of food earthworms preferred and were now just beginning to set up experiments to try to determine what the earthworms liked best.

The last group was trying to set up a transparent environment for the earthworms so that they could study what earthworms do in various types of soil.

In this study and inquiry into the life of an earthworm, Mr. Harper's students learned about the basic needs of a particular organism, the basic structures and functions of this organism, its life cycle, and some features of animal behavior. They simulated the role of a scientist by generating questions, planning and conducting experiments, measuring and recording data, identifying patterns in data, and reaching conclusions about some of the basic concepts and principles underlying the life sciences.

An Example of Becoming Expert Practitioners in a Field of Study

Mrs. McQuerry is a middle school teacher who uses every opportunity she can to engage students in problem-based activities that introduce or extend the learning process in meaningful ways. She looks for newspaper and journal articles that highlight important concepts that her students are learning in their curriculum and tries to turn these ideas into problems for her students to solve. She has found that this way of teaching motivates her students and assists them in seeing the relevance of what they are learning to the reality of life. A project that her students recently worked on has been published in a book called *Nuclear Legacy* (McQuerry, 2000). This book was written by students from two communities: Richland, Washington, home of the Manhattan Project; and Slavutych, Ukraine, home of the workers at the Chernobyl site. *Nuclear Legacy,* written in English and Ukrainian, is an example of authentic collaboration between cultures that captures a perspective on nuclear culture as seen by the first post-Cold War generation and gives us insight into what may be possible for our global future as nuclear cultures now work together. Student perceptions of the history of their communities and hopes for the future of our world tell the nuclear story from the perspective of those who will inherit its legacy.

This project became a way to help Ukrainian and American students connect what they were learning in school to a real product that would be valuable outside the walls of the classroom. The book includes firsthand accounts by young people of the 1986 Chernobyl nuclear accident and interviews with scientists and engineers who worked on the 1940s' Manhattan Project in the United States. In this book, students of two countries explore the history, present, and future of their nuclear communities and discuss with fresh voices their hopes for the future.

The study began in a one-semester elective course at Hanford Middle School in Richland, Washington, where students are given an opportunity to pursue a passion and given instruction in the inquiry method of research. This project was one of several conducted by the students. Each student is expected to become an active researcher by writing a project plan, taking and organizing notes, and conducting original research. In this class, Mrs. McQuerry provides guidance to students as they select projects of interest. Students interact with practicing professionals and design projects that require them to use the skills and modes of inquiry that fit particular disciplines. The class culminates with a presentation before a committee of "experts."

In summary, learning experiences arranged by the teacher for the Curriculum of Practice may focus on an inquiry that is student generated or teacher constructed. In all cases, general methodologies, domain-specific skills and thinking skills are taught to the students and then used by students in their inquiries. The goal in writing this section is to create opportunities for students to be the scientists, sociologists, poets, artists, historians, cartographers, mythologists, and so forth and to apply the skills these professionals use to construct knowledge and to make sense of their experiences. Figure 6.6 summarizes some of the key skills of the Curriculum of Practice—including examples from habits of mind, the comprehensive skills of research and problem solving, specific skills of disciplines, and thinking skills.

Resources in the Curriculum of Practice

Students and teachers use a variety of resources to accomplish the learning goals within a Curriculum of Practice unit. Resources should appeal to a wide range of readers and their interest levels. In gathering resources for an instructional unit, educators should locate books, journals, artifacts, photographs, artwork, electronic information, community members, experts in the field, primary and secondary source documents, and methodological guides (how-to books) used by practicing professionals in a variety of disciplines. Additionally, resources may include the equipment or tools that are used by scholars in the field to conduct their research.

Pictures and slides of students completing inquiry-based projects are helpful when trying to orient students to the role that they will play in the investigation. Children's literature, such as *Tibet: Through the Red Box* (Sís, 1998) or *Starry Messenger: Galileo Galilei* (Sís, 1997), can be used to introduce students to the value of conducting research and the significance of the work that is produced by scholars and experts. Additionally, magazines, such as *Discover, Scientific American, Nature, Scholastic Magazine,* and *Consumer Reports,* can assist educators in finding interesting topics that might be turned into problem-based investigations or ideas that can be used to generate interest that may lead to student-generated projects.

Products in the Curriculum of Practice

Students will create a variety of short-term and long-term products (e.g., journals, student forums, service, performances, problem solutions, explanations, publications, performances, exhibits, and reflections) that will provide evidence of increased student understanding of the application of principles and concepts in a particular field, research procedures, new discoveries made about an area of study, and the implications and significance of their research findings. These products offer an endless array of opportunities for assessing student progress, growth over

Figure 6.6. Some Key Process Skills in the Curriculum of Practice

Time management
Organization
Decision making
Learning to learn
Quotation
Paraphrasing
Goal setting
Evaluation
Self-motivation
Critique of ideas and processes
Scholarship/scholarliness
Drawing on the known while thinking originally
Determining when to ask questions and what kind
Establishing and maintaining integrity of ideas
Having a vision versus accepting the status quo
Determining when to fight and when to relinquish
Maintaining focus without rigidity
Developing and using skills of collaboration
Developing and using skills of independence
Using specific methods and tools of research
Recognizing problems
Refining problems
Analyzing data
Reporting research findings
Seeking and using feedback

time, and adjusting student instruction in order to promote student success and technical expertise within a field of study.

While it is appropriate to select the types of products students will create, it is important that the students create products that are close approximations of the types of products that practicing professionals create in their fields. Because students are acting as real inquirers and scholars, their products address real problems and real questions and involve transformations rather than summaries of existing ideas or information. Students should be provided with opportunities to select those products that resemble the work of scholars and that best match where they are as learners.

It is also important to have students present their products to a significant audience. Audiences provide students with an opportunity to share our findings and understandings. Audiences also provide us with direct feedback from others who are interested in our work. These conversations may encourage further research. The key here is to locate authentic audiences—those who are interested in the students' work, those who might benefit from the results of the students' findings, and those who can provide expert-like evaluations that can assist students in improving upon their knowledge, understanding, ideas, working processes, and skills.

Extension Activities in the Curriculum of Practice

Inquiry-based learning activities might lead to other questions to be studied in other subject-area classes. A teacher can follow up on student-generated ideas by networking with other colleagues to provide places for these ideas to be explored. Activities created for students using the Curriculum of Practice can become interdisciplinary projects that are tied together through a universal theme, principle, or concept. For example, Mrs. McQuerry could collaborate with the science department so students can design science fair projects; a social studies teacher who might ask students to present some part of their projects or investigations for the History Day celebration; and the art and technology departments, which may decide to work with the students on the design and layout of products they create.

Further extensions can be designed to have students interact or work with researchers, college professors, or community experts who can provide methodological support and assistance to the students. It is possible for teachers to ask writers, archaeologists, sociologists, biologists, mathematicians, or community members, who have specific interests, for assistance in creating these units for their students. These professionals can help generate problem-based experiences that might be incorporated into a teacher's unit of study, provide methodological guidance in helping students learn the procedures to conduct research, to write books, to graphically illustrate important ideas, or even to provide the resources and materials that will be needed by the students to conduct their investigations.

While it is possible that these types of learning experiences are new to the students, it is also possible that this type of teaching may be new to the teacher designing or implementing this Curriculum of Practice. Seeking assistance in creating these learning experiences provides an exciting adventure for both the teacher and the students and makes teaching come alive! Seeking assistance often leads to surprising events, as it did for Mrs. Anderson, a fourth grade teacher.

Mrs. Anderson's students had just finished a unit on fables. She had invited Mr. Alvera, a university English professor, to the school to present his research on fables in other countries and how they compare with fables in our own country. In the middle of his presentation, a student named Sam raised his hand and said, "I read one of these fables to my mom and dad and when I asked them what they thought the moral of the story was, they both had a different answer. Why would this be?"

Surprised by this question, Mrs. Anderson turned to Mr. Alvera and asked him if he could respond to Sam's inquiry. After careful reflection, Mr. Alvera responded, "Sam, this is an interesting observation. I don't know if we know the answer to this question."

Sam, being persistent, replied, "Don't you think we should find out?" By this time everyone was interested in the exchange that was taking place between Sam and Mr. Alvera. Mrs. Anderson then turned to Mr. Alvera with a surprised look on her face and stated, "I don't have any idea how we would do this. Do you?"

This conversation continued during recess, with Mr. Alvera suggesting that he thought he could be of assistance in setting up this project for the students. He had some university students that he was working with in a children's literature class, and he agreed to present this idea to them at their next class meeting.

After meeting with the university students and Mrs. Anderson, Mr. Alvera arranged to have his students work with her students to design an experiment that would allow the students in her classroom to investigate the following question: Does gender play a role in how fables are interpreted? He taught the students how to set up the experiment, his students served as assistants in this project to transcribe the interviews the students had conducted with males and females after they read a selected fable out of a book, and Mrs. Anderson learned firsthand what it meant to be flexible and to follow the lead set by questions asked in the classroom. Out of this experience grew many more collaborative projects designed by Mrs. Anderson and other experts in her community.

Student Grouping in the Curriculum of Practice

Depending on student experience with inquiry-based activities, a teacher can use a variety of grouping practices within the classroom setting. Early on, teachers may feel more comfortable having all students work on one inquiry-based unit as a benchmark teaching unit. Later, small groups and individuals will learn how to establish and conduct their own inquiries. Using this incremental approach, teachers can introduce students to the experience of conducting research rather than assuming students have those skills.

In the Curriculum of Practice, students should learn how to assume the role of the professional, learning how to work independently as well as collaboratively, and to self-regulate their learning behaviors. Skills of independence, collaboration, and self-regulation must be taught. We teach for this by arranging guided independence prior to more complete independence, by ensuring that students are taught how to collaborate effectively and helped to address issues that arise when collaboration efforts are bumpy, and by helping students set goals for their work and assess their progress according to those goals.

Figure 6.7 illustrates one simple format that students can use to support their learning goals. Journals and group planning sheets can also be used to document their progress.

Teachers should use flexible grouping practices throughout the unit. Groupings should be responsive to the students' learning styles, readiness levels, and cognitive and affective development so that optimum learning can occur. In some cases, a group of students can manage the work on its own with little assistance, whereas other students need structured support and regular guidance from the classroom

Figure 6.7. Sample Student Planning Form

Student Planning Record

Name_____   Date _____

Inquiry_____   Class_____

The tasks I worked on today:

_____   _____

_____   _____

_____   _____

                Activity   Completion

Evaluation:

_____   I completed my goals.

_____   I used my time wisely.

Next time, I plan to:

_____

_____

_____

         Activity   Materials or resources I'll need

---

teacher. At some point in the unit, a teacher will need to work with the whole class to teach a methodological skill (e.g., how to generate open-ended questions for an interview or how to set up a museum-quality exhibit). At other times, some students will be comfortable with a particular skill (e.g., finding Web sites on the Internet or finding the mean of a data set), and others will need additional instruction on that skill. Sometimes, teachers will have a reason to assign student groups, and sometimes, it is ideal for students to compose group membership. Sometimes, students will work more effectively alone, and sometimes, they might need the support and partnership of peers. In all cases, students should be encouraged to support each other in their work.

Modifications Based on Learner Need, Including Ascending Intellectual Demand

Curricular experiences using the Curriculum of Practice acknowledge that students require a wide variety of assistance, reference materials, and examples to help them reach an understanding of the concepts and principles they are examining or acting on. Teachers who provide learning experiences of this nature share some common characteristics:

▶ They work in a way that mirrors experts in a discipline as they seek answers to questions in order to expand their knowledge and understanding.

▶ They are knowledgeable about their students' interests, cognitive and affective development, physical attributes, motivation, and learning styles, which helps them to plan and differentiate student learning options.

▶ They orchestrate discourse among their students to create a community of scholars who will learn from each other. Classroom environments are respectful of children's voices and encourage all students to make their learning known.

▶ At all stages of the unit, they match their actions to the particular needs of their students. At times, they will provide additional instruction, modeling, or examples for students to guide their understanding and skill. At other times, they will demand more rigorous grappling by students, deciding when and how to guide learners to new levels of sophistication in their thinking and work.

▶ They know when they don't know, yet are willing to investigate with the students to determine a method of finding out. They recognize that they, too, are becoming more comfortable with understanding how knowledge is constructed so that they can provide experiences that are rich and meaningful to their students.

▶ They recognize that on some days the learning experiences don't go as planned. They are able to revise their plans with their students and begin the process again.

As students become more expert-like, or more expert in their work with a Curriculum of Practice, teachers may need to employ strategies of ascending intellectual demand in order to ensure continuous intellectual ascent in these students—even in a curriculum as inherently rich and complex as the Curriculum of Practice. As is the case with the Core Curriculum and the Curriculum of Connections, there are some "generic" methods of increasing the challenge level for students. Those are listed in Chapter 4, Figure 4.8. Additional paths to ascending intellectual demand that are particularly relevant to the Curriculum of Practice are

Figure 6.8. Some Paths to Achieving Ascending Intellectual Demand in the Curriculum of
Practice Parallel

- Encourage students to distinguish between approaches that seem relevant in tackling authentic problems of the discipline and those that are less relevant.
- Call on students to develop a language of reflection about problems and scenarios in the field.
- Devise tasks and products that cause students to develop, through application, personal frameworks of knowledge, understanding, and skill related to the discipline.
- Have students test those frameworks through repeated field-based tasks and refine them as necessary.
- Have students compare standards of quality used by practitioners, connoisseurs, and critics in the field to standards of quality typically used in school as they relate to problem solving in that field.
- Guide students in establishing their own goals for work at what they believe to be the next steps in quality for their own growth and to assess their own work according to those standards.
- Make it possible for students to submit best-quality exemplars of their own work to experts in a field for expert-level feedback.
- Have students work on problems currently posing difficulties for experts in the discipline.
- Structure products and tasks to require students to engage in persistent, prolonged, written reflection about their own work and thinking in the field, with analysis and critique of those patterns as they evolve.
- Call on students to compare and contrast their own approaches to discipline-based dilemmas, issues, or problems with those of experts in the field.

---

provided in Figure 6.8. These generally involve students working more at an expert level rather than engaging in expert-like work.

Summary

The components of instruction that comprise the Curriculum of Practice Parallel are the same as for the other parallels, but the characteristics and emphasis vary slightly because of the teacher's desire to orchestrate experiences through which students can construct understanding in much the same way a professional constructs understanding. The ability of teachers to develop and guide such a curriculum requires a sophisticated set of judgments about the content, students, learning, and teaching. Creating a network of educators (colleagues, parents, students, and experts in the community) is one way to increase professional sophistication.

An Example of the Curriculum of Practice

Once again we revisit Lydia Janis, our fictionalized teacher, and the Civil War unit she's been constructing for her fifth graders. Here she uses the Curriculum of Practice to develop a curriculum that will extend her students understandings of the time period. Her focus will be on having her students work as practicing historians as they become acquainted with the Civil War. Although her goal is not predominately focused on absorption of facts about the time period, students will nonetheless come away with critical information about the time period as well as with a framework of understanding and a set of authentic skills.

In much the same way that biographies and autobiographies touch our lives, history can reveal compelling stories that explain how individuals lived their lives long ago. Historical accounts share with us the fears, perspectives, and experiences that change people as they live their lives during times of conflict. After reading the examples in this chapter, Lydia decided that she wanted to try writing a unit based on the idea that the students would assume the role of historians to document the lives of individuals who experienced the events during the Civil War. She carefully thought through how the Curriculum of Practice would help her in accomplishing this goal.

Increasing an Understanding of Historical Research

Prior to identifying goals for students as practitioners, Lydia called the local historical society to see if its staff could assist her in understanding how historians conduct their work and what type of skills and methods of thinking they use. Mrs. Esquith, the Director, helped her understand that historians are dependent on documents and written records that have been left behind and are often contained in special collections, libraries, or the National Archives. By drawing on such a variety of sources, historians are able to develop rich and detailed descriptions about what they are studying. These documents give historians a time perspective, which is essential in understanding and describing what happened in the past. Usually, historians like to interview individuals who have firsthand experience in what is being studied by conducting interviews or using surveys and questionnaires; however, when those people are gone, they use what artifacts they leave behind.

With Mrs. Esquith's help, Lydia was able to understand the role that she wanted her students to play during this unit; she could begin thinking about the goals of this unit; and she could begin the process of locating some of the resources that the students would use to gather their data.

Identifying the Content/Standards Goals of the Unit

Lydia next reviewed her district's curriculum framework, the textbook adopted by the school, the *National Standards for History*, and other curriculum resources.

She highlighted the standards that most closely paralleled what she wanted the curriculum unit to address.

First, she knew that she needed to engage students in reading about the time period, to interact with narrative accounts that would provide the students with an understanding of the time period through the eyes of those who lived it. She knew that her students enjoyed reading historical fiction and often remarked that the individuals in the past were courageous, faced difficult hardships, and experienced things that they would never experience in their lifetime. The latter comment was the one that she was most interested in pursuing with the students during this unit. Lydia wondered if she could design an inquiry-based unit that might help students see the relationship between their world and the world lived by those during the Civil War.

Second, she wanted to design the unit so that students would deepen their understanding of the time period accurately by using diaries, journals, photographs, and other historical documents that could provide an accurate account of what life was like during the Civil War. By having her students analyze these documents, she would create situations for them to identify various viewpoints of those whom the war affected. Using these documents would help the students compare and contrast the varying points of view, document how the war affected various lives, and realize that lives change in significant ways that help to shape a course of events that eventually affects future generations.

Her third goal was to encourage students to continually raise questions about their findings and research, to identify new questions that could lead to future research projects, and to create a climate that closely approximates that of historians and sociologists. She would teach them how to look for evidence, question the evidence, and gather and record data to answer their questions.

From this thinking, Lydia developed a set of understandings or principles that would help guide the development of her lessons. These were the ideas that she felt were enduring over time and could help her create learning experiences to assist students in constructing and deepening their own ideas about this time period. Her content/standards goals read as follows:

Students will understand that:

▶ As a nation becomes more diverse, so do the perspectives of its members.

▶ A person's point of view is influenced by cultural, social, economic, political, and religious factors.

▶ Differing viewpoints can lead to conflict.

▶ Conflict can lead to changes in the social, economic, political, or religious order.

▶ Successful historical research involves answering questions, using reliable and valid sources to answer these questions, analyzing and looking for patterns in the data, and drawing conclusions.

From this list, Lydia generated a series of questions that would be added to a list of questions that the students would generate prior to the start of her unit. These questions would guide the students' research and would make the understandings listed above more user friendly and more inquiry based for her fifth grade students.

▷ What was life like for those who lived during the Civil War?

▷ What perspectives (points of view) did people hold during this time period?

▷ Did these perspectives (points of view) ever change?

▷ How are these perspectives (points of view) different and similar?

▷ What influences these perspectives (points of view)?

▷ How did the war affect the lives of those who lived during the time?

▷ How were the experiences of these individuals similar and different?

▷ How do historians find out the answers to their questions?

▷ How do the experiences of the past affect my life?

These questions would help to initially facilitate the learning process, but Lydia would also encourage students to develop their own questions that might lead to future studies. She hoped that by interacting with the stories, documents, and diary and journal entries, students would begin to identify other questions; questions that were personally meaningful to them.

Gathering the Resources

Lydia began by developing a list of those whose lives would be studied in this unit and a preliminary list of resources that her students could use to gather information to answer their questions. She wanted to locate historical fiction, primary documents, art, magazines, newspapers, books, music, diaries, and journals. She wanted this unit to be of interest to the students, and she knew that she wanted to bring history alive by providing students with an opportunity to interact with the words, sounds, and images of real people from long ago (see Figure 6.9).

Determining the Teaching Methods, Identifying a Strategy for Designing the Learning Activities and Products, and Designing the Assessment

Lydia decided she would present a series of problem-based tasks to the students to guide their historical research. First, she would ask the students to each assume the role of a character from the Civil War time period, documenting the character's

(Text continues on page 197)

Figure 6.9. References for Lydia's Civil War Research Project in the Curriculum of Practice

Historical Fiction Books	Description
Charley Skedaddle Patricia Beatty (William Morrow, 1987) Role: Drummer Boy, Union Army	Charley Quinn, a former member of a New York City street gang, is determined to enlist as a soldier in the Union Army to avenge the death of his brother.
Jayhawker Patricia Beatty (William Morrow, 1991) Role: Abolitionist	At age twelve, Elijah Tulley has an experience that he will never forget. Radical abolitionist John Brown visits his home and blesses him and his sisters. Elijah is forever committed to abolishing slavery, and he becomes even more passionate about the cause when his father is killed while attempting to free some slaves from a Missouri plantation. He becomes a spy for the Union Army, reporting their activities to his fellow abolitionists, or Jayhawkers.
Turn Homeward, Hannalee Patricia Beatty (William Morrow, 1984) Role: Confederate	This story is based on a story of the displacement of Georgia mill workers during the Civil War. Twelve-year-old Hannalee Reed works in a Georgia textile mill. When General Sherman's troops pass through her town, they burn the mill, round up all the mill workers, and send them to work in the North. Hannalee is separated from her younger brother and her friend, but she is determined to find them and return home. She escapes from the Kentucky household where she is forced to work as a servant and sets off on a daring adventure that brings her face to face with the horrors of war.
With Every Drop of Blood James Lincoln Collier and Christopher Collier (Delacorte Press, 1994) Role: Confederate	Johnny hopes for a chance to avenge his father's death at the hands of the Yankees. When he hears about a supply convoy leaving for the Confederate capital of Richmond, Virginia, he decides to join in the effort. Before the wagons get very far, Yankee soldiers attack it, and Johnny is shocked to find himself taking orders from a young African American soldier who takes him prisoner. The friendship that forms between them makes Johnny question the point of the war as well as his own beliefs about African Americans.
Lincoln: A Photobiography Russell Freedman (Clarion Books, 1987) Role: President	This is a detailed and balanced account of the life and career of Abraham Lincoln. Illustrated with a wealth of photographs and prints, the biography gives readers a close look at the complex and fascinating man who led the nation through one of its darkest hours.
Across Five Aprils Irene Hunt (Follett Press, 1964) Role: Both Perspectives	Nine-year-old Jethro, who lives in southern Illinois, has an idealized view of war based on stories from history books about dramatic battles and their glorious heroes. When the Civil War breaks out, however, painfully dividing his family as it divides North and South, Jeth must confront the many confusing and horrifying realities of war. At age 10, his father ill and his older brothers off fighting in the war, Jeth becomes the man of the household. *Across Five Aprils* spans the four long years of the war, during which Jethro is transformed from a boy into a young man.

(Continued)

Figure 6.9. Continued

Historical Fiction Books	Description
Escape from Slavery: The Boyhood of Frederick Douglass in His Own Words Michael McCurdy, Editor, (Alfred A. Knopf, 1994) Role: Abolitionist	Skillfully selected excerpts from Frederick Douglass's autobiography paint a vivid portrait of the great abolitionist. The story of Douglass's childhood provides a close look at slavery from the perspective of the enslaved, and the account of his escape and subsequent career is both dramatic and inspirational.
The Story of Booker T. Washington Patricia and Fred McKissack (Children's Press, 1991) Role: Slave	This book provides a brief overview of the life of Booker T. Washington, with many photographs and other illustrations.
The Boys' War Jim Murphy (Clarion Books, 1990) Role: Confederate and Union Soldiers	Many of the soldiers who fought on both sides of the war were not men but children. Jim Murphy's book is an account of the war from the perspective of these young soldiers. It contains many quotations from the boys' journals and letters as well as photographs of the soldiers and the battlegrounds where they fought and died. The book captures their firsthand experiences of war, from the thrill of enlistment through the horrible reality of combat.
Shades of Gray Carolyn Reeder (Macmillan, 1989) Role: Both Perspectives	The war has left 12-year-old Will Page without any immediate family: his father and brother were killed by the Yankees; his sisters died of an epidemic spread from a Union encampment near his Virginia home; and his mother died of grief over these losses. Will reluctantly goes to live with his Uncle Jed and his family, who refuse to fight for the Confederate Army. With his anger directed toward the Union Army, Will comes to understand that the moral issues involved in the decision to fight were not as clear-cut as he thought and that good people can have honest disagreements.
Harriet Tubman M.W. Taylor (Chelsea House Publishers,1991) Role: Abolitionists	Part of the Black Americans of Achievement series, this biography tells the incredible life story of the architect of the Underground Railroad, which helped hundreds of slaves make their way to freedom. The text is augmented with many photographs and drawings that bring the text to life.
Up From Slavery Booker T. Washington (Doubleday, 1963) Role: Slave and Political Activist	The great political activist and educator tells the story of his life in his own words. Washington was born into slavery and freed under the Emancipation Proclamation, after which he devoted his life to helping African Americans make a place for themselves in the economy and society of the United States. The full text of *Up From Slavery* is also available online.

Till Victory Is Won: Black Soldiers in the Civil War Zak Mettger (E. P. Dutton, 1984) Role: African American Soldiers	The story of African Americans and their involvement in the Civil War. Initially, in 1861, they were not allowed to fight. Eventually, they would gain the right to fight, and this book tells of their struggles and the stunning contributions they made on the battlefields as soldiers and on the waters as sailors. The book is based on firsthand accounts, with photographs and drawings that illustrate how blacks influenced the outcome of the war and the decades that followed.
Soldier's Heart Gary Paulsen (Bantam Books, 1998) Role: Union	A story of a 15-year-old boy who enlists in the Minnesota Volunteers not as a flag bearer or drummer, as many young boys did; Charley lied about his age and took on the combat role. Charley isn't concerned with freeing the slaves, he just wants to teach those Rebels a lesson for daring to break up the Union.
For Home and Country: A Civil War Scrapbook Norman and Angel Bolotin (Lodestar Books, 1994) Role: All	Visual information that concentrates on the social effects of war.

Historical Documents

The American Civil War Homepage	Images of the wartime, biographies, music, women in the Civil War, newspapers, and some images of war time.
National Archives and Records Administration (NARA)	This site contains reproducible copies of primary documents from the holdings of the National Archives of the United States.
Library of Congress: American Memory http://memory.loc.gov/amme m/cwphtml/cwphome.html	This site contains photographs and historical documents that can be used by the students to locate information about the Civil War and other time periods.

perspectives from the historical fiction books. They would be asked also to record the feelings, images, and words that help identify what these perspectives were and how these perspectives changed throughout the story. Second, they would be asked to gather as much information as possible about the lives of these characters or individuals like them by using historical references, such as photographs, diary entries, journals, music, and any other resources they could find in the library or on the Internet. These references would be used to provide evidence of these perspectives and to document changes to support their original findings gathered from their text.

Third, Lydia identified the types of skills and methodologies required to assist the students in analyzing these documents, recording notes, and drawing conclusions about these data. These skills and methodologies would be the focus of some of her lessons. These included explaining the steps of historical research, generating research questions, taking notes, distinguishing between primary and secondary sources, establishing the validity and reliability of sources, analyzing print and nonprint sources, and drawing conclusions from data. She would also help them work through the steps of research, modifying assignments for students who needed more support or who needed more challenge. Lydia created a chart to help her students work through the research process (see Figure 6.10). They often referred to this chart to keep them on track during the research process.

Then Lydia decided to create a contract (see Figure 6.11) that would outline the procedures for student investigations during their study. She found this contract useful—all the students could refer to it throughout the study. Lydia would encourage students working at a high level of knowledge and independence to develop their own work plans rather than following the one prescribed in the contract.

The nature of Lydia's learning contract for the students actually addresses several key curricular components. The contract not only includes a number of learning activities (e.g., reading the historical novel and gathering data on the character they are developing) but also includes short-term products that give evidence of student understanding (e.g., the double-sided notebook entries and completed data sheets). These short-term products are also assessment vehicles for Lydia as she tracks student understanding and growth throughout the contract period. In addition, the rubric in the contract guides both students and their teacher in assessing progress during the contract period and assessing the quality of the students' culminating products. In fact, completion of Items 8 and 9 on the contract results in culminating products that show students' grasp of essential understandings in the unit as well as their skill in working like historians. This latter emphasis is, of course, a central goal for the Curriculum of Practice Parallel.

Developing Extension Activities

Lydia knew it would take the students from three to four weeks to complete this unit of study. She would build some of the teaching and learning activities into her reading and writing classes so that she could address two sets of standards simultaneously. This would provide the necessary time to explore this unit in depth.

To extend the lessons, numerous people were identified to assist her in helping the students become better researchers. With the help of a parent volunteer, Lydia was able to locate a Civil War buff in the community who helped her teach the students how to analyze historical documents. She also found a museum director who taught the students how to analyze historical photographs. Numerous parent volunteers agreed to assist her students in their work, and Lydia welcomed them into the learning community. The most exciting individual she found was Jon Botter, the graphic artist at her local newspaper. He was glad to help the students study political cartoons. Since Lydia had found many of these cartoons on the Internet, Jon was

(Text continued on page 205)

Figure 6.10. Research Steps for Lydia's Students

Research Steps

Define the Research Problem
Begin with a problem that is puzzling. A puzzle is not just a lack of information but a gap in our understanding. You need to ask: What is the problem that we are investigating?

Review the Evidence
Review the available evidence in the field. Researchers need to sift through whatever related research exists to see to see how useful it is for their purpose. You need to ask: What have others found out about this problem or topic that might help me understand what I need to study?

Make the Problem Precise
Researchers try to clarify the problem they are studying. Sometimes, they ask questions in order to reach a better understanding of the thing that they are studying. At other times, they develop hypotheses or educated guesses that can be written in such a way that the material gathered will provide evidence either supporting or disproving it. You need to ask: What new questions or hunches do I have that need to be investigated?

Work Out a Design
As researchers, we need to decide how we are going to collect data. In some cases, we will use surveys, interviews, questionnaires, document analysis, and observations. At other times, we will set up experimental research studies. You need to ask: What methods can I use to investigate my questions or to test my hypotheses?

Carry Out the Research
At this point, we will be collecting and recording data, contacting people to help us with our research, and solving some of the unforeseen difficulties that can easily come up as we conduct our study. You need to ask: What do I need to do first? How am I doing on my research? Have I planned accordingly? Do I need to gather other information?

Analyze the Results
Based on the evidence you have gathered, you will identify patterns and themes in your research. You need to ask: What have I found out in my research?

Report the Findings
You will need to decide how to report your data. You will need to choose a product to help you share this information with an audience and to share with them the new questions that you have about this topic. You need to ask: What is the significance of my work? How do these findings relate to my questions?

Figure 6.11. Civil War Contract

Civil War Contract

Have you ever wondered what it would be like to have lived during the Civil War? In the next few weeks, you and your teammates will be trying to accurately portray what this time period was like by becoming historical researchers. With your partners, you will assume the role of an individual who lived during this time. You will read a historical fiction book to understand how it must have felt to be alive during this time period. In order to complete this project you will need to ask yourself some questions, read the text to answer the questions that we will generate together, and document the feelings, perspectives, and changes that occur for your characters over time. If you want to know how it felt to be part of those events, you will also need to read the diaries, letters, and other artifacts that people who are like them left behind.

1. **Determine Your Role:**
   Abolitionist
   Slave
   Confederate Soldier
   Union Soldier
   Black Soldier
   Woman in the War
   Child in the War
   President

2. **Generate Questions to Guide Your Research**

You might consider questions like these:

- What was life like for those who lived during the Civil War?
- What perspectives (points of view) did people hold during this time period?
- Did these perspectives (points of view) ever change?
- How are these perspectives different and similar?
- What influenced these perspectives (points of view)?
- How did the war affect the lives of those who lived during the time?
- How were the experiences of these individuals similar and different?
- How do historians find out the answers to their questions?
- How do the experiences of the past affect my life?

3. **Read a Historical Fiction Book**

You can select from some of the books that I have gathered for you or use others after we visit the library. Remember to select one that is appropriate for you as a reader. The important thing is that you feel comfortable reading it and that it provides you with a way to study the type of individual you are investigating.

4. Record the Data

You will use your notebook to record the answers to your questions. You can list your questions on the left-hand side of the notebook, and on the right-hand side of the notebook, you can record the answers to your questions that you find in your book. You will want to record pictures, images, your thoughts, and evidence from your book to support these answers. Good historians record what they are thinking, too, so feel free to capture your own thoughts and questions as you read.

Your research notebook will look like this:

Left-Hand Side

What was life like for my character?

Right-Hand Side

Will lived on a farm in Illinois. It looked like....

5. Gather Evidence From Historical Documents

You will need to locate historical documents to analyze to see if your perceptions of this time period are accurate. Use the Internet and any other sources to answer your questions. You will need to use many data sheets to help you record your findings.

Data Recording Sheet Questions	What You Found Out
Who wrote this document?	
Who's speaking in this document?	
What is the source?	
When was the information recorded?	
What kind of document is this? (diary, journal, poetry, government document, photograph)	
What is the document about?	
What did this document help you to find out?	

(Continued)

Figure 6.11. Continued

6. Analyze the Results of Your Findings

Now it is time to analyze your findings. Using the information that you have gathered, you will need to look for some patterns in your data. You will need to ask yourself some tough questions about your data and record these ideas in your journal. Do you see any patterns with respect to what your character's life was like? What were your character's viewpoints of the war? Did these viewpoints change over time? What influenced these changes?

7. Compare Your Findings to Other Findings

Sit with another group of students in your class who studied other individuals during the Civil War. Compare your findings with their findings. Use a Venn diagram to compare the similarities and differences between your two groups.

8. Report Your Findings

Decide how to report these findings to other people. The results of your hard work need to be shared with an audience so that they can learn from you. Will you write an article for publication? Will you share this information by creating a play or perhaps orally presenting it in the form of a documentary? Use the list of products to guide your creation.

9. Apply What You Have Learned to Your Life

It is often said that events in the past change future generations and the lives they lead. What does this mean? You will work with other students in the class to decide what this means. Your group will be made up of students in all the roles that were investigated during this study. Look in magazines and newspapers and think about your own life, then ask yourself these questions: Is there evidence today that our lives are different because of the Civil War? Are the conditions of our lives so different from the conditions of the lives of those who came before us? Why do people change? How do people change? Did they have the same concerns? Did they worry about similar things? What changes took place in their lives that compare to changes in your lives?

   You will need to think about these questions and any others that our class generates. Your group is responsible for investigating this idea. Your group will determine how best to show the meaning behind this statement.

10. Assess Your Learning Rubric for Conducting the Historical Research Study

During your study, we will use a rubric to modify or make changes to your research study so that you can continue to improve it along the way. At times, I will ask you to complete a self-evaluation of the work you are doing, and at other times, we will use the rubric on the next page to guide the quality of your work.

*Student Researcher:*_____

Attributes	The Distinguished	Apprentices	Novices
Research Questions	Use all of the questions to guide their research; develops new questions to guide the research	Use most of the questions that they found interesting and testable; don't develop any new questions to research	Use a few questions to guide the study; don't develop any new questions to explore
Gathering the Data	Use a variety of resources; developed an accurate and extensive bibliography; use sophisticated data gathering methods to further explore their ideas	Use many resources; developed an adequate bibliography; try to revise their study but experienced difficulty in carrying out the research	Use a few resources; used sources to find information more than to shape thinking
Recording the Data	Keep complete and accurate records, including supplementary data, in their notebooks and on data sheets	Keep complete and accurate records in their notebooks	Some records are complete and some partially complete in notebooks and on data sheets
Analyzing the Data	Are skilled at using descriptive research methods to identify themes and make inferences	Are developing a use of descriptive research methods to find themes and make inferences	Show early attempts at using descriptive research to find themes and make inferences
Interpreting Findings	Explain data; accurate, logical explanations	Explain data; accurate, logical explanations	Make some explanations of data
	Sophisticated and thorough interpretation of events through perspective of those living in that setting. Interpretations and explanations are supported by the data	In-depth interpretation of events through perspective of those living in that setting	Show basic interpretation of historical events through perspective of those living in that setting

(Continued)

Figure 6.11. Continued

Attributes	The Distinguished	Apprentices	Novices
Reporting the Findings	Address most of the questions explored. Inferences are explained using the data found. Use skills of evaluation as well as synthesis and analysis. Support claims with clear research evidence from valid sources.	Address some of the questions explored. Some inferences made, although minor errors may exist. Comprehension on an inferential level, and the key skills are analysis and synthesis. Support some claims with research evidence.	Address a few questions explored. A few inferences are made. Answers deal with material on a concrete, literal level
Significance of the Findings	Make full meaning of the information and incorporate it into their own life by generating examples	Make partial meaning of the information and incorporate it into their own life by generating examples	Make some meaning of the information but do not incorporate it into their own life by generating examples
Conceptual Understanding	Identify relationships between the concepts of change and perspective that are sophisticated. Could identify causal relationships between the two concepts by providing examples. Move beyond answering the main question(s) identified for the research study.	Identify relationships that mostly focus on the answers to the main question(s) identified for the research study. Relationships that are explained are descriptive only.	Identify a few relationships that have some connection to the questions.
Products	The performance or product is highly effective. The ideas are presented in an engaging, polished, clear, and thorough manner. The performance or product is developed with an audience in mind.	The performance or product is effective. The ideas are presented in a clear and thorough manner, showing awareness of the audience.	The performance or product is complete, providing some evidence of planning, practice, and consideration of audience.

able to use some of them to help the students take some of the cartoonists' ideas and create cartoons that depicted the time period.

She also found out that some of her students had generated other interesting questions to explore during this unit. These questions were integrated into the unit so that the students could conduct follow-up research based on their new inquiries.

Planning for Student Grouping

By having the students work in groups based on their interests, the students would support each other, as real-world team members often do when they are grouped based on shared interest. Lydia also helped the students know the work that they were doing was meaningful. In fact, she would have the students begin to consider how their work might be shared with a wider audience. She prepared carefully, yet created an environment where dialogue was stressed, questioning was promoted, reworking plans was a common procedure of the day, and very important work would be shared and celebrated in the end. This resulted in a variety of student groups in addition to the interest-based investigations. Often, students worked alone on their contracts. At times, they met in small groups with the teacher to fine-tune research skills or to talk about formats for their culminating products. Sometimes, students elected to attend these small-group coaching sessions, but sometimes, they were asked by the teacher to come to one or more of the sessions. Often during the unit, students asked a peer to help them with locating resources, interpreting materials, or editing their work. Of course, there were also times when the teacher led the whole class in direct instruction, sharing information, or troubleshooting for their contract work.

Groupings had a "fluid" feel during the unit, with students reconfiguring themselves in a variety of ways to ensure success with their activities and products. In addition, the teacher varied groupings in response to her own evolving sense of student interests and readiness levels.

Modifications in Response to Student Need, Including Ascending Intellectual Demand

There were many considerations that Lydia thought through before she started this unit. She decided that the format of designing the contract would assist her in providing an environment where she could attend to the differences in her students. She could use multiple texts to support the varying reading levels of the students. The contract was purposefully designed to allow some students to be guided step-by-step through the process while more confident learners, who loved the complexity of working on many tasks at once, could move at their own pace and in a sequence they found comfortable.

Lydia knew there were some students for whom the research project needed to be modified to provide a greater level of challenge. Depending on student familiarity with research, it was possible to enable these students to complete this project differently. She brainstormed a list of options that would allow some students to move into more complex types of research that would help them escalate their learning. She considered several options for her students, knowing that her ultimate goal was to teach students how to work much like professionals in the field and to function as scholars. Opportunities for increased intellectual demand for these advanced students include the following:

1. Interview someone who is an expert in history or sociology to identify problems or questions that need to be explored in these disciplines. After you have met with them, identify a new research topic that might be of interest to you. You will need to complete a management plan that articulates your idea, develop a set of research questions, gather the resources, and begin to identify how to analyze the data. (Students could then plan their own studies and, with the assistance of a mentor, develop projects that more approximate their readiness level.) (Identifying relevant and original research; problem finding; developing their own standards of quality, and assessing their work according to those standards)

2. Learn how to use surveys, conduct oral histories and interviews, and develop questionnaires to assist you in your research. Use these methods of research to research a question that you find thought provoking. (Learning advanced research skills; distinguishing between more relevant and less relevant approaches to addressing problems)

3. Submit your research findings to experts in the field so that you can receive some feedback. Use this feedback to make improvements in your research. You can also submit your research for publication. (Seeking feedback from experts to refine their research)

4. Locate experts who are willing to have you become part of a study in an area of mutual interest. (Escalating their involvement in the field)

5. Network with community businesses to conduct original research for them. Perhaps the museum needs someone to collect oral histories, interview older people, or even develop exhibits for their displays. (Identifying problems; planning research; identifying solutions)

6. Compare your findings with others in the field. Collaborate on ways to work together on a project. Design a telecollaborative project. (Persistent and ongoing reflection about their own work as compared to others; identifying other issues that need to be explored)

7. Locate and use advanced research documents, books, and articles in your research. (Advancing the complexity of the research process)

8. Read original research written by experts to advance your knowledge of a particular field. (Learning the standards of quality in the field; understanding how research is critiqued)

9. Manage your own research study, determine a schedule for your work, and plan accordingly. (Guiding their own research agenda; learning how to self-regulate; setting priorities)

10. Identify student-relevant problems that need to be solved. Use these problems to design a research project that you find interesting. (Problem-finding; relevance of research to self)

Looking Back and Ahead

The Curriculum of Practice Parallel is derived from and extends the Core Curriculum. Its main purpose is to help students function with increasing skill and confidence as professionals in a field would function. It exists for the purpose of promoting students' expertise as practitioners of the discipline. Therefore, its goals focus on the teaching of those specific research skills that will assist learners in identifying problems; generating questions; using methods and techniques to gather, document, and analyze data; reaching conclusions; creating meaningful products that are like those produced in the field; and sharing the findings with authentic audiences.

More important, the Curriculum of Practice assists students in moving core knowledge into a new level of abstraction and application. It deepens understanding by asking students to test ideas in new situations, identify patterns or relationships that exist between and among concepts, and elaborate on these experiences by comparing old ideas with new ones. The type of understanding developed in the Curriculum of Practice is one that enables students to use knowledge flexibly or in new ways. By using the skills and methods of the practitioner, a student should be able to demonstrate new levels of understanding, because it is through the use of these skills that new understanding will emerge.

In its relation to the Curriculum of Connections, the Curriculum of Practice assists students in making connections in a scholarly manner. The tools and techniques that are used by the students can assist them in accurately testing the strength of these connections in real life. Many connections can be further developed by using data analysis techniques to identify the validity of these connections, the limit to these connections, and the likelihood that the same connections can be applied to all situations.

The relationship between the Curriculum of Practice and the Curriculum of Identity is apparent. As adults we want our children to have lives that are personally meaningful. Our hope is that they can fill their lives pursuing fields of study that match who they are in disposition, philosophy, character, and interest. The Curriculum of Practice creates contexts in which to practice and/or study these roles in order to find out if certain disciplines match who the student is as an individual.

The relationship between and among all the parallels in the Parallel Curriculum Model facilitates an integrated and multidimensional approach to understanding a discipline. One approach is not more important than the other. Each may serve a different purpose, but in combination they provide learners with a more comprehensive understanding of how a discipline relates to their lives. In fact, the Curriculum of Identity explored in Chapter 7 has a particular and unique focus on helping young learners use the disciplines they study to learn not only about those disciplines but about themselves as well.

7

The Curriculum of

Identity Parallel

Lydia Janis was struck by the knowledge of a particular student in her fifth grade class. His name was Jacob, and whenever she talked about wars in class, Jacob displayed an unusual storehouse of information about battles, weapons and arms, the people involved with the war effort, and the historical context. She was surprised when, during the unit on the American Revolution, he said that guerilla tactics were used by the Colonists, that the tactics had been used and refined by Native Americans, and that the Colonists' adopted warfare tactics helped them to win the Revolutionary War. She recalled vividly Jacob's comments about this early American war. "The Battle of Lexington was particularly deadly for the redcoats because Minutemen ambushed them on Lexington Road. The Minutemen hid behind walls, hedges, and trees and picked off the redcoats with their muskets," he said in a matter-of-fact tone one day in class during a discussion of Paul Revere's ride.

Lydia wondered about Jacob and his flourishing interest in war and history. She wondered where it came from, who nurtured it, and what he would grow up to be. She envisioned him as a professor of history or perhaps an author. She found herself wondering, too, about what other experiences this young boy would have in school that might lead him to become a history scholar. In fact, she wondered how school-related experiences contributed to the development of all children's abilities and talents.

Equally important, she realized that none of her previous standards and objectives dealt with the issues of student identity. Where, she wondered, did these important pieces fit into her curriculum? She knew that there must be more layers of possibility in her curriculum than even the facts, concepts, principles, and skills covered in the other parallels. "Could the knowledge objectives alone "trigger" the development of children's abilities and talents?" she pondered to herself.

It was at this moment that Lydia began another journey. In some ways, it was similar to the journeys that she had traveled while remodeling her Civil War unit: highlighting the key concepts and principles about the Civil War for the Core Curriculum Parallel; taking time to help her students see connections across disciplines, cultures, and time in the Curriculum of Connections Parallel; and planning how to incorporate the skills and methodology of the historian into her unit in the Curriculum of Practice Parallel.

Yet she knew this journey would take her down a different road because she was no longer dealing only with knowledge and skills previously covered. The things Lydia was thinking about now were more associated with students' likes and dislikes, interests, abilities, attitudes, values, and ways of working. She remembered a graduate course she had taken many years ago that addressed Bloom's taxonomy. David Krathwhol had worked with Bloom to create an accompanying volume to the well-known *Taxonomy of Educational Objectives: Cognitive Domain* (Bloom et al., 1956). This second volume considered an affective taxonomy (Krathwohl, Bloom, & Masia, 1964). She also remembered that *Connecticut's Common Core of Teaching* (Connecticut State Department of Education, 1999) spoke directly to the critical need for teachers to get to know their students and how they learn. Most recently, Lydia recalled reading *Understanding by Design* (Wiggins & McTighe, 1998), in which the authors alluded to the importance of self-knowledge.

"What an intriguing way to think about curriculum," Lydia mused to herself. "This is one of the first times that I have started to think about my curriculum by thinking about the strengths my students bring to classroom . . . their learning strengths: interests, abilities, how they like to learn, how they like to express themselves." She thought back to Jacob, her history buff. "Maybe this journey will help me to understand how I can help him and others understand themselves better by looking at the work of historians."

This chapter is arranged in a format similar to those preceding it. It contains: (1) a definition of the Curriculum of Identity, (2) a rationale for using this approach for curriculum development, (3) a description of characteristics for each of the curriculum components within the Curriculum of Identity Parallel, (4) an example of developing a Curriculum of Practice, (5) techniques for modifying the components of the Curriculum of Identity based on learner need—including provisions for ascending intellectual demand, and (6) an explanation of the relationship of this framework to the other three curriculum parallels described in prior chapters.

What Does Identity Mean in the Curriculum of Identity?

Of all the curriculum approaches described in this book, the Curriculum of Identity Parallel is likely the one least familiar to readers. Like the other parallels in the Parallel Curriculum Model, the Curriculum of Identity Parallel is a lens through which educators can view the curriculum design process. The focus for this parallel, however, is different because students are at the heart of this curriculum design process. They are at the center because the intent of this parallel is to help students find themselves—their identity—in and through curriculum.

Figure 7.1. A Metaphor for the Curriculum of Identity

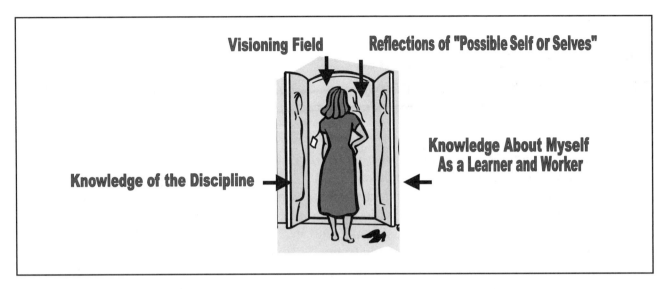

It is helpful to think about the Curriculum of Identity as a three-way mirror that continually provides different kinds of "reflective" feedback to the student (see Figure 7.1).

Of course, the mirror is a metaphor for the feedback provided by teachers, teaching and learning activities, experts in the targeted field, as well as the student him- or herself. One side of the mirror, titled Knowledge of the Discipline, provides the student with feedback about his or her knowledge in a targeted field of study. The other side panel of the mirror, called Knowledge About Myself As a Learner and Worker, provides the student with a different perspective: reflection and feedback about his or her abilities, preferred ways to communicate, learning and working preferences, and goals as they relate to those required of practicing professionals in the field.

The center panel of the three-way mirror, the front or forward-facing panel, is the Visioning Field. It is the mirror through which the student assesses the "degree of fit" between her- or himself and the discipline, both now and in the future. Using the composite image reflected in the center panel—derived from both side panels—the student perceives possibilities in the center panel and uses the Reflections of Possible Self or Selves in the center section of the mirror to make continual adjustments in his or her life course. The student modifies his or her course according to answers to many questions such as, for example, "Do I like what I am learning? Who are the professionals who use this information in their daily lives? Would I want to become like these professionals?" Depending on the answers to these questions and many others like them, a student will be either satisfied and continue with his or her original orientation or unsatisfied with the fit and make modifications to his or her life course. Naturally, the depth of students' insights will vary by developmental stages, as will any accompanying changes in career paths. Yet even young children express facets of their identity. They have unmistakable interests, express likes and dislikes, and, when left to their own devices, engage visibly in goal-oriented activities.

Why Should We Be Concerned About a Student's Identity?

Ever since the human race began, its members have been trying to answer the questions "Who am I? What is my purpose? How do I come to understand myself and my role in the world?" Research and theories put forth in the past century are testimony to the importance of identity as a factor in the learning process. Maslow (1970) suggests that the highest human need is self-actualization. Self-actualization, he proposes, is based on the intrinsic motivation that is derived from learning. Csikszentmihalyi (1990) describes the trancelike quality of those deeply involved in optimal learning. Such experiences, he reports, provide a sense of discovery and a sense that the person involved is transported to a new reality. It pushes the person to higher levels of performance and consciousness. In fact, such experiences transform the self by making it more complex. The growth of self, he says, is the key to this sort of absorption in learning (Csikszentmihalyi, 1990). Thus both Maslow and Csikszentmihalyi see a direct link between the quality of learning experiences and the transformational power they hold for the learner.

Recent knowledge about the brain gives convincing evidence for the need to connect learning with an individual's emotions, a facet of identity. According to work by Jensen (1998), we learn more effectively and efficiently when learning is associated with personal feelings: "Emotions drive the threesome of attention, meaning, and memory. The things that we orchestrate to engage emotions in a productive way will do 'triple duty' to capture all three" (p. 94). In order to understand who we are, we need to understand critical components of ourselves as learners and workers: our likes and dislikes for particular phenomena, for example, as well as our values.

Finally, the literature on learning-style differences is replete with recommendations to provide students with opportunities to learn in their preferred modes of learning. This literature suggests that students learn more effectively and perform more capably when they are allowed to learn and demonstrate their learning in preferred modes.

Thus a large body of literature and research exists about identity and how it is formed across the life span. Scholars and researchers continue to find critical links between identity, identity formation, and learning (see Figure 7.2). Specifically, learning is enhanced when it takes into consideration aspects of a student's identity: interests, values, preferred way of communicating, personal goals or life mission, envisioned contribution made to a field or discipline, and so forth. Enhanced learning may lead to increasing levels of intrinsic motivation, the forerunner of self-actualization. In turn, intrinsic motivation fuels learning, and the cycle continues. Put simply, the Curriculum of Identity holds promise for society at large. With proper attention to nurturing students' identities through curriculum and instruc-

Figure 7.2: Identity and Learning

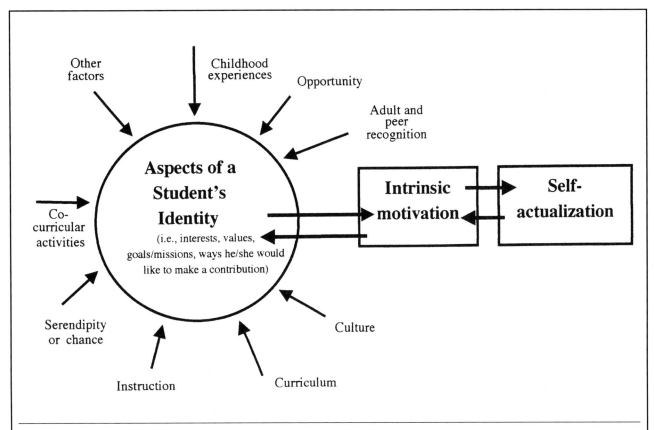

tion, teachers may be able to assist more students to lead creatively productive and satisfying lives while they learn and find meaning in the fundamental information, ideas, and skills of a discipline.

Beyond the clear benefit that the Curriculum of Identity Parallel holds for society at large, it also directly benefits teachers and students. It benefits teachers because it:

1. Reminds us that the focus of our work is students, who share with us space and opportunity to learn during critical, formative periods of time in their lives
2. Makes teaching more enjoyable as we get to know students personally
3. Provides specific techniques for learning about the identity of individual students
4. Illuminates critical learning differences among students
5. Pinpoints where teachers need to make adjustments in the curriculum and instruction to accommodate those learning differences
6. Lessens the likelihood of the one-size-fits-all curriculum
7. Helps make student learning more efficient and effective

The Curriculum of Identity benefits students because it:

1. Encourages exploration and mastery of required content in a highly motivating context
2. Decreases anonymity
3. Reduces student alienation
4. Encourages a student's systematic examination of and reflection on his or her learning strengths (e.g., abilities, interests, learning-style preferences, expression style preferences)
5. Engenders opportunities for a student to think about the fit between his or her learning strengths and all aspects of a discipline, including cognitive aspects as well the day-to-day life of practicing professionals, their long-term goals, the sacrifices, commitments, responsibilities, and contributions that are required
6. Illuminates student progress and development in both the affective and the cognitive realm
7. Highlights student growth areas; targets possible "next steps" in the journey toward creative productivity in a field
8. Clarifies for a student, over time and at increasing levels of specificity, the degree of "fit" between his or her learning and work profile and the targeted field or domain
9. Informs decision making
10. Increases the likelihood of creative productivity across the life span

Figure 7.3 lists some of the focusing questions that guide both teacher and student work in the Curriculum of Identity. It is through pursuit of answers to these questions that curriculum helps students come to understand themselves as they study a particular discipline.

What Are the Key Features and Characteristics of Curriculum Components Within the Curriculum of Identity?

The components of the Curriculum of Identity are the same that underlie each of the other curricula in the Parallel Curriculum Model. The Curriculum of Identity has a different look, however, because in the design process, the teacher emphasizes some components more than others and modifies aspects of components in order to accomplish the goals and purposes of this particular parallel. Each of the components is discussed on the following pages. Readers may wish to use Figure 7.4 to support their learning about the components of the Curriculum of Identity. This visual representation can be used as a graphic organizer for this next section of the chapter.

Figure 7.3. Some Focusing Questions of the Curriculum of Identity

- What do practitioners and contributors in this discipline think about?
- To what degree is this familiar, surprising, and/or intriguing to me?
- When I am intrigued by an idea, what do I gain from that, give as a result of that, and what difference does it make?
- How do people in this discipline think and work?
- In what ways do those processes seem familiar, surprising, and/or intriguing to me?
- What are the problems and issues on which practitioners and contributors in this discipline spend their lives?
- To what degree are those intriguing to me?
- What is the range of vocational and avocational possibilities in this discipline?
- In which ones can I see myself working?
- What difficulties do practitioners and contributors in this discipline encounter?
- How have they coped with the difficulties?
- How do I think I would cope with them?
- What are the ethical principles at the core of the discipline?
- How are those like and unlike my ethics?
- Who have been the "heroes" of the evolving discipline?
- What are the attributes of the "heroes"?
- What do I learn about myself by studying them?
- Who have been the "villains" of the evolving discipline?
- What are the attributes of the "villains"?
- What do I learn about myself by studying about them?
- How do people in this discipline handle ambiguity, uncertainty, persistence, failure, success, collaboration, compromise?
- How do I handle those things?
- What is the wisdom this discipline has contributed to the world?
- How has that affected me?
- To what degree can I see myself contributing to that wisdom?
- How might I shape the discipline over time?
- How might it shape me?

1. Content/Standards in the Curriculum of Identity

While most states now have standards for students in the disciplines, we do not have the same kind of well designed, coherent documents that set forth expectations for identity formation among young people. We do, however, have some guidance from documents such as the Secretary's Commission on Achieving Necessary Skills Report (SCANS Report) (U.S. Department of Labor, 1992), emerging documents

(Text continued on page 219)

Figure 7.4. Curriculum Components of the Curriculum of Identity

Component	Modification Techniques
Content/ Standards	• Determine the concepts, principles, skills, methodologies, and dispositions (e.g., interests, attitudes, beliefs, and expression style preferences) of practicing professionals in the discipline you will teach. • Consider objectives from the Secretary's Commission on Achieving Necessary Skills (SCANS) Report, which address essential workplace skills. • Target the concepts, principles, skills, methodologies, and dispositions from the world of the practicing professionals that best match the goals and purposes of the curriculum unit. • Work with students to gather and analyze data from their learning and work profiles. Create charts that display the students' learning and work profiles. Identify patterns and trends in the class profile. Make note of individual profiles as well. • Make appropriate accommodations in the unit to address patterns in students' learning and work profiles (e.g., address students' interests, encourage students' opportunities to work in their preferred learning or expression style) and to reflect consistently on what they learn about themselves through their work.
Assessment	• Create longitudinal rubrics to identify the stages of talent development in students in a variety of content areas. Use the rubric to note the evolution of student abilities in the classroom, determine where each student is on the novice to expert continuum, and decide on strategies that can be used to guide the student to the next level of proficiency. • Utilize assessment formats that require student reflection (e.g., goal statements, reflective essays, longitudinal portfolios, journals, and personal discoveries). • Provide for choice in assessment tasks. • Provide students with time to document and analyze their own learning and work profile over time and identify emerging patterns and trends. • Ensure systematic opportunities for students to reflect upon their past, present, and future selves. • Share with parents or a significant adult where each child is in his or her development. Explore with them the ways that they can contribute to development of student interests and abilities at home.
Introduction	• Provide students with a graphic organizer of the all fields within a discipline so that they can visualize the range of work done by practitioners within a discipline. • Share with students an array of products that professionals in the discipline produce (e.g., in history: fiction and nonfiction books, newspaper articles, photographs, timelines, maps, videos, charts, journals, letters, and telegrams).

Introduction	• Read aloud to students about famous and infamous people who have contributed to the field (e.g., *The Lighthouse Keeper's Daughter* by Arielle North Olsen; *Eleanor* by Barbara Cooney). Books that portray the famous people at the approximate age of the students are especially powerful.
	• Introduce a timeline of important turning points in the discipline that includes the names and contributions of eminent people of both genders and a variety of cultures within the field. Seek students' answers to questions such as: What did it take to become this person? What might he or she have been like as a fifth grader? In what ways am I like this famous person when he or she was my age? In what ways am I different? What parts of this person's work would interest me? What parts would I not enjoy?
	• Brainstorm personal characteristics of practicing professionals within the field both now and at earlier ages. Call upon students to compare their own interests and abilities to those of practicing professionals.
	• Share revealing audio-clips, segments of documentaries, and newspaper articles about important moments and the people who shaped those moments.
Teaching Methods	• Generate questions for students' written reflection and discussion throughout the unit to assist students in thinking about the knowledge that practitioners in the field use, problems they address, ways they work, personality traits, career development, personal and work goals, and so forth and what students can learn about themselves through examining these elements.
	• Use independent investigations to provide students opportunity to study research on, contributions of, and working modes in the discipline.
	• Use shadowing experiences and mentorships to provide students with firsthand opportunities to learn about the day-to-day routines, values, and beliefs of professionals in the field.
	• Use problem-based learning to enhance students' awareness of problem-solving abilities employed in the field.
	• Use simulations to engage students in reflecting on the issues and problems of the discipline.
	• Use visualization techniques to assist students in reflecting on past, current, and future selves.
Learning Activities	• Have students use a multiple-step process to identify, research, and plan to solve a problem that requires a novel solution.
	• Help students formulate questions that they want to answer.
	• Ask students to use appropriate criteria to select the best possible alternative in making decisions.
	• Ask students to rank, prioritize, and sequence the steps involved in an independent investigation.

(Continued)

Figure 7.4. Continued

Component	Modification Techniques
Learning Activities	• Help students develop or refine the ability to set appropriate goals for their work, use those goals to guide their work, modify the goals as work progresses, and assess their work according to their goals. • Help students develop the skills of introspection and the ability to compare and contrast their own personal characteristics and goals with those of the practicing professional.
Grouping Strategies	• Use individual conferences to discuss student interests, reflection, growth in learning and work profiles, and to forward student learning related to competencies in both content and personal reflection. • Use small groups for (1) interest-based explorations related to the curriculum content, (2) analysis of the class learning and work profile, (3) debriefing activities, and (4) extension activities. • Use pairs for think-alouds that support students' reflection and self-assessment, students' analyses of their learning and work profiles for emerging themes and patterns, and students' editing. • Work with large groups of students to provide an overview of the unit, introduce the learning and work profile, hear guest speakers, and participate in field experiences.
Resources	• Locate school and community members who are practicing professionals in careers related to the unit of study. Invite them to be guest speakers and mentors for students. • Locate biographies, at appropriate reading levels, of historical and contemporary practicing professionals. • Provide students with segments of audiotapes, documentaries, or newspaper articles that chronicle significant events in the lives of people who have contributed to a field. • Provide students with a wide variety of products created by practicing professionals in the discipline. Provide time for students to examine the collection and ask questions.
Products	• Provide students with regular opportunities to analyze and reflect on products that reflect the work of practicing professionals. • Encourage students to create portfolios of their best work samples. Provide opportunities for students to assess the growth reflected in the chronology of their portfolio pieces. • Ensure that students have the opportunity for self-assessment using rubrics that have been designed for products and performances. • Provide students with systematic opportunities to reflect on who they are becoming as learners and workers. Call on them to put their thoughts in journal entries, reflective essays, collages, tape-recorded reflections, and so on.

Extensions	• Provide opportunities for students to be involved with simulations related to the curriculum unit and their interests.
	• Make available supplementary videotapes on related topics.
	• Provide opportunities for students to visit with local experts and other professionals in related areas.
	• Ask the gifted education specialist to assist in locating a speaker to talk about cutting-edge research questions and state-of-the art research techniques in their work and the discipline.
	• Ask the library media specialist for assistance to locate Web quests related to the curriculum topic.
	• Find students a shadowing experience, internship, or mentorship when appropriate.
	• Help students find community-based opportunities to investigate the work of practitioners in the discipline.
Modification Based on Learner Need, Including Ascending Intellectual Demand	• Be aware that students are at different levels of development with respect to the content goals of the unit, interest in the discipline, and ability to be introspective.
	• Provide support for students who may have potential in the field, but who have not yet displayed interest in the topic and/or discipline.
	• Provide different levels of support to scaffold students' acquisition of content and skills related to their emerging sense of identity.
	• Provide an array of materials to accommodate students' interests, prior experiences, reading abilities, and ability to draw inferences (for example, in a mapping unit: copies of historical maps, star charts, maps of the ocean floor, town maps, road maps, topographical maps, relief maps, political maps, population maps, floor plans, treasure maps, maps of the ocean floor)
	• Support increasing levels of student independence in self-assessment regarding goals.
	• Assess students' current level of awareness of generic working skills such as time management, ability to work in a team, leadership skills, responsibility, sociability, and so forth as they relate to practitioners in the discipline and to self.

from state departments of education that focus on character education, and state Codes of Professional Responsibility. The following are goals for students from selected documents that support the intent of the Curriculum of Identity.

Self-Esteem:

The student believes in own self-worth and maintains a positive view of self; demonstrates knowledge of own skills and abilities; is aware of impact on others; and knows own emotional capacity and needs and how to address them.

Sociability:

The student demonstrates understanding, friendliness, adaptability, empathy, and politeness in new and ongoing group settings. Asserts self in familiar and unfamiliar social situations; relates well to others; responds appropriately as the situation requires; and takes an interest in what others say and do.

Self-Management:

[The student] assesses own knowledge, skills, and abilities accurately; sets well-defined and realistic personal goals; monitors progress toward goal attainment and motivates self through goal achievement; exhibits self-control and responds to feedback unemotionally and nondefensively; is a "self-starter." (U.S. Department of Labor, 1992)

Students will assume primary responsibility for learning, including identifying their needs and setting reasonable goals. (Connecticut State Department of Education, 1998)

The following quotation addresses the professional responsibilities of teachers with respect to the development of the characters of their students.

The professional teacher, in full recognition of his or her obligation to the student, shall (a) recognize, respect and uphold the dignity and worth of students as individual human beings . . . (f) assist students in the formulation of value systems and worthy, positive goals. (Connecticut State Department of Education, 1998b, 1999)

Based on the intent of these and other documents, we can develop a short, beginning list of standards to serve as the underpinnings for the Curriculum of Identity.

Students will be able to:

1. Understand the components of a learning and work profile (i.e., abilities, interests, learning-style preferences, skills, goals or mission statements, and extracurricular activities) and document their learning and work profile over time

2. Reflect upon their learning and working profiles, identify significant themes in their learning and work, note changes over time in these profiles, and make predictions about how their profiles might change in the future

3. Develop an accurate sense of what the daily lives of practicing professionals are like (e.g., the work hours, the extent of collaboration among peers, the extent of field work, the nature of lab work, the extent to which one is required to interact with the public, the problems, issues, the nature of ambiguity, the persistence, the failures, and the successes)

4. Assess the degree of fit between their own conceptions of day-to-day living with the actual day-to-day life of the practicing professional

5. Identify how components of their learning profiles align with those of the practicing professional in one or more discipline(s)

2. Assessments in the Curriculum of Identity

Exemplary assessment tasks for any of the curriculum parallels discussed in this book are varied, closely aligned with learning goals, and diagnostic in nature. In order for assessment tasks to be effective for teachers and students working within the context of the Core Curriculum, the Curriculum of Connections, the Curriculum of Practice, and/or the Curriculum of Identity, the assessment tasks need to be adapted to address the goals and purposes of each curriculum parallel.

To align assessment tasks with the goals and purposes of the Curriculum of Identity, we can remodel our assessments in four different ways. First, we select and generate a list of assessment formats that require student reflection. Second, we address the need for student choice with respect to assessments and products. Choice accommodates students' emerging and developing interests. Third, we look at the role of self-assessment within this curriculum parallel and propose two ways that practitioners can incorporate this practice. Finally, we look at longitudinal rubrics that address the talent development process and help us visualize student growth over time.

Review the assessment formats included in Figures 4.4 and 4.5 in Chapter 4. Close examination reveals that some of the formats are more likely than others to require student reflection (e.g., conversations, essays, concept maps, and performances). Each of these formats may require students to think about who and where they are as learners and workers. For example, a 12th-grade English teacher who is incorporating author study within a poetry unit might ask his students to write an essay about personal sacrifices that famous authors have made using a prompt such as this:

Identify the personal sacrifices Robert Frost made in his evolution as a poet and why he was willing to make them. Then, explain the personal sacrifices you would be willing to make in order to achieve a similar level of accomplishment in your selected field. In what ways are your goals and willingness to sacrifice to reach them like and unlike Robert Frost's?

Other assessment formats that align with the introspective nature of the Curriculum of Identity include goal statements; reflective essays; photographic essays that chronicle a student's passage from novice toward expert; a journal, a log of insights, discoveries, and/or thinking; and longitudinal portfolios. These assessment formats call upon students to reflect on their work and their role in that work. Used purposefully and systematically, these reflective assessment tasks provide students with insights that will help them make appropriate adjustments in their learning, work, and/or career orientation.

Besides reflection opportunities that can clarify students' emerging sense of self, students also need recurring opportunities to explore their developing interests.

Teachers can structure opportunities for interest exploration when they provide students with multiple assessment formats.

Let's look at a third-grade example. Mrs. Greene is toward the end of her unit on number sense and is working on the concept of place value. She has read aloud to her students *How Much Is a Million?* written by David Schwartz and illustrated by Steven Kellogg (1985). To assess her students' understanding of the immensity of a million, she calls upon her students to complete the following task either individually or in small groups:

Think about a favorite object, like a toy or a piece of sports equipment, a favorite food, like M&Ms or gum drops, or a favorite activity, like shooting baskets or jumping rope. Using a calculator to help you, tell me:

How much 1,000,000 of your objects might weigh, or
How long 1,000,000 of your objects would be lined up side by side, or
How tall 1,000,000 of you objects might be when stacked one on top of the other, or
How long it might take you to complete your favorite activity 1,000,000 times

Write about your findings or draw a picture to illustrate your answer.

Students naturally focused their work around their interests. One small group of students focused their solutions around a basketball and another around a soccer ball. Lots of students were interested in the candy. One student's favorite candy bar was Snickers, and he figured out how tall 1,000,000 of them would be when stacked together, one on top of another. Mrs. Greene was especially pleased when Ben and Tanesha, who invariably disliked math, showed some enthusiasm for the task. They tried to figure out how much a million buckets of water would weigh, which was the amount of water they thought it might take to fill up the community swimming pool.

Choice with respect to assessment tasks serves two important purposes. First, choice provides students with the opportunity to gravitate to an interest area and deepen their understanding of the subject as well as their role within it. Equally important, choice provides reluctant students with a pleasurable way to engage in a discipline that has been less than satisfying. The choice may even provide reluctant students with a new way to connect with a discipline.

Another way we can align our assessment practices with the Curriculum of Identity is to incorporate opportunities for students to assess their own work and learning. Self-assessment is a powerful tool. It is the ability to be reflective, to understand one's role as a learner and where one is developmentally with respect to a set of learning objectives.

How can students become astute assessors of the nature and quality of their work? The following features should be part of every classroom in order to help students develop the capacity to reflect meaningfully on their work:

▶ Students are familiar with the performance standards.

▶ Students have the opportunity to participate in developing the criteria by which work/performances will be assessed.

▶ Students have the opportunity to understand what the criteria mean and how they will be applied to their work.

▶ Students are provided with time to reflect on their work and draw conclusions about themselves as learners.

▶ Students are provided with time to talk about their conclusions with a peer or adult.

▶ Students are provided with thoughtful feedback about their conclusions, from peers and the teacher, to enhance the accuracy of their reflection and quality of their work.

One strategy teachers can use to promote reflection is called "Think Aloud." To use this strategy, students work in pairs, with one student playing the role of a thinker and the other of a listener. The teacher poses self-assessment questions (see Figure 7.5). Thinkers verbalize what goes through their minds as they answer the question. Listeners pay full attention and may ask clarifying questions in order to understand the thinker's thoughts. Next, the teacher conducts a debriefing period in which responses are shared and considered. Think-alouds conducted in this fashion reveal an array of important data: what students learned, what was easy about a task or performance (their strengths), what was difficult (their weaknesses), remaining misconceptions, how students feel about themselves as learners in this content area, and how well they can reflect upon their own work and themselves as learners. The strategy allows focus on both key content and student awareness of their roles as learners.

In addition to the opportunity for self-assessment on single products and performances, all students need periodic opportunities to reflect and "take stock" of themselves as learners and workers. This kind of reflective activity serves to forward a student's vision of possible selves discussed earlier in this chapter. Reflection about three different selves is required from a student to clarify his or her possible self. Students need opportunities to think about their "past self" or "past identity." The past self is the person the student perceives that he or she was last month, last summer, or last year, for example. It is a reference point by which a student measures change, as is noted in the two examples that follow.

Carmen: I used to like dinosaurs. Now, I think I like wild animals better.

Rosa: When I was little, I always wanted to be a doctor. But now I realize that I really don't like being around sick people. I think I need to think about other careers in which I can help people.

Figure 7.5. Examples of Self-Assessment Questions for the Curriculum of Identity

- What did I learn?
- What was easy for me?
- How might I describe my strengths?
- What was still confusing for me?
- What questions do I have that might clear up my confusion?
- Who might help me?
- Did I like being involved with this work?
- What aspects were particularly interesting?
- Would I like to continue doing this kind of work in _____ (content area)? Why or why not?

Reflection can also concern the "current self," the vision the student has of oneself at the current time.

Sherita: I think I learn best when I talk to others. I know for sure that I don't like learning from my social studies textbook!

Hazel: I am not a good silent reader. Every time my teacher tells us to read in class, I nearly fall asleep.

Finally, reflection can also be about a "future self," the vision that the student has of him- or herself in a time that has yet to come.

Lia: I have always had an interest in astronomy. I know that some day I will be involved with space exploration, but I am still not sure of the area. I won't be an astronaut, but I might like to be an engineer.

Bruce: I want to be in medical research and be the one to make a breakthrough in cancer research. I have always thought about the kind of contribution I can make to the world, and this one seems a good fit for me.

Students need regular opportunities to reflect on all their past, present, and future selves throughout their K-12 experience. With regularly scheduled opportunities to reflect on who they are and who they are becoming, students will find both the academic content through which they see themselves and the emergence of their own self-awareness give school a new dimension of meaning. Reflection puts students in an active role and engages each of them as the "vision maker."

The last technique that we will use to remodel our assessments for the Curriculum of Identity involves the creation of longitudinal rubrics. This curriculum parallel, which stresses development of individual capacity, requires teachers to be talent trackers. They need to be able to identify the behaviors that characterize a young mathematician, a budding scientist, a young artist, or the next Gwendolyn Brooks.

Furthermore, teachers need to be able to assist students' growth in their emerging strength areas. For these reasons, teachers benefit from longitudinal rubrics that not only help them spot emerging abilities in their classroom but also provide concrete ideas for helping a student move to the next level on the continuum of development.

Figure 7.6 provides an example of a longitudinal rubric that teachers can use to spot and nurture talent in one content area, history. It is representative of rubrics teachers can create for the various content areas.

The figure contains three columns. The first column, "Stage," does not represent the age or grade level of the student. Instead, the numbers represent the escalating stages toward expertise in history. The second column contains descriptors of likely student behaviors at each level of talent development. The descriptors are by no means comprehensive but have been selected because they are representative. The final column includes actions that a teacher or parent can initiate to support advancement of the student's growth process in the area of strength. The actions merely sample and serve to "jump-start" our thinking about the varied ways we can support the advancement of abilities in young people.

This instrument and similar forms in other content areas are effective tools for teachers who are serious about developing their students' identity. The continuum supports teachers in their efforts to identify emerging preferences and abilities in their classrooms and helps them support students' learning assets (e.g., interests, abilities, and goals) with activities that will lead, step-by-step, to satisfying and productive lives.

Teachers can support development of student preferences and abilities when they use assessment tasks that require students to reflect on their role in a discipline; provide choice with respect to assessments and products; call on students to evaluate their own work; provide students with opportunities to reflect on their past, current, and future selves; and use longitudinal rubrics to keep track of students' developing talents. In this way, teachers work dually with the content for which they and their students are responsible and with the emergence of self-identity in learners through the vehicle of that content.

3. Introductory Activities in the Curriculum of Identity

The purpose of each element in an introduction, (for example, focusing question, needs assessment, teaser or hook, rationale, objectives, and students' interests) remains the same across all of the four curriculum parallels. What changes in the Curriculum of Identity is the focus of each element based on the particular goals of this parallel. These changes are discussed below.

In a high-quality curriculum, focusing questions highlight or underscore essential concepts or principles. Focusing questions, when referred to throughout the curriculum, remind teachers and students about the major purposes of the lessons and help students reflect on, gauge, and quantify their growth. In a unit about explorers, for example, focusing questions might include these: Why do people

Figure 7.6. Longitudinal Rubric for Spotting and Nurturing Talent in History

Stage	Student Behavior	Possible Action to Forward Talent to the Next Stage
1	Jose asks numerous questions about people and events from the past.	Read books to Jose about famous historical people; share historical book titles with his family so they can read to him, too.
2	As a seven-year-old, Jose spent much longer than any of his Grade 1 classmates looking at a diorama depicting the Battle of Lexington and Concord.	Investigate local and regional historical sites; provide names of some sites he and his family can visit.
3	When offered the opportunity, Jose enjoys visiting historical sites, touching historical artifacts, and reading nonfiction and fiction texts about historical topics.	Help Jose gather information about historical sites and artifacts; enlist the support of the library media specialist and technology specialist to get additional resources for him.
4	When given options about projects, Jose generally chooses alternatives that address some aspect of history.	Provide extension activities for Jose on topics that he enjoys; suggest other related explorations he may find equally, or even more, appealing.
5	As a young adolescent, Jose is beginning to make a conscious effort to attend classes, read books, and, in general, increase his knowledge of and skills regarding historical topics and methods.	Discuss the discipline of history with Jose; talk about the methodology of the field; explore course offerings; encourage his parents to work with the guidance counselor to select appropriate history courses.
6	Jose prefers and seeks out the company of peers who also enjoy history. He likes working with these students on class projects. He uses free time in scouting and community projects that address historical issues or needs.	Use community resources to determine local projects and issues related to history; use the Internet to locate other resources and projects.
7	Jose begins to think he might be a future historian. While he enjoys every aspect of his studies and work in history, he knows he has much to learn to become a practitioner.	Locate internships for Jose that will provide an in-depth look at the skills and methodologies required of the practicing professional.
8	Jose begins to make short-term and long-term plans for professional growth. Often, he forgoes leisure activities in order to advance his personal and professional expertise.	Locate a mentorship for Jose. Look for regionally or nationally based organizations that have members like Jose, such as historical societies; encourage Jose to become an active member.
9	Jose is thinking and working like a practitioner in the field; he is developing a knack for finding interesting questions, unexplored topics, discrepant information, and controversies in history.	Encourage and support Jose's frequently intense work on topics that compel him. Assist with resource acquisition. Enlist professionals to advise him and provide feedback on the nature and quality of his work.

10	Jose enjoys his association with colleagues who like to discuss abstract ideas, who enjoy unearthing unanswered questions, and who derive satisfaction from exploring possible answers to unanswered questions.	Help Jose apply for grants and fellowships; encourage his attendance and participation in local, regional, and national-level conferences and reading of professional-level materials.
11	Jose works with colleagues, a mentor, and alone to investigate, research, and problem solve in history.	Encourage and nurture Jose's research, writing, and presentation skills.
12	Jose realizes that history fulfills him and that history must be the focus of his life's work. His behaviors, life plans, and career will revolve around this discipline. He feels actualized by the knowledge and skills he uses; he sees his life in and through history.	Encourage Jose to publish his own work in journals and other related publications.

explore? What impact does exploration have on humankind? Does exploration strengthen or weaken a society?

To incorporate aspects of the Curriculum of Identity into a curriculum, a teacher may add one or two additional focusing questions for students. These questions would be cast differently than those in the other parallels because they address the role of the student within the discipline and elicit a personal response. Within the context of the explorers unit, above, they might include any of the following:

1. Who are contemporary explorers?
2. What were they like as students? How did they spend their time? What were their interests? How did they first become interested in geography, maps, and navigation?
3. How do they spend their time at work? On what sorts of questions and issues do the spend their time?
4. In what ways do the interests and values of the contemporary explorers reflect or differ from your own?
5. In what other ways are you like the contemporary explorers?
6. In what other ways are you different from them?

In a high-quality, comprehensive curriculum unit about explorers, a teaser or "hook" might include a videotape of a blast-off into space; a copy of a personal correspondence from Marie Curie; segments of an interview with Robert Ballard, famous underwater explorer; writings and recordings from the Freedom Riders in the 1960s and 1970s and again at the turn of the new millennium; pioneers in computer technology; or pictures of frontiers over the course of history. Any one of these teasers could serve to engage and motivate the students in a general way about explorers across time.

Within the context of the Curriculum of Identity, the hook or teaser will take on an introspective or personal focus. In the same Curriculum of Identity unit on explorers, a teacher may elect to play a recording of Neil Armstrong's words as he walked on the surface of the moon: "That's one small step for man, one giant leap for mankind." As a follow-up, the teacher might ask students to engage in a small group discussion around the following prompt: What personal characteristics did Neil Armstrong possess that enabled him to take the first steps on the lunar surface in 1969? What similarities are there between Armstrong's characteristics and your own? Within a few minutes, students would have the opportunity to create a personal connection with the unit and be drawn into the discipline.

The rationale is another element of high-quality introductions. The rationale makes clear to students the importance of the topic. Keeping the focus on identity, a teacher might engage students in small group discussions around the following introspective questions:

1. What are the "frontiers" for your generation in the 21st century?
2. If you became an explorer in the 21st century, what might your contribution or legacy be?
3. In what ways are explorers important to you? To humankind?

A fourth element in an introduction concerns the performance standards. Within the framework of the Curriculum of Identity, teachers will share with students the performance standards that relate to self-knowledge, including, for example, these:

1. Students will develop an appreciation for the personal characteristics of explorers across time.
2. Students will be able to compare their own personal qualities with those of explorers, past and present.

It is important to point out that not all elements in an introductory set of activities have to be replaced to align Curriculum of Identity. Teachers may elect to infuse reflective opportunities into just one or two of the elements. Teachers need to assess their students' needs, the nature of the curriculum unit, and their time frame and then make reasonable decisions regarding which introductory components to re-model in order to invite students' reflective thinking.

4. Teaching Methods in the Curriculum of Identity

Earlier in the book, we described teaching activities as existing along dual continua: direct to indirect methods with high to low levels of teacher or peer support. Teachers have an important task in matching teaching methods to learning goals and students' learning needs. While all types of teaching methods may be employed in the Curriculum of Identity, those that readily lend themselves to the acquisition of self-knowledge include methods that provide students with the opportunity to (1) take on or otherwise closely examine the role of the practicing professional and (2) reflect on and construct self-knowledge. Coaching, demonstration/modeling, visualization, role-playing, cooperative learning, jurisprudence, simulations, inquiry- based instruction, problem-based learning, shadowing experiences, mentorships, independent study, and independent investigations are teaching strategies that effectively and efficiently promote the goals and purposes of this curriculum parallel (see Figure 3.7 in Chapter 3).

Readers will note that the teaching strategies most appropriate for the Curriculum of Identity cluster toward the indirect end of the teaching strategies continuum. Within this cluster of teaching strategies, however, a wide range still exists. Visualization, one of the more direct methods, might be employed frequently by teachers in this curriculum parallel to help students move back and forth across their past selves, present selves, and future selves.

Other strategies especially appropriate to the Curriculum of Identity include simulations, shadowing experiences, and mentorships. These methods hold great promise for students seeking insights into personally meaningful future paths. As students explore day-to-day activities of professionals, the problems and dilemmas of experts, and the texture of professional interactions that characterize a professional's role, these latter inductive teaching strategies efficiently and effectively forward student self-awareness.

5. *Learning Activities in the Curriculum of Identity*

High-quality Curriculum of Identity learning activities foster cognitive engagement: analytic, critical, and synthetic thinking. They require students to perceive, process, rehearse, store, and transfer new knowledge and skills that have been introduced in the teaching activities. While all thinking skills are important, those learning activities that draw on executive processing skills and creative thinking are especially important for the goals and purposes of the Curriculum of Identity because of their capacity to promote student reflection and analysis (see Figure 3.8 in Chapter 3).

The executive processing skills are essential. To understand the day-to-day life of the professional, the student needs to develop processing skills required in any field or discipline. These include goal setting, formulating questions, developing hypotheses, generalizing, problem solving, decision making, and planning. When students are afforded these kinds of thinking opportunities, they can actually "feel" what it like to be the practicing professional and have a much clearer sense about what it means to be a historian, an anthropologist, a musician, a mathematician, an artist, or an environmental scientist, for example.

In a similar fashion, creative thinking skills are important. In today's workplaces, people function in diverse teams on complex problems that require creative thinking. Practicing professionals must use their imaginations freely, combine ideas or information in new ways, and make connections between seemingly

Figure 7.7. Some Additional Process Skills Key to the Curriculum of Identity

---

- Relating self to others
- Introspection
- Balancing self-acceptance and self-critique
- Developing perspective on events
- Establishing a personal compass for decision making
- Determining significance
- Prediction
- Deducing and inducing logically
- Seeing self in varied contexts
- Self-affirmation
- Developing courage
- Reading and using contextual cues
- Learning from experience
- Pursuit of wisdom

---

unrelated ideas. It is not surprising that the SCANS report (U.S. Department of Labor, 1992) lists creative thinking, decision making, and problem solving, in that order, as the most needed skills in our country's workforce. Figure 7.7 suggests other process skills of particular relevance to goals of the Curriculum of Identity.

6. Grouping Strategies in the Curriculum of Identity

Teachers who work with a Curriculum of Identity will use many grouping patterns. Teachers will employ one-on-one conversations with learners to help each one with a variety of skills, questions, and issues related to his or her work. Certainly, it is necessary for students in the Curriculum of Identity to work alone in order to reflect on evolving insights about self in relation to the discipline. On the other hand, there will be times when discussions in a pair or small group provide a useful sounding board for insights. In some instances, it will be helpful for students to work in small groups where students share interests, preferences, goals, and ideas in order to confirm, extend, or question a particular line of thought. In other instances, it should be more instructive to work with peers whose interests and perspectives differ as a means of expanding thought. Peer editing can be especially helpful when students are involved in writing reflective essays or preparing letters of introduction, for example. Further, small group instruction will play a role, too, in managing interest-based activities, debriefing sessions, differentiation, and extension activities. Finally, teachers will use large group instruction to give directions, introduce and host guest speakers to "jump-start" students' thinking, or provide an overview of the unit, a lesson, or the students' learning and work profiles. Whole-class discussions can also help build a sense of a shared journey toward understanding what it means to find one's place in a complex world.

Figure 7.8. Resources That Support Student Learning in the Curriculum of Identity

Resources		
Human	*Non-Human*	
	Print	*Nonprint*
Older students	Biographies	Artifacts
Younger students	Diaries/Journals/Logs	Photographs
Other students in the classroom	E-mails	Videotaped interviews
Parents	Personal letters	Personal belongings
Other teachers	Personal correspondence	News clips
Community members	Unpublished manuscripts	Audiotaped conversations
Content area experts	Notes	Documentaries
Other school personnel	Personal scrapbooks	
University personnel	Memoirs	
Business personnel	Data sets	
Service organization personnel	Web sites	
Professional groups		
Avocational groups		

7. Resources in the Curriculum of Identity

Exemplary resources for the Curriculum of Identity are those that provide students with revealing glimpses into the personal lives and daily activities of practicing professionals. They afford students the opportunity to learn the obvious, such as the career paths and the major contributions of selected individuals. At the same time, they afford students the opportunity to learn the little known, but critical, facets about an individual's life, such as the events and colleagues that provided support during crucial episodes, the personal challenges famous people faced, and how they resolved the challenges. When students are able to visualize the human side of older, more accomplished people, it is easier for them to draw parallels between those people's lives and their own.

Examples of resources that can offer students these kinds of unique perspectives include human resources and non-human resources (see Figure 7.8). These kinds of revealing resources are readily available in museums and newspapers and on Web sites.

The critical task that teachers face is to ensure alignment among the learning goals, the learning tasks, the resources, and students' unique learning needs (e.g., reading level, learning preference, and interest areas). The following example illustrates the issue of alignment. History of Science is a science content standard category in many states' curriculum framework documents. A common performance standard, Grades 9-12, might be this: "The student will recognize that changes in science usually occur as small modifications and result in incremental understandings of the world." To accomplish this learning goal, a high school teacher might assign the following learning task:

> Select a person from the accompanying list of men and women in science. In a presentation format of your choice, describe the contribution of your scientist and the impact of his or her legacy on the field. Highlight the challenges, setbacks, and successes that he or she faced in order to leave a legacy to the scientific world. Use at least five references, at least three of which must be primary source material (e.g., letters, photographs, personal correspondence, and audio- or videotapes).

To ensure appropriate learning materials for the wide range of learner interests in the classroom, the teacher needs a variety of primary and secondary source materials on the targeted scientists. Additionally, the teacher would have to ensure a range of reading levels among the print resources to accommodate students' diverse reading needs within each interest area.

8. Products in the Curriculum of Identity

Teachers can draw on a variety of authentic product formats in order to help students understand the nature of products required of practicing professionals and what goes into the creation of those products (see Figure 3.9, Chapter 3). It goes without saying that products or performances should be chosen with care to (1) align with the targeted learning goals, (2) have the capacity to reveal the targeted knowledge or skill, (3) reflect the work of the practicing professional, and (4) invite student reflection in ways that produce insights about personal traits, goals, preferences, values, and ways of working compared with those same traits in those who work in or are reflected in the discipline.

Students should be afforded regular opportunities to select the format for their products. A critical component of a student's identity is his or her expression style preference. For example, some students prefer to express themselves visually; others prefer to express themselves in writing. Still others prefer to express themselves through a multimedia format. When students are provided with the opportunity to choose the way they want to express themselves, they naturally gravitate to their favored format, thereby strengthening both their capabilities within a medium and a sense of their particular strengths and interests.

Self-assessment is also a powerful facet of product assignments. When products are accompanied by quality rubrics and thoughtful teacher feedback and guidance, the self-measuring process becomes an integral part of products and performances and can "trigger" students' awareness of their place on the novice-expert growth continuum and the next steps required to move ahead in the discipline.

9. Extension Activities in the Curriculum of Identity

Teachers can effectively use extension activities to forward a student's self-knowledge through exploration of key content. Extension activities in the Curriculum of Identity would include individual and small group investigations derived from the curriculum unit and students' interests. They might be designed to provide participating students with opportunities to interact with practicing professionals who would share not only their work with students but also their day-to-day activities and philosophies. Extension activities could enable students to learn about the lives and work of practitioners by reading journals or diaries, using the Internet, interviewing, viewing related videos, and so on. Students might also be interested in simply reading biographies or autobiographies or examining work samples or critiques of the work of experts in fields related to the unit's content goals and student interests. Extension activities might also include introspective writings in which authors reflect on the same sorts of questions about themselves that the young learners will encounter in the Curriculum of Identity. Such writings are available for all ages and reading levels and can be helpful to students in understanding how it sounds when others carry on a sort of interior monologue about their interests, goals, likes and dislikes, abilities, learning patterns, and so on. Put simply, extension activities in this parallel provide students with compelling glimpses of who they are and who they might become.

At some point in a final reflection about a student's extension activity, a teacher needs to ask the student what new questions the student now has related to his or her interests, skills, values, goals, and so forth. A student's answer to this question is a "tip off" to where he or she might need to go next in thinking and exploration. When teachers take the student's questions seriously and act upon them to ensure follow-up, they once again forward a student's emerging sense of identity.

10. Modification in Response to Learner Need, Including Ascending Intellectual Demand in the Curriculum of Identity

By its very nature, the Curriculum of Identity is responsive to learner variance. In this parallel, students may prepare personal profile inventories and watch the profiles change over the years. This provides a unique opportunity for students to identify emerging patterns and themes and develop individual learning goals around a deepening awareness of fit within one or more disciplines. Even within this flexible framework, however, there is a need for teachers to provide students with varying opportunities for continuous movement toward expertise within a field or discipline.

At the heart of the Curriculum of Identity is a desire to help students think about themselves and their goals in the context of the disciplines that organize human knowledge. Certainly, in all grades there are students who are already passionate about science, art, literature, mathematics, history, or music. In those same classrooms are students who have never thought of themselves as mathematicians or artists, for example, but who would do so with appropriately focused, supported, and inviting learning experiences. There are also in those classes, however, students whose struggle with school will make it difficult for them to relate to the notion of self as a geologist, biographer, cartographer, and so on. To open the window of opportunity for self-reflection a bit wider, teachers may respond to learner variance by having students reflect on themselves in relation to the topic they are studying rather than the discipline in which it is housed. One such example, given earlier in this chapter, is the teacher having her students reflect on themselves as explorers rather than as the historians who study and write about the explorers. It is our belief that, appropriately supported, many students would benefit from seeing themselves as early scholars or practitioners in a discipline and reflecting on what those experiences reveal to them about themselves. An approach to modifying the Curriculum of Identity in response to learner need, however, is "opening up" the window through which students are invited to view themselves so that the teacher uses both the disciplines and appropriate objects of study within the discipline to help students think about themselves. Thus one student might find it more interesting and challenging, for example, to reflect on oneself as a biographer, whereas another would find it more interesting and challenging to reflect on oneself as a soldier, or hero, or pioneer about whom the biography is written.

Similarly, because students' interests and capacities develop differently, learning opportunities tailored to individuals or small groups of students will, as in the other parallels, require attention to student reading levels as well as their depth of knowledge and interest in a topic or discipline. Some additional, basic approaches to increasing intellectual demand are the following:

- ▶ Use longitudinal rubrics to help student and teacher locate and respond to a student's level of proficiency on a novice to expert continuum within a topic or discipline

- ▶ Vary the resources (i.e., non-human and human) that students use. Non-human resources vary in reading difficulty, complexity, and/or the degree of inference required. Human resources vary as well because individuals have different levels of expertise within a field or domain.

- ▶ Increase the complexity of questions or problems with which students work and on which students reflect. Within each discipline are cutting edge problems, questions, and issues. Students can begin their search for themselves in a curricular area by being involved at a "junior level." As they demonstrate increased interest and commitment to selected fields, they can take on increasingly more complex problems.

- ▶ Ask students to develop their own rubrics or scales to assess the proficiency of products in a topic or discipline that holds a special interest for them (e.g., a watercolor, a dance, an essay, a debate, a professional article, a science experiment, a map).

Other, more complex approaches to ascending intellectual demand are listed in Figure 7.9.

At this point, we turn our attention away from the structural components of this parallel and focus on their application. In the next section, we see how our fictionalized teacher Lydia Janis remodels her Civil War unit to align with the goals and purposes of the Curriculum of Identity.

Figure 7.9. Some Paths to Achieving Ascending Intellectual Demand in the Curriculum of Identity

- Looking for and reflecting on "truths," beliefs, ways of working, styles, and so on that typify the field
- Looking for "roots" of theories, beliefs, and principles in a field and relating those theories, beliefs, and principles to the time when they "took root" in one's own life
- Looking for and reflecting on the meaning of paradoxes and contradictions in the discipline or field
- Conducting an ethnography of a facet of the discipline and reflecting on both findings and personal revelations
- Engaging in long-term problem solving on an intractable problem in the discipline that causes the student to encounter and mediate multiple points of view and reflecting systematically on the experience
- Researching and establishing standards of quality work as defined by the discipline, applying those standards to the student's own work in the discipline over an extended time period and reflecting systematically on the experience
- Collaborating with a high-level professional or practitioner in the field in shared problem solving and reflection
- Challenging or looking for limitations of the ideas, models, ways of working, or belief systems of the discipline
- Looking for parallels (or contrasts) in personal prejudices, blind spots, assumptions, habits, and those evident in the field
- Studying and reflecting on one discipline by using the concepts, principles, and modes of working of another discipline, reflecting on the interactions and insights gained

An Example of the Curriculum of Identity

Lydia has noted Jacob's developing interest in history. She is wondering who Jacob will become over the course of the next 20 years, what her role is in helping Jacob develop his interests, whether Jacob is unusual, or whether each student has a unique set of interests and abilities she can help nurture. She wonders also how a teacher blends a need to ensure student mastery of designated content and awareness of an evolving self.

Lydia wasn't quite sure where to start. She looked over her content standards. They helped her achieve clarity about the knowledge, concepts, principles, and skills of her curriculum. There was nothing in the standards, however, related to students' interests, abilities, or values.

Lydia's thoughts returned to her students. She sensed that the Curriculum of Identity had to incorporate students' development as people as well as content development. How would she know enough about her students to begin intelligently to take them into account in her planning?

Figure 7.10. Categories in Ed's Student Profile Survey

1. **Abilities/Subject Area preference** (i.e., reading, writing, spelling, mathematics, social studies, science, art, or music)
2. **Product Preferences/Expression Style Preference** (i.e., reports, talking, projects, art work, pictures or charts, displays, acting, or helping others)
3. **Learning Preference** (i.e., talking with others, listening to a speaker, reading, watching or viewing, games, computers, pretending, or making something)
4. **Grouping Preference** (i.e., working alone, working with a partner, working in a group, or working with an adult)
5. **General Interest** (i.e., performing arts, creative writing or journalism, mathematics, business or management, athletics, history, social action, fine arts and crafts, or science, and technology)
6. **Specific Interest** (i.e., a special section where students can list high-interest topics they already have)
7. **Cocurricular Activity** (i.e., lessons and activities outside school)
8. **My Goal for the Year** (i.e., a personally meaningful objective)

That afternoon, after the close of school, she walked down the hall to talk with Ed Lester, the gifted education specialist. He showed her some student profile surveys and explained how he used them. She spent a great deal of time talking with him about the profiles.

"There are many advantages to using surveys like these," Ed shared. "First, they help me collect important information about students' learning strengths. Second, I use the information contained in the profile to analyze how I can optimize the 'fit' between the students and instruction. For example, I always provide opportunities for students to pursue an area of interest. Often, I encourage students to work in a preferred learning style (for example, by talking with others, listening to a speaker, reading) or in a preferred grouping (for example, working alone, with a partner, or with a group). I also use the document in a conference with each student. Together we review the profile, analyze how it has changed over time, and discuss ways we can further the student's interests, abilities, goals, or questions."

Ed continued, "I combine what is on the learner profile with what I have come to know about each student firsthand. Then, using a longitudinal rubric to help me, I try to figure out where the student might 'fit' on the novice-expert continuum in his or her preferred content area, like math or science." Ed pulled out a folder and took out the longitudinal rubric for history (see Figure 7.6). "Jacob, you see, is someplace around Stage 4 or 5 on this history continuum. Once I locate his approximate place on the scale, it is much easier for me to determine possible next steps that will advance him toward expertise."

Lydia decided she'd begin with the learner profile surveys. She'd tally what she learned from the surveys to get a rough sense of the distribution of characteristics *across* her students as well. Figure 7.10 notes the categories in Ed's student profile surveys.

Lydia was compelled by the power the profiles held for her students and her instruction. First, she thought, the learning and work profile would help her gather important baseline information about her students. She would certainly know her students better after she collected these kinds of information. In turn, she could better help her students reflect on themselves as learners. Second, if she could capitalize on her students' abilities and interests, she knew that she would be able to increase their motivation for learning. She always found teaching more rewarding when students were engaged with the lessons she taught. She thought, too, that if her students were really engaged, their academic achievement should increase as well.

When she got home, Lydia laid Ed's profile survey on her dining room table. She didn't feel confident enough to collect or use all the information that Ed described. She looked at the document and said to herself, "I think I'll begin by asking students about their interests, their abilities, and how they like to learn best."

Lydia decided to create a much simpler one-page profile that she felt comfortable using with her students. She planned to talk with students first before they completed any information on the profile. She wanted to explain the importance of the document and how she planned to use the information that they provided to alter some of the components of her instruction in the upcoming unit on the Civil War. Figure 7.11 illustrates Lydia's survey.

She liked her format where everything fit on one page. She included the most essential learning characteristics she could think of: student interests, their abilities, their preferred ways to learn, and their expression style preferences. She was especially pleased with the two-column format that encouraged students to think about themselves now and in the future. Lydia knew her fifth graders did not often think of their "future selves." This learning and work profile should begin to prompt their thinking about who they might like to become, a key goal of the Curriculum of Identity.

After the fifth graders completed the survey, Lydia tallied the results for the class (see Figure 7.12). While there was quite a bit of diversity among her students, she was excited about the new information she had. After some reflection about her students and content goals, she decided to make five adjustments in her upcoming Civil War unit compared with the unit she created earlier using the Core Curriculum Parallel. First, she would change her introduction to orient students to many ways people can be historians. Second, she would invite two guest speakers to talk about their work as historians. Third, she would focus on students' specific interests and abilities through interest-based groups and extension activities. Fourth, she would have the students work as historians at some points in the unit. Finally, she would have the students reflect systematically on how their study teaches them about themselves. These changes would allow her to continue the unit's focus on her required content goals while also making an opportunity for students to use the work of historians to learn more about themselves.

In addition, Lydia thought about the power that authentic products might hold for her students. She decided to bring in products designed by historians to invite her students into the study of history. She found copies of some photographs taken at the time of the Civil War, copies of political cartoons from the time period, pictures of museum exhibits about the Civil War, copies of newspaper articles written about Civil War battles, a film and video about the Civil War, and grade-level fiction

Figure 7.11. Lydia's Learning and Work Profile Survey

Subject Areas	I Like This	I Want to Become Good at This
Reading		
Writing		
Spelling		
Mathematics		
Social Studies		
Science		
Art		
Music		
PE		
Other		

Preferred Ways To Learn	I Like This	I Want to Become Good at This
Talking With Others		
Reading		
Viewing		
Games		
Computers		
Pretending		
Making/Doing		
Working Alone		
Working With a Partner		
Working in a Group		
Working With an Adult		
Choices and Options		
Detailed Directions		

and nonfiction books about this time in history. During her unit introduction and throughout the unit she would share these products with her students. She would talk with them about historians and make clear that historians share their knowledge about the past in different ways, all of which contribute to our understanding

Figure 7.11. Continued

Showing How I Learn	I Like This	I Want to Become Good at This
Reports		
Talking		
Projects		
Artwork		
Pictures/ Charts		
Displays		
Acting		
Helping Others		
Media		
Other _____		

My Interests	I Like This	I Might Like This
Performing Arts		
Creative Writing/ Reading		
Mathematics		
Business		
Athletics		
History		
Social Action		
Fine Arts		
Science		
Technology/ Video Games		
Other _____		

of people and events. She hoped this approach to introducing the unit would help her students begin the process of considering the work and lives of historians.

Lydia added some new resources to her unit to direct it toward the goals of the Curriculum of Identity. She planned to invite two practicing professionals in areas related to the Civil War to speak to her class. The work of Willis Taylor, a local historian, and Sam Gelston, a newspaper reporter, centered on history. Mr. Taylor was

Figure 7.12. Lydia's Class Tally of Student Profile Surveys

Subject Areas	I Like This	I Want to Become Good at This
Reading	///	
Writing	////	
Spelling	///	
Mathematics	//	
Social Studies	////	
Science	̷H̶T̶	
Art	̷H̶T̶ /	
Music	///	
PE	̷H̶T̶ ///	
Other		

Preferred Ways To Learn	I Like This	I Want to Become Good at This
Talking With Others	̷H̶T̶	
Reading	̷H̶T̶ //	
Viewing		
Games	̷H̶T̶ ///	
Computers	////	
Pretending		
Making/Doing	//	
Working Alone	//	
Working With a Partner	̷H̶T̶ /	
Working in a Group	̷H̶T̶ ///	
Working With an Adult	///	
Choices and Options	̷H̶T̶ ̷H̶T̶ //	
Detailed Directions	////	

known for his long-standing interest in the stories from local homeowners who had convincing evidence that their homes were used as stations on the Underground Railroad. She wanted Mr. Taylor to be able to share with students (1) his stories about homes in town that had been part of the Underground Railroad Network, (2) how he had collected his stories—his methodology as a historian, (3) how students could

Figure 7.12. Continued

Showing How I Learn	I Like This	I Want to Become Good at This
Reports	/	
Talking	///	
Projects	ЖНГ ////	
Artwork	////	
Pictures/ Charts	ЖНГ //	
Displays	ЖНГ	
Acting	/	
Helping Others	////	
Media	///	
Other _____		

My Interests	I Like This	I Might Like This
Performing Arts	///	///
Creative Writing/ Reading	///	///
Mathematics		
Business		
Athletics	ЖНГ /	ЖНГ //
History	//	//
Social Action		
Fine Arts	////	
Science		//
Technology/ Video Games	////	ЖНГ
Other _____		

work as historians to learn about their families, school, or community, (4) his day-to-day life as an historian, and (5) how his work as a historian has changed both him and their town. Mr. Gelston, a reporter for the local paper, had covered the war in Vietnam. She wanted him to (1) describe for students what wars are like, (2) tell them about the job of a war correspondent, (3) explain how he became interested in his job, and (4) say why he believes being a journalist and historian is a good match for him.

Lydia's third change in the Core Curriculum Unit to change its focus to a Curriculum of Identity involved use of interest-based small group work and extension activities. She began immediately to plan these elements of her curriculum. To get started, she reviewed the learner profiles—specifically the section on students' interests. "How can I accommodate all these interests in a Civil War unit?" she wondered.

She thought about the different ways historians share their knowledge. She drew a diagram like the one in Figure 7.13. Down the left side of the page, she placed the interests of her students as reflected on their profile surveys, as well as the number of students with the interest. In the top of the right area of the chart, she wrote her question about addressing student interest. In the rest of the chart, she wrote down aspects in the unit that matched her students' interests. She knew that students' interests were a powerful indicator of their emerging sense of self.

Lydia thought about the elements she should consider in her planning. What she needed to do was construct learning tasks for students that focused clearly on the major information, concepts, principles, and skills she needed to teach but to use students' interests as a context for learning the content or a format for products through which students expressed what they learned. For example, some of Lydia's students were interested in art. To tap into that interest, she might ask students to observe paintings from the Civil War period to see how they depicted events and conditions students were learning about and also to reflect on ways in which artists can play the role of historian. To address the interest of students who particularly enjoy video games and sports, Lydia could have students use appropriate Web sites to learn about military strategies in a key battle they would study in class and to examine ways contemporary historians are using Internet technology to preserve history. She would plan some of these interest-based activities as small group tasks through which all learners would work toward the same learning goals but do so in a variety of formats. Other interest-based options would become part of the extension activities Lydia would offer to her fifth graders.

The last modification Lydia made to her unit to accommodate the Curriculum of Identity was extension activities. She planned these activities for students with a special desire to learn more about a topic that interested them. The extension activities, she knew, would arise from activities in the unit that prompted interesting student questions.

Lydia continued with her plans for the Civil War unit and completed the arrangements for her two guest speakers. She asked Willis Taylor to visit the class near the beginning of the unit to pique her students' interest in the Civil War. She asked Sam Gelston to come about halfway though the unit because she wanted her students to have a basic understanding about the two different perspectives during the war that would pave the way for his talk about potential bias in newspaper accounts.

She was not surprised at the rapt attention her students provided both guest speakers. Although shy at first, the students warmed quickly to both Mr. Taylor and Mr. Gelston.

Figure 7.13. Lydia's Chart to Align Civil War Content With Students' Interests

Students interests and co-curricular activities	*What aspect of this unit on the Civil War might align with students' interests?*
Music 3 students	African American spirituals, Fife and Drum Corps music
Reading 3 students	Historical fiction and nonfiction
Sports 6 students	Battle strategies, war tactics
History 2 students	Primary source documents, multiple viewpoints, videos and films, letters
Art 4 students	Political cartoons, pen and ink drawings, daguerreotypes, engravings, paintings
Video Games 4 students	Simulations, Civil War reenactments

Lydia took time after each speaker left to talk with her students about what they heard. She used three different types of questions to help her students connect the content of the presentation with the Civil War and the attitudes, values, and skills of each presenter. She made a point to introduce her students to the visualization process in this debriefing. If students were to see themselves as future historians or war correspondents, they needed to be able to imagine these experienced adults as youngsters who were once very much like themselves. Figure 7.14 lists some of Lydia's questions for follow-up discussions.

To ensure that her students reflected on their own interests, goals, values, and preferences in comparison with those of the speakers, Lydia gave her students a brief reflective assignment at the conclusion of the last speaker's presentation. They used the following prompt:

Look over the learning profile that you completed recently. Based on what you know about yourself, explain what kind of a war correspondent or historian you might become. Write about yourself first as a historian then as a war correspondent. In what ways would each of these roles be interesting to you? Not interesting? How well would each role cause you to use your interests, goals, and strengths? In what ways is each role a poor fit for your interests, goals, and strengths?

Figure 7.14. Questions for Student Reflection in the Curriculum of Identity

Category	Question
Thinking Back	1. In two or three sentences, summarize what you just heard about: the Underground Railroad, the Civil War, the job of the historian/journalist. 2. What information did you already know? 3. What was new to you? 4. What kinds of skills and personality traits does the historian/war correspondent need to develop to be "good" at what he/she does? 5. What other things does it take to be a good historian? A good war correspondent?
Thinking About Similarities	1. Visualize Mr. Taylor and Mr. Gelston when they were fifth graders. What interests, goals, and skills might they have had? 2. In what ways are your interests, personality traits, goals, and skills like Mr. Taylor's? Mr. Gelston's? 3. What do these similarities tell you about yourself?
Thinking About Differences	1. Visualize Mr. Taylor and Mr. Gelston again when they were in fifth grade. 2. How are your interests, personality traits, goals, and skills different from theirs? 3. What do these differences tell you about yourself?

Lydia was not surprised at Jacob's paragraphs. He stated up front that he was sure he wanted to be a historian. She was a bit surprised by William's paper. He was a young man who remained an enigma to her. He was so quiet that Lydia often wondered what he was thinking about in class. His paper was serious in tone. William said he thought war correspondents were heroic because they risked so much to bring back important stories for people to read. Lydia made a mental note to follow up with William.

Lydia didn't have to wait long for her opportunity to speak with William. Later that week, she explained to the class what an extension activity was and made a few suggestions of options that could help them learn more about the life and work of historians. She also encouraged the students to develop their own ideas for extension activities based on questions they had or ideas that were interesting to them in their study of the Civil War to this point. Later, she asked who wanted to pursue an extension activity related to the Civil War. Four students raised their hands, and one was William. She asked to see the small group of students just before recess that afternoon.

Lydia worked with Jacob first. In talking with him, she learned of his particular interest in weapons. They decided he would try to find a historian to interview whose work related to weaponry in the Civil War. An Internet interview was one option.

Shauna and Beth wanted to read more about young women who fought as soldiers during the war. They had heard Lydia talk about the book *Girl in Blue* by Ann Rinaldi, a story about Sarah Wheelock who disguised herself as a boy and worked as a male nurse in the Civil War. They would read some additional historical fiction about women in the Civil War and also learn about how the authors of the books did their research to write historical fiction. William wanted to read more diary entries and newspaper accounts written by or about Union and Confederate soldiers. He didn't know yet quite what he wanted to do with what he learned but thought he might like to write some original poems. Lydia suggested he could look at poems based on history and see how those writers used the subject matter of history to write poetry. She has a clearer sense now that William's thoughts were more intense and deeper than those of many students his age.

Lydia shared the students' ideas for extension activities with Ed. He volunteered to help both Lydia and the students. He recommended that Lydia send the students to his room once a week during social studies so he could help them plan their investigations. Lydia felt relieved. She was glad to work with the students on their ideas but knew Ed had materials and experiences that would help them as well.

For example, Lydia was delighted when Ed shared a project self-evaluation form with her (see Figure 7.15). In particular, she liked the way it required students to reflect on their new learning, as well as the prompt that asked them to think about new questions they might have.

Figure 7.15. Ed's Student Self-Assessment Form

ASSESSING MY LEARNING

Please fill in the information about your project. Then read each question below. Rate yourself on a scale from 1 to 5, with 1 being the lowest and 5 being the highest. Explain your answers.

Name:_____

Project Title:_____

Goal 1:_____

Goal 2:_____

Goal 3:_____

1. How well did you achieve your goals?   1 2 3 4 5

_____

_____

_____

2. How well did you learn new information and ideas? (Please explain below.)   1 2 3 4 5

_____

_____

_____

(Continued)

Figure 7.15. Continued

3. How well did you learn new skills? (Please explain below.)   1   2   3   4   5

_____

_____

_____

4. How well did you use new tools or methods? (Please explain below.)   1   2   3   4   5

_____

_____

_____

5. How well did you learn new things about yourself? (Please explain below.)   1   2   3   4   5

_____

_____

_____

6. What part of your work makes you the most proud?

_____

_____

_____

7. If you had to do your project over again, what would you change and why?

_____

_____

_____

8. How does your work show that you have grown or improved in some way?

_____

_____

_____

9. What new question do you have? How can I help you begin to find your answer?

_____

_____

_____

An additional adaptation Lydia included in her revised unit was a whole-class product that would allow students to work as historians on a common product. Based on the presentation by Willis Taylor about local involvement in the Underground Railroad, Lydia would lead her students to research that portion of their community history through the use of a variety of primary and secondary resources.

Mr. Taylor agreed to provide suggestions for their work and give them feedback as they progressed. Ultimately, students would develop a brochure on houses in their town that once served as stations on the Underground Railroad. The brochure would be targeted at young visitors to the historic houses and would include a section on students as historians. Even though this product would not require exhaustive research, it would give students a shared experience with doing historical research, drawing and supporting conclusions based on what they learned, and communicating accurate and informative data in an interesting way. This shared experience would also provide a great laboratory for group reflection on the methods and contributions of historians, the traits and interests required to be a historian, and how these elements helped them understand their own strengths and interests.

The final adaptation Lydia made in the Curriculum of Identity unit on the Civil War was taking care to ensure that students regularly considered the roles of varied kinds of historians and their products and contributions, and to link those learning experiences with student reflection on what they learned about the Civil War, the work and contributions of historians, and their own profiles. She had already built some of these reflections into introductory activities, student profile surveys, particular learning activities including visits with the guest speakers, the interest and extension activities, and the community history product. She would take care to use brief class discussions, student journal entries, and small group sharing to focus consistently on this aspect of the unit.

Lydia looked back at her work on the Curriculum of Identity. She was proud of her progress and of the emphasis on student identity that she had incorporated in the Civil War unit. The five major changes she had made to her unit—the introduction, two guest speakers, interest-based groups and extension activities, the shared community history project, and continual reflection on student's thinking about their own profiles as learners and workers through the lens of the historian—aligned her curriculum with the goals of the Curriculum of Identity.

Adapting the Components of the Curriculum of Identity Based on Learner Need, Including Ascending Intellectual Demand

Lydia knew the Curriculum of Identity unit was abstract and entered new territory for most of her students. In reflecting on students' differences in readiness to learn and degree of sophistication as a learner, she knew she needed to consider two questions. First, how would she support the success of students for whom introspection and abstract thinking were difficult? Second, what would she do to ensure challenge for those students who found even the level of complexity and ambiguity in this unit to be insufficiently challenging.

For students needing extra help and support, she would certainly make sure to have a variety of media available in resource materials and to make certain there were plenty of materials in a range of readability suited to her students for whom reading continued to be difficult. She would also model and provide sample responses to abstract questions to give students images of the sorts of thinking called for in activities requiring reflection. Lydia could also lead small group discussions in which students could formulate their responses with teacher guidance and peer input. Further, she could begin with these students by emphasizing questions with more concrete answers, such as ways historians express themselves and descriptions of their working environments. She would also be attentive to indications of student interest in and comfort with topics in the unit. It might be, for example, that some students would find it more comfortable to think about themselves in relation to soldiers, farmers, merchants, or conductors in the Underground Railroad than in relation to the work of the historian. If this proved to be the case, she would encourage the students to make comparisons that worked for them. After all, the goal of the Curriculum of Identity is self-discovery. If that happens through one lens better than another, so be it.

For students whose thinking "pushed against the edges" of her unit's requirements, Lydia would provide more complex resources, emphasize the use of primary documents, and present resources that reflected widely divergent perspectives on the content or on what it means to work as a historian. She might also take a lead from the Curriculum of Connections and have the students study similarities and differences among historians, their methods, and their contributions in several time periods or in countries with differing cultures or types of government. Certainly, she would meet with these students to set criteria for their products and personal reflections that genuinely tested their skills. Two related goals she would use for these students were (a) being certain students saw truly expert-level criteria for historical writing and products and (b) having students articulate some of their own goals for personal excellence in research, writing, and production. The gifted education specialist and the two guest speakers could also help with this advanced level of standards setting. Finally, she might introduce these students to critiques of historians and famous people who were important in the unit. It could be useful to very deep thinkers to confront the reality of criticism as a part of life—even the lives of those whom we think of largely in terms of success and praise.

Lydia reflected back on her work with the Curriculum of Identity and was convinced her time had been well spent. First, she felt she knew her students personally much more than in past years of her teaching. Now, when she looked at the faces in front of her, the students were much better defined in her thinking. She had a better sense of the abilities and dreams of her students. She also had a clearer sense of how she could help nurture those abilities and dreams. She truly felt that she had reached a turning point in her career. Until recently, she envisioned herself simply as a teacher. Now, she also saw herself as a steward entrusted with the evolving identities of 26 remarkable young people.

Lydia also saw clear evidence that students were more cognizant of their own interests, abilities, and working preferences. She was still amazed at conversations among her students in which they shared interests and insights with one another. Provided with consistent opportunities to reflect on their interests, abilities, values, and goals in relationship to practicing professionals, she felt confident that the students would make more confident and informed decisions in their lives.

It was also evident that student motivation in her class was very high. Students were highly engaged with the guest speakers, small group tasks, personal reflections, and community history project. Somehow, the combination of personal relevance in the subject matter and the expectation to work and think like professionals gave the class a new sense of dignity.

Lydia knew she was not yet through learning about the possibilities of curriculum. In fact, she was eager for the next challenge. It occurred to her that, like her students, she was moving along a continuum toward expertise, and she liked the feel of it.

Looking Back and Ahead

The Curriculum of Identity Parallel is unique among the other parallels in the Parallel Curriculum Model. Whereas the other parallels focus on facts, concepts, principles, skills, and connections, the Curriculum of Identity Parallel extends the focus to include affective components: interests, appreciations, values, attitudes and, eventually, a life outlook.

In spite of the different focal points of the four parallels, they are all tightly entwined. Understanding the essential framework and meaning of a discipline is key to making meaning across disciplines, to practicing in a discipline in an authentic way, and to examining the goals and practices of a discipline to one's own development. Likewise, to practice in a discipline is to understand it better. To connect the discipline with self strengthens connections one might make within and across disciplines in varied times, places, cultures, and so on.

In fact, the interconnectedness of the four parallels in the Parallel Curriculum Model points to their potential flexibility for teachers designing curricula for individuals and groups to address a range of purposes. The next and final chapter takes a brief look at additional ways to use the model in curriculum design.

8

Making Decisions About the Use of the Parallel Curriculum Model

The primary purpose of this book is to introduce readers to four parallel approaches for designing a curriculum that has promise for enhancing learning for virtually all learners and to suggest, in the context of the parallels, a way of addressing the learning needs of students advanced on a continuum of learning. To that end, the book has introduced the Parallel Curriculum Model, suggested an "anchoring" framework of basic curricular elements, and then illustrated how each of the four parallels in the Parallel Curriculum Model can be used to build a curriculum on that framework of basic curricular elements.

To aid readers in comparing and contrasting the four parallels, we elected to illustrate five curriculum units on the same topic and in the same grade and classroom, using first the Comprehensive Curriculum Framework and then the four parallels of the Parallel Curriculum Model. We would be remiss, however, if we stopped our exploration of the Model with the impression that each parallel is useful only for constructing full curriculum units. In fact, the parallels invite teachers to use multiple lenses on a topic or discipline within a single curricular unit. In other words, it is not only possible to construct effective units using multiple parallels within the same unit but often wise to do so.

Units that employ more than one parallel would: give students multiple perspectives on the same content, reach more students because of the capacity of such units to tap into a range of interest areas, and provide reinforcing learning experiences that enhance student capacity to retain, retrieve, and use the content they study. In fact, the name "Parallel Curriculum Model" envisions that teachers might often move simultaneously among multiple parallels in the process of designing a curriculum. It is possible to use this sort of flexible approach to curriculum design using more than one parallel because all of them are rooted in a conceptual understanding of a topic and/or discipline.

The Core Parallel ensures that students focus on the facts, concepts, principles, and skills that are essential to the content they are studying. The other three parallels are rooted in the same conceptual approach but offer students a chance to (a) see the concepts, principles, and skills at work in other contexts (Curriculum of Connections); (b) understand how experts in a field do their work (Curriculum of Practice); and (c) extend their understanding of themselves by comparing their own skills, perspectives, and goals to those of experts in the disciplines and/or people studied through the disciplines (Curriculum of Identity). In each instance, teachers and students draw upon the fundamental information, ideas, and methods of the discipline—but do so with different emphases, depending on the parallel or parallels that shape the curriculum.

The purpose of this final chapter, then, is to explain ways of using the Parallel Curriculum Model other than as an approach to developing curriculum units based on a single parallel. In addition, the chapter briefly presents guidelines for making decisions about use of the Parallel Curriculum Model.

Flexible Options for Using the Parallel Curriculum Model

There are many ways to draw upon the four parallels in the Parallel Curriculum Model in the curriculum design process. This section of the chapter examines only a small sampling of approaches. There is no "right order" for introducing the parallels. There is no "correct number" of parallels to use in a lesson, a unit, or a course of study. The parallels can be used to develop curriculum for individuals, small groups, and entire classes. Teaching in the parallels can be deductive or inductive. The parallels can be used as a catalyst to discover student abilities and interests or in response to student abilities and interests. We encourage teachers and other curriculum designers to think about their current curriculum and consider additional ways in which the parallels can help them make that curriculum more coherent, compelling, relevant, and memorable.

The Parallels as Support for Thematic Study

In many classrooms, teachers work to help students connect content that might otherwise seem disjointed to young learners. Thematic study is one useful approach to helping students grasp the interconnectedness of knowledge. In a thematic study, it is the theme itself that is the focus of students' thought and reflection rather than a particular topic. Although students study multiple topics during a thematic study, they do so in large measure to illustrate the theme.

In a thematic unit, the four parallels of the Parallel Curriculum Model offer rich ways of exploring the central theme. For example, in an elementary classroom, a teacher might focus much of her curriculum and instruction on the theme of "change." In one fourth grade classroom, for example, a teacher finds the theme implicit in students' study of weather in science, the westward migration in social studies, and biography and autobiography in language arts. In addition, students reflect on the theme of change when they think about what happens in math when moving from one operation to another, in music when keys and rhythms change, and so on. Thus, during the third quarter of the year, the teacher focuses her curriculum on the theme of "change" and guides students to explore the theme at work in a range of topics.

The teacher might use all four parallels of the Parallel Curriculum Model in her curriculum plans. For example, using the Core Curriculum Parallel, she would establish a definition of change, identify key principles related to change, and introduce students to the key skills they need to work in each of the discipline areas specified by her standards document and textbooks. Using the Curriculum of Connections Parallel, she would conduct periodic lessons in which students compare and contrast the concept of change in the various content areas they are studying. Using the Curriculum of Practice Parallel, the teacher would ask students to use the methods of a practitioner in one of the disciplines to observe and report on a significant change that is currently taking place in that discipline. Drawing on the Curriculum of Identity Parallel, the teacher would ask her students to do an illustrated autobiographical sketch in which they compare their own interests and perspectives to those of an expert in one of the disciplines they have studied.

In this instance, the teacher used the four parallels "in service of" the theme she selected to unify her students' work in potentially disparate subject areas. It would, of course, be possible for her to use several, but not all, of the parallels for a similar purpose (see Figure 8.1).

Parallels to Build From a Common Foundation

Any of the parallels can serve as the foundation or starting point of a study on which other parallels are taught. For example, an art teacher has her students work

Figure 8.1. Using the Parallels to Support a Thematic Study

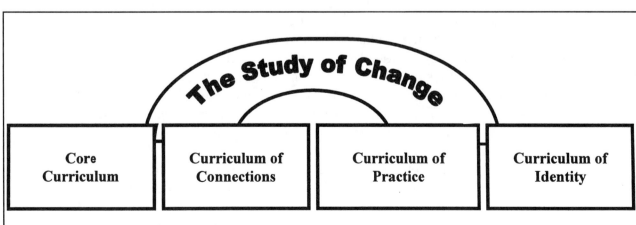

as graphic designers to identify and solve a graphic design problem in an interest area such as theater, music, museums, medicine, or sports. For the greater part of a month, she works with her students in the Curriculum of Practice to orient them to the nature of graphic design as an expert sees it, methods of graphic designers, problem identification and solution strategies, and so on. As the study progresses, she uses the other three parallels to extend and reinforce important ideas and skills. For example, in a series of lessons using the Core Curriculum, she works with her students to identify key concepts and methodologies of graphic design in the work of contemporary graphic artists. In a lesson drawn from the Curriculum of Connections, she shows students examples of graphic design from a range of time periods and cultures. She then asks her students to use their knowledge of the concepts and methods of design, as well as of technology and culture, to hypothesize the time period and culture that the designs represent. In a two-day lesson using the Curriculum of Identity, students select a graphic design from a broad array of options and discuss ways in which both the design and design process used in creating their selection is metaphorical for them as people and artists. While the teacher has designed the majority of the unit based on the goals of the Curriculum of Practice, she has used the other parallels to help students think about their work more expansively.

It is possible for any of the parallels to serve as the foundation for a unit and for any or all of the other parallels to diversify and extend the unit. Figure 8.2 suggests only two possibilities.

A Layered Approach to Using the Parallels

A teacher might want to "layer" her or his curriculum so that a student studies a topic or standard through successive "layers." This approach can serve as an amplification of a pivotal idea, helping students understand the utility and portability of what they study. For example, a high school history teacher plans for a standard that requires students to understand the causes and effects of the American Revolution. At successive points in her students' study of the American Revolution, she uses the lessons from the Core Curriculum to introduce fundamental facts about the time period; the concepts of "conflict," "conflict resolution," "revolution," and "cause and effect"; and the skills of comparing and contrasting, document analysis, and providing credible evidence for positions. Later, as illustrations of the concept of "revolution" at work, she uses lessons from the Curriculum of Connections to have students use a range of documents to analyze causes and effects of revolutions in art, politics, and technology—comparing causes and effects of those revolutions to causes and effects of the American Revolution. Still later, she uses lessons from the Curriculum of Identity to have students simulate a conflict resolution scenario, examine their own processes and abilities as arbiters, and predict roles and issues that will occur for those seeking to resolve conflicts between England and the colonies during the American Revolution. Ultimately, the teacher uses the Curriculum of Practice to have students work in groups to analyze primary and secondary documents related to the end of the American Revolution, find common themes that

Figure 8.2. Building a Unit From a Common Foundation and Extending the Study With Other Parallels

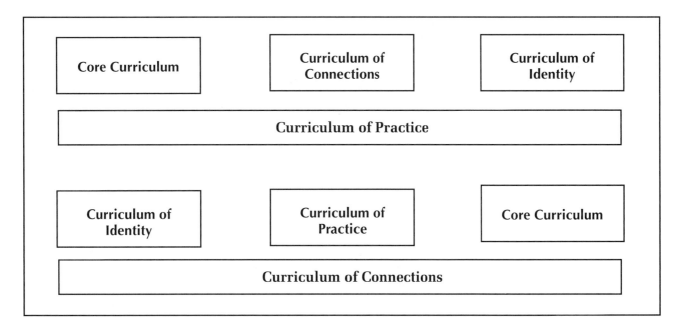

illustrate how the time period was shaped by conflict and conflict resolution, and present findings in a class symposium during which each group will both present their findings and respond to finding of other groups in the role of historian.

In this instance, the standards related to causes and effects of the American Revolution is the focal point of instruction. Helping students work through successive "layers" of understanding prompted by experiences in the four parallels allows for multiple exposures to both concrete information related to and meaning of the standard. Figure 8.3 illustrates the layered approach to teaching a standard or topic.

Using the Parallels for Varied Purposes Within a Single Unit

At earlier points in the book, we have illustrated the potential of the parallels in the Parallel Curriculum Model to extend learning in a unit for any student—including at an ascending level of intellectual demand for learners who are advanced. There are, however, many other purposes effectively addressed by using one or more of the parallels in curriculum design.

A teacher can think about one or more of the parallels as a vehicle to introduce students to a topic or concept, as a way to support or illustrate new learning, as a means of forging new student understandings, as a format for a culminating product or assessment, and so on. In such instances, a parallel offers a shorter term lens for examining a topic, standard, or idea in a longer term exploration of that content. For example, an English teacher decides to use the Curriculum of Connections to introduce a novel-based unit on justice and injustice. To do so, she forms interest-based groups to examine ways in which the concepts of justice and injustice currently relate to race, gender, handicapping condition, and/or age in the areas of medical

Figure 8.3. A Layered Approach to Teaching a Standard or Topic Using the Parallels

Standard: Students will understand the causes and effects of the American Revolution

CORE CURRICULUM
Students are introduced to key facts, concepts, principles, and skills of the topic and discipline.

CURRICULUM OF CONNECTIONS
Students study the causes and effects of revolutions in art, politics, and technology and comparisons with causes and effects of the American Revolution.

CURRICULUM OF IDENTITY
Students simulate conflict resolution, comparing their own perspectives and abilities as conflict arbitors to those in the same roles during the American Revolution.

CURRICULUM OF PRACTICE
Students work as historians, analyzing documents to find themes related to ways in which conflict and conflict resolution shaped the time period of the American Revolution. Students present and critique presentations in a symposium format.

care, housing, education, or sports. As students work together, they begin to formulate a sense of the complexity of the concepts themselves as well as ways in which people's perspectives affect their views about justice and injustice. By introducing the concepts across groups and topics, the teacher has captured the interest of students and has begun to build a bridge between students' own world and a pair of abstract concepts.

This same teacher, however, may prefer to use one or more of the parallels to support new learning at some point in the unit. Students in the unit are reading Harper Lee's (1960) *To Kill a Mockingbird* and have been discussing ways in which power and privilege can shape one's sense of justice. This idea is new to students, many of whom are just beginning to examine these sorts of issues in their lives. The teacher decides to use a learning experience from the Core Curriculum Parallel to help students develop a deeper understanding of the relationship between power and justice. First, she leads the class in developing several assertions or hypotheses about that relationship (for example: "A person's position of power in a group affects that person's perspective on justice." "Both physical and mental power can become tools of justice and injustice."). Students then examine the novel for confirming or refuting evidence of the assertions. Next, she asks students to work individually or in groups to diagram or map the relationship between power and justice/injustice. Finally, she leads students to develop a set of principles about the relationship between power and justice/injustice that they believe they can support. They will continue to examine, revise, and add to these principles as the unit continues. In a novel study that is topic and theme based, the teacher has nonetheless used the Core Curriculum lens to help students identify, define, and explore concepts important to the unit. She has also helped them generate a sort of concept map examining relationships among concepts, and develop principles that will both focus and deepen their study in the novel unit.

This same teacher might elect to use only one of the parallels to help her students forge a new understanding. In this instance, she decides to ask her students to select the character in *To Kill a Mockingbird* with whom they most identify and to write an interior monologue from that character's perspective at an interesting point in the novel. Next, she asks them to do the same kind of writing from the perspective of the character with whom they find it most difficult to identify. Finally, she introduces the students to the title of Mary Catherine Bateson's (1989) *Composing a Life* and asks students to reflect on what the novel and interior monologues show them about how they are composing their own lives. Students can develop their response in an annotated drawing, song, or interior monologue of their own. Here, the teacher has used a learning experience from the perspective of the Curriculum of Identity to help the students discover the power of literature to help them reflect on their own lives.

Finally, the teacher might elect to use one of the parallels to provide a culminating learning experience for her students. She may have taught the unit to that point without drawing on any of the other parallels, or may have done so to introduce the unit, support new student understandings, forge new student understandings, and/or extend the basic unit through interest groups, homework options, independent investigations, and so forth. To provide a culminating experience, the teacher decides to use the Curriculum of Practice. She introduces students to the research method of ethnography, teaching them its basic purposes, principles, and methods. Students also examine excerpts from published ethnographies, ethnographers' notes, and ethnographers' reflections on analyzing their data. The culminating product assignment for the unit asks students to play the role of ethnographer over a period of two weeks in a setting of their choice. Their goal is to create a brief piece of ethnographic writing that evokes an authentic and informed sense of place, time, character, and significance reminiscent of Harper Lee's work. A goal of the product includes having students review key elements of fiction—but also using them and doing so with the keen eye and ear of a good writer. The product rubric provides guidance for students in the use of ethnography to inform their writing, as well as other requirements for quality in their work. Figure 8.4 suggests some of the

Figure 8.4. Using the Parallels for Varied Purposes Within a Single Unit

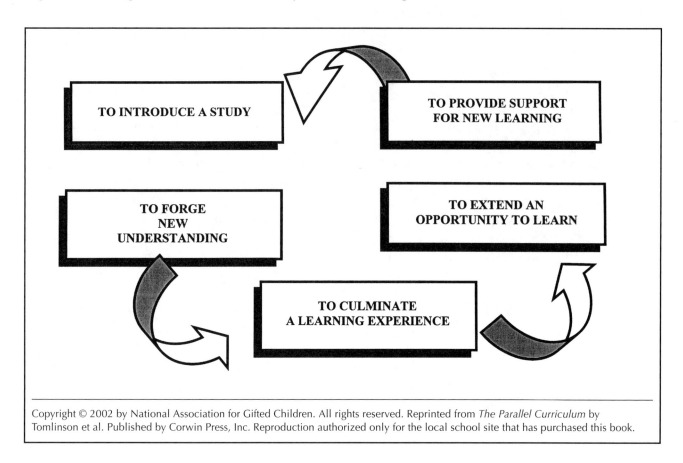

purposes for which one or more parallels from the Parallel Curriculum Model might be used as teachers design curriculum.

Designing Individual Learning Pathways Using the Parallel Curriculum Model

Many students—particularly those who are highly advanced as learners, those who are particularly creative, and those who have strongly developed interests in particular topics—benefit from an "individual pathways" approach to curriculum design. In this approach, teacher-student interactions reveal the relationship between what students currently know and what they need to know in order to attain their goals as learners, scholars, or experts in an area. A student's interests, learning preferences, and specific abilities can also shape decisions about pathways to curriculum.

In a classroom with an "individual pathways" approach to curriculum design, there are still teacher-directed lessons and goals or standards that must be achieved in order to ensure student competence and success. The teacher and individual students also work together, however, to determine which components of the Parallel

Curriculum Model the student will use at a particular point as well as the order in which that student will work with the components.

This use of the Parallel Curriculum Model has great potential to "tailor" the curriculum for students whose needs and interests make the standard curriculum an uncomfortable fit. This will be the case for some students in almost every setting, even when the standard curriculum is high level and meaning-rich. Figure 8.5 provides one illustration of an individual pathways approach to curriculum design using the Parallel Curriculum Model.

Figure 8.5. Using the Parallel Curriculum Model to Develop Individual Pathways

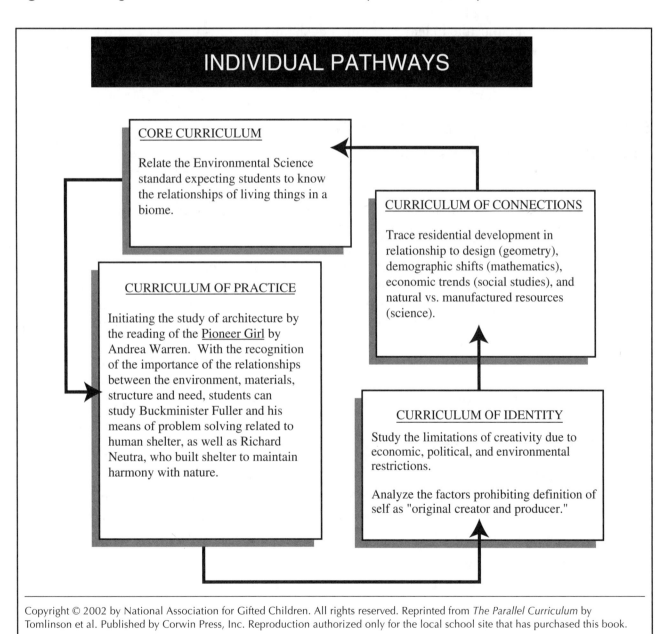

INDIVIDUAL PATHWAYS

CORE CURRICULUM

Relate the Environmental Science standard expecting students to know the relationships of living things in a biome.

CURRICULUM OF PRACTICE

Initiating the study of architecture by the reading of the Pioneer Girl by Andrea Warren. With the recognition of the importance of the relationships between the environment, materials, structure and need, students can study Buckminister Fuller and his means of problem solving related to human shelter, as well as Richard Neutra, who built shelter to maintain harmony with nature.

CURRICULUM OF CONNECTIONS

Trace residential development in relationship to design (geometry), demographic shifts (mathematics), economic trends (social studies), and natural vs. manufactured resources (science).

CURRICULUM OF IDENTITY

Study the limitations of creativity due to economic, political, and environmental restrictions.

Analyze the factors prohibiting definition of self as "original creator and producer."

Extending Your Options Using the Parallels

This section of the chapter has suggested several ways teachers might use one or more of the parallels from the Parallel Curriculum Model to enhance curriculum planning. When using one or more of the parallels as a guide for planning a lesson, product, unit, or course of study, the goal of the Parallel Curriculum Model is to promote student learning that is engaging, authentic, meaningful, relevant, memorable, and useful to the student. To that end, we would encourage teachers to examine many possible configurations and uses of the various parallels to guide a broad range of learners in continual growth toward expertise in a discipline. The suggestions here are just a sampling of possible ways to think about and work with the Model. When using the Model as a tool to think about curriculum, however, it is important for educators to make informed decisions about its use—as would be the case with any curricular decision making. In the next section of the chapter, we'll take a look at some significant elements in that decision-making process.

Making Decisions About Use of the Parallel Curriculum Model

While teachers may sometimes make curricular decisions intuitively, solid decisions are usually grounded in sensitivity to elements that govern the degree to which the decision is a good fit for the context in which the curriculum will be used and the goals that the curriculum is to serve. Thorough exploration of all the factors that should shape curricular decision making would require an additional book. The following brief sections, however, provide an overview of some key factors that should shape decisions about curriculum. These factors include: the learning goals designated for students to achieve, the nature of the students who will use the curriculum to achieve those goals, the teacher who will teach the curriculum, the context in which the curriculum will be taught, and the teaching of the curriculum to achieve maximum benefit.

The Nature of the Learning Goals

A curriculum is a plan to achieve important learning goals. It is critical, then, that whatever plan a teacher develops be likely to guide students to the desired outcomes. Among questions a teacher should ask when deciding whether to use the Parallel Curriculum Model, and if so, which parallel(s) are these:

▶ What are the learning goals the curriculum must address, including local and state standards, textbook goals, and teacher-determined goals?

▶ What is the essential core of knowledge and understanding reflected in the learning goals?

▶ What other expectations do I hold and do others hold for the education of students who will study this curriculum?

▶ In what ways could the Parallel Curriculum Model help me focus and clarify content for my students?

▶ Which specific learning goals would the model address effectively? Are there goals that would not be well served by using the model?

Early and careful thought about the match between the full range of goals for the curriculum and the potential of the Model to support achievement of those goals will provide teachers with a compass for curriculum planning. Such considerations also begin to help a teacher understand which portions of the Parallel Curriculum Model would be most effective in developing a particular segment of curriculum.

The Nature of the Students

Curriculum plans should be made with full awareness of the students whom the curriculum is designed to teach. Among questions about students that are significant in making decisions about curriculum are:

▶ What is the general developmental level of my students?

▶ What sorts of experiences are they likely to bring to this study?

▶ What is the span of student readiness that the curriculum must address?

▶ What interests are likely to be represented in my students?

▶ What are the cognitive profiles of my students? How do they learn best?

▶ What are the likely personal learning goals of my students in regard to this topic?

▶ What sorts of learning experiences can I anticipate will be inviting, engaging, memorable, useful, and meaningful to my students?

▶ In what ways could the Parallel Curriculum Model help my particular students achieve the specific learning goals and other expectations for them?

▶ Are there parts of the Model that would likely be more effective with particular learners and my class(es) as a whole? Less effective?

In teaching, as in many other human endeavors, knowing the "audience" for what we do is profoundly important. Easy as it is to think about curriculum as though it were separate from the students who will study it, that approach is likely doomed for students and teacher alike. Much of what we know about learning suggests that the curriculum must fit the learner—not the other way around.

The Nature of the Teacher

High-quality teaching is evolutionary. Good teachers grow as much as their students every year—if not more. That fact suggests that teachers, like students, are "ready" for different challenges at different points in their development. Just as it is necessary to ask whether a particular curriculum plan is appropriate for given students, it's critical to ask whether the curriculum plan is a good match for the teacher(s) who will teach it as well. Among questions helpful in that regard are the following:

▶ At what level of professional development is the teacher?

▶ How well does the teacher know the subject matter of the unit?

▶ To what degree does the teacher know what constitutes the essential core of the content?

▶ How willing is the teacher to extend his or her knowledge of the subject matter?

▶ How well does the teacher know his or her students?

▶ How effective is the teacher in addressing a range of learner needs?

▶ How comfortable is the teacher in using a range of instructional methods?

▶ How effective is the teacher with managing student groups?

▶ In what ways could the Parallel Curriculum Model support the effectiveness of the teacher(s) who will teach this unit?

A rich and challenging curriculum can encourage teacher growth, just as it can support student growth. On the other hand, if the curriculum plan is "too far ahead" of a teacher's current knowledge and skill, results for both teacher and students are likely to be predictably poor. If the curriculum is the blueprint to achieve important learning goals, the teacher is the architect who must transform the plan into a three-dimensional reality. The plan, then, must match the skill and will of the architect.

The Context of the Curriculum

The curriculum on paper is a different matter from the curriculum in a real world shaped and constrained by elements like time, materials, space, and so on. The real-world context of the school and classroom suggests important questions for the consideration of curriculum designers.

▶ How much time is available for this study?

▶ Into what "blocks" is the available time arranged?

▶ What books and other materials are available for the study?

▶ What access do I have to colleagues who can offer support in designing or teaching the curriculum?

▶ What sorts of community resources can I access as I plan and teach the curriculum?

▶ In what sort of learning space(s) can the unit be taught?

▶ In what ways could the Parallel Curriculum Model be a good match for the context in which the curriculum will be taught?

▶ Are there elements of the context that are not a good match for all or part of the Model?

Teaching the Curriculum

Beyond, and related to, knowledge of goals, students, teacher, and context, there are still many decisions to be made about how to teach the curriculum using a particular model. Among questions helpful to teachers in making appropriate curricular decisions in this area are the following:

▶ What is likely to be the most effective order in which to teach the important information, ideas, and skills (for example: chronological/sequential, simple to complex, concrete to abstract, example to principle, or principle to example)?

▶ What is the relative importance of the various parts of my curriculum, and how do I allocate time within the curriculum to reflect the relative importance?

▶ Which teaching and learning methods are the best match for the nature of the students and the nature of the learning goals?

▶ Do I want to teach inductively, deductively, or using a combination of approaches?

▶ When is it most effective for me to be on "center stage" in the curriculum, and when is it most important for my students to be in that position?

▶ How can I use one part of the curriculum to reinforce information, ideas, and/or skills in another part of the curriculum?

▶ How will I assess student growth and needs throughout the unit?

▶ What grouping patterns will I need to use to reach my students?

▶ What personalized learning opportunities will I need to provide during the study based on my students' needs?

▶ In what ways can the Parallel Curriculum Model be useful in answering questions about how to teach the curriculum?

We believe the Parallel Curriculum Model has great potential to enhance teaching and learning in many settings. We know, however, that the Model will not always be the best approach for all students and teachers, in all contexts, with all learning goals. We understand also that when it *does* provide a fruitful way to think about curriculum design, it is more a description of a rich curriculum than a rigid template for curriculum design. The Model thus calls for flexible application to ensure a match between learning goals, students, teachers, context, and decisions about how to arrange the curriculum.

The questions we have posed here about learning goals, students, teachers, the learning context, and organizing and teaching the curriculum are significant, but they are also only a small sampling of questions that thoughtful teachers ask continually. The goal of such teachers is continual refinement of their professional practice—a goal that calls for both the flexibility of practice and the reflective decision making recommended by this chapter.

Looking Back and Looking Ahead

Planning curriculum and instruction are central to the profession of teaching. In fact, learning to create and teach artful curriculum is a career-long process for high-quality teachers—and perhaps we never really arrive at the zenith of our possibilities. Nonetheless, the curriculum we develop mirrors our professional growth, and as we continue our professional development, the image in the mirror matures along with the teacher. We are hopeful that this book is both a challenge and an encouragement to teachers as they do the hard work of developing a curriculum that reshapes them, even as it reshapes the world of their students.

This book began and ends with the premise that a curriculum is a catalyst for helping young people progress steadily, but vigorously, along a continuum toward expertise in the disciplines by which humans organize knowledge. The Parallel Curriculum Model is rooted in the beliefs that all learners must construct meaning from what they study and that learning becomes more engaging, relevant, durable, transferable, and purposeful as students understand the key concepts, principles, and skills of the disciplines, come to see those concepts and principles as the connective tissue that binds the universe of knowledge, apply the understandings and skills in ways that empower them as thinkers and producers of knowledge, and see the disciplines as a way to understand themselves both now and in the future. All students deserve an education in classrooms devoted to delivering those things. Such classrooms are catalysts for the emergence and recognition of talent and incubators of students' possibilities.

Teachers in the highest quality classrooms also recognize, however, that there is not a single best pace of instruction, that excellence is defined by extending each individual's reach rather than by adhering to a group norm. Thus teachers in these classrooms are continually in search of each learner's next step in a learning sequence that never ends. Teachers in these classrooms vigorously support each learner in taking his or her own next step—and then the next, and the next, and so on.

We hope this book and the model it presents will also serve as a catalyst for the development of possibilities in teachers as they read about the Parallel Curriculum Model, argue about it, try it out, and adapt it. In the end, teachers construct knowledge as their students do—by seeking meaning, making connections, putting ideas to work at a high level of professional quality, and reflecting on what their work teaches them about themselves—even as it teaches the young people they serve.

References

Amabile, T. M. (1983). *The social psychology of creativity.* New York: Springer-Verlag.

Ausubel, D. P. (1968). *Educational psychology: A cognitive view.* New York: Holt, Rinehart & Winston.

Bandura, A. (1977). Self-efficacy: Toward a unifying theory of behavioral change. *Psychological Review, 84,* 191-215.

Bateson, M. C. (1989). *Composing a life.* New York: Atlantic Monthly Press.

Beatty, P. (1984). *Turn homeward, Hannalee.* New York: Morrow.

Beatty, P. (1987). *Charley Skedaddle.* New York: Morrow.

Beatty, P. (1991). *Jayhawker.* New York: Morrow.

Bloom, B., Englehart, M., Furst, E., Hill, W., & Krathwhol, D. (1956). *Taxonomy of educational objectives Handbook I: Cognitive domain.* New York: Longmans Green.

Bolotin, N., & Bolotin, A. (1994). *For home and country: A Civil War scrapbook.* New York: Lodestar.

Bourman, A. (1996). *Meeting of minds.* Portland, ME: Walch.

Brandt, R. (1998). *Powerful learning.* Alexandria, VA: Association for Supervision and Curriculum Development.

Brown, M. (1949). *The important book.* New York: Harper & Row.

Bruner, J. S. (1960). *The process of education.* Cambridge, MA: Harvard University Press.

Bruner, J. S. (1966). *Toward a theory of instruction.* Cambridge, MA: Harvard University Press.

Burns, D. E. (1993). *A six-phase model for the explicit teaching of thinking skills.* Storrs: University of Connecticut, National Research Center on the Gifted and Talented.

Collier, J. L., & Collier, C. (1994). *With every drop of blood.* New York: Delacorte.

Collins, M., & Amabile, T. M. (1999). Motivation and creativity. In R. J. Sternberg (Ed.), *Handbook of creativity* (pp. 297-312). New York: Cambridge University Press.

Connecticut State Department of Education. (1998a). *The Connecticut framework: K-12 curricular goals and standards.* Hartford, CT: Author.

Connecticut State Department of Education. (1998b). *Regulations concerning state education certification, permits, and authorization.* Hartford, CT: Author.

Connecticut State Department of Education. (1999*). Connecticut's common core of teaching.* Hartford, CT: Author.

Costa, A., & Kallick, B. (2000). *Discovering and exploring habits of mind.* Alexandria, VA: Association for Supervision and Curriculum Development.

Csikszentmihalyi, M. (1990). Flow: The psychology of optimal experience. New York: Harper & Row.

Csikszentmihalyi, M., Rathunde, K., & Whalen, S. (1993). *Talented teenagers: The roots of success and failure.* New York: Cambridge University Press.

Delpit, L. (1995). *Other people's children: Cultural conflict in the classroom.* New York: New Press.

Dewey, J. (1938*). Experience and education.* New York: Macmillan.

Dunn, R., & Griggs, S. (1995). *Multiculturalism and learning style: Teaching and counseling adolescents.* Westport, CT: Praeger.

Erickson, H. L. (1998). *Concept-based curriculum and instruction: Teaching beyond the facts.* Thousand Oaks, CA: Corwin.

Feldman, D. (1992). Has there been a paradigm shift in gifted education? In N. Colangelo, S. G. Assouline, & D. L. Amronson (Eds.), *Talent development: Proceedings from the 1991 Henry B. and Jocelyn Wallace National Research Symposium on Talent Development* (pp. 89-94). Unionville, NY: Trillium.

Fleischman, P. (1996). *Dateline: Troy.* Cambridge, MA: Candlewick.

Freedman, R. (1987). *Lincoln: A photobiography.* New York: Clarion.

Gagné, R. M., & Briggs, L. J. (1979). *Principles of instructional design* (2nd ed.). New York: Holt, Rinehart & Winston.

Gardner, H. (1993). *Frames of mind: The theory of multiple intelligences.* New York: Basic Books.

Grigorenko, E., & Sternberg, R. (1997). Styles of thinking, abilities, and academic performance. *Exceptional Children, 63,* 295-312.

Hoemann, G. (2001). *The American Civil War homepage.* Retrieved July 11, 2001 from internet.

Howard, P. J. (1994). *An owner's manual for the brain.* Austin, TX: Leornian.

Hunt, I. (1964). *Across five Aprils.* River Grove, IL: Follett.

James, W. (1885). On the functions of cognition. *Mind, 10,* 27-44.

Jensen, E. (1998). *Teaching with the brain in mind.* Alexandria, VA: Association for Supervision and Curriculum Development.

Krathwohl, D. R., Bloom, B. S., & Masia, B. B. (1964). *Taxonomy of educational goals. Handbook II: Affective domain.* New York: Longman.

Lee, H. (1960). *To kill a mockingbird.* New York: Harper & Row.

Levy, S. (1996). *Starting from scratch.* Portsmouth, NH: Heinemann.

Library of Congress. (2000). *Selected Civil War photographs.* Retrieved July 11, 2001 from

Mahoney, A. S. (1998). In search of the gifted identity: From abstract concept to workable counseling constructs. *Roeper Review, 20*(3), 222-226.

Mansilla, V. B., & Gardner, H. (1998). What are the qualities of understanding? In M. S. Wiske (Ed.), *Teaching for understanding: Linking research with practice.* San Francisco: Jossey-Bass.

Marzano, R. (1992). *A different kind of classroom: Teaching with dimensions of learning.* Alexandria, VA: Association for Supervision and Curriculum Development.

Maslow, A. H. (1970). *Motivation and personality* (2nd ed.). New York: Harper & Row.

McCurdy, M. (Ed.). (1994). *Escape from slavery: The boyhood of Frederick Douglass in his own words.* New York: Alfred A. Knopf.

McKissack, P., & McKissack, F. (1991). *The story of Booker T. Washington.* Danbury, CT: Children's Press.

McQuerry, M. (2000). *Nuclear legacy: A collaborative research study with middle school students.* Columbus, OH: Battelle Press.

Mettger, Z. (1984). *Till victory is won: Black soldiers in the Civil War.* New York: E. P. Dutton.

Murphy, J. (1990). *The boys' war.* New York: Clarion.

National Academy Press. (1996). *National science education standards.* Washington, DC: Author.

National Archives and Records Administration. (2001). *NARA.* Retrieved July 11, 2001 from <http://www.nara.gov>

National Center for History in the Schools. (1996). *National standards for history.* Los Angeles: Author.

National Research Council. (1999). *How people learn: Brain, mind, experience, and school.* Washington, DC: National Academy Press.

Paulsen, G. (1998). *Soldier's heart.* New York: Bantam.

Phenix, P. H. (1964). *Realms of meaning.* New York: McGraw-Hill.

Reeder, C. (1989). *Shades of gray.* New York: Macmillan.

Renzulli, J. (1977). *The enrichment triad model: A guide for developing defensible programs for the gifted.* Mansfield Center, CT: Creative Learning Press.

Renzulli, J. S., Leppien, J. H., & Hayes, T. S.(2000). *The multiple menu model: A practical guide for developing differentiated curriculum.* Mansfield Center, CT: Creative Learning Press.

Schlechty, P. (1997). *Inventing better schools: An action plan for educational reform.* San Francisco: Jossey-Bass.

Schwartz, D. M. (1985). *How much is a million?* New York: Lothrop, Lee & Shepard.

Sís, P. (1997). *Starry messenger: Galileo Galilei.* New York: Farrar, Straus & Giroux.

Sís, P. (1998). *Tibet: Through the red box.* New York: Farrar, Straus & Giroux.

Sternberg, R. J. (1985). *Beyond IQ: A triarchic theory of intelligence.* New York: Cambridge University Press.

Sullivan, M. (1993). *A meta-analysis of experimental research studies based on the Dunn & Dunn learning styles model and its relationship to academic achievement and performance.* Unpublished doctoral dissertation, St. John's University.

Taba, H. (1962). *Curriculum and practice.* New York: Harcourt, Brace & World.

Taylor, M. (1991). *Harriet Tubman.* Broomall, PA: Chelsea House.

U.S. Department of Labor. (1992). *What work requires of schools: A SCANS report for America 2000.* Washington, DC: Government Printing Office.

Vygotsky, L. S. (1962). *Thought and language*. Cambridge: MIT Press.

Vygotsky, L. S. (1978). *Mind in society*. Cambridge, MA: Harvard University Press.

Washington, B. T. (1963). *Up from slavery*. New York: Doubleday.

Wassermann, S. (1988). Play-Debrief-Replay: An instructional model for science. *Childhood Education, 64*, 232-234.

Whitehead, A. N. (1929). The rhythm of education. In A. N. Whitehead (Ed.), *The aims of education*. New York: Macmillan.

Wiggins, G., & McTighe, J. (1998). *Understanding by design*. Alexandria, VA: Association for Supervision and Curriculum Development.